D1191261

GIS Worlds

Creating Spatial Data Infrastructures

IAN MASSER

ESRI PRESS

REDLANDS, CALIFORNIA

ESRI Press, 380 New York Street, Redlands, California 92373-8100

Copyright © 2005 ESRI
All rights reserved. First edition 2005.
10 09 08 07 06 05   1 2 3 4 5 6 7 8 9 10

Printed in the United States of America

Library of Congress Cataloging-in-Publication Data
Masser, Ian.
GIS worlds : creating spatial data infrastructures / Ian Masser.—1st ed.
      p. cm.
   Includes bibliographical references and index.
      ISBN 1-58948-122-4 (pbk. : alk. paper)
      1. Geographic information systems. 2. Information storage and retrieval systems—Geography. I. Title.
G70.212.M289 2005
910'.285—dc2   2005004162

Ask for ESRI Press titles at your local bookstore or order by calling 1-800-447-9778. You can also shop online at www.esri.com/esripress. Outside the United States, contact your local ESRI distributor.

ESRI Press titles are distributed to the trade by the following:

In North America, South America, Asia, and Australia:
Independent Publishers Group (IPG)
Telephone (United States): 1-800-888-4741
Telephone (international): 312-337-0747
E-mail: frontdesk@ipgbook.com

In the United Kingdom, Europe, and the Middle East:
Transatlantic Publishers Group Ltd.
Telephone: 44 20 8849 8013
Fax: 44 20 8849 5556
E-mail: transatlantic.publishers@regusnet.com

GIS Worlds

Creating Spatial Data Infrastructures

Contents

Contents . . . vi
List of boxes . . . viii
List of figures. . . xi
List of tables . . . xiii
Foreword . . . xiv
Preface . . . xvi
Acknowledgments . . . xxi

CHAPTER 1   *An introduction . . . 1*
Why GIS is valuable . . . 6
The objectives of this book . . . 12
Setting the scene . . . 16

CHAPTER 2   *The diffusion of national SDIs:*
Innovators and early adopters . . . 23
The diffusion of innovations model . . . 26
Innovators or early adopters . . . 30
Comparative evaluation . . . 38
Characteristics of the innovators/early adopters . . . 48

CHAPTER 3   *The diffusion of national SDIs:*
The early majority . . . 55
Profiles of Europe, the Americas, Asia and the Pacific, and Africa . . . 58
Comparative evaluation . . . 80
Characteristics of the early majority . . . 90

CHAPTER 4   *The evolution of SDIs in the United Kingdom . . . 93*
The impact of the Chorley Report . . . 96
The National Geospatial Data Framework . . . 100
The current state of SDI development in the United Kingdom . . . 104
Some general lessons from the United Kingdom experience . . . 120

Contents

CHAPTER 5   *Implementing multilevel SDIs in the United States, Australia, and Canada* . . . 127

The United States . . . 130

Australia . . . 144

Canada . . . 156

Comparative evaluation . . . 168

CHAPTER 6   *SDI bodies at the regional level:*

The European Umbrella Organisation for Geographic Information . . . 179

The development of EUROGI . . . 188

Some current activities . . . 204

A profile of EUROGI's national GI association members . . . 208

An exchange of letters . . . 214

CHAPTER 7   *SDI bodies at the global level:*

The global spatial data infrastructure . . . 221

The evolution of the GSDI . . . 224

The GSDI Association: A profile . . . 240

Evaluation . . . 248

CHAPTER 8   *Conclusions* . . . 253

Shifts in SDI development . . . 256

The diffusion of SDIs . . . 258

The evolution of SDIs . . . 262

Implementing multilevel SDIs . . . 264

The hierarchy of SDIs . . . 268

Final remarks . . . 272

References . . . 276

List of acronyms . . . 286

Index . . . 290

Box 2.1   The Australian Spatial Data Infrastructure (1998) . . . 32

Box 2.2   The U.S. National Spatial Data Infrastructure (1998) . . . 33

Box 2.3   Qatar's National Geographic Information System (1998) . . . 33

Box 2.4   Portugal's Sistema Nacionale de Informacao Geografica (1998) . . . 34

Box 2.5   The Netherlands National Geographic Information
             Infrastructure (1998) . . . 34

Box 2.6   Indonesia's National Geographic Information System (1998) . . . 35

Box 2.7   Malaysia's National Land Information System (1998) . . . 35

Box 2.8   The Korean National Geographic Information System (1998) . . . 36

Box 2.9   The Japanese National Spatial Data Infrastructure (1998) . . . 36

Box 2.10   The Canadian Geospatial Data Infrastructure (1998) . . . 37

Box 2.11   The United Kingdom's National Geospatial Data
             Framework (1998) . . . 37

Box 2.12   Infraestructura Colombiana de Datos Espaciales (ICDE) . . . 52

Box 2.13   South Africa's National Spatial Information Framework . . . 52

Box 2.14   Hungary's National Spatial Data Strategy . . . 53

Box 3.1   The National SDI of the Czech Republic . . . 65

Box 3.2   The Finnish National Spatial Data Infrastructure . . . 65

Box 3.3   Chile's Sistema Nacionale de Informacion Territoriale . . . 69

Box 3.4   Mexico's IDEMEX . . . 69

Box 3.5   The Indian National Spatial Data Infrastructure . . . 74

Box 3.6   Nepal's National Geographic Information Infrastructure
             Program . . . 74

Box 3.7   Ghana's National Framework for Geographic Information
             Management . . . 79

Box 3.8   The Kenyan National Spatial Data Infrastructure . . . 79

List of boxes

Box 4.1   The Future Search method . . . 109

Box 4.2   Profile of Mick Cory, Chief Executive, Ordnance Survey
Northern Ireland, Belfast . . . 110

Box 4.3   Profile of Gesche Schmid, ICT and Information Manager,
Medway District Council, Chatham, Kent . . . 118

Box 4.4   What happened to the other ten national SDIs surveyed in 1998? . . . 125

Box 5.1   Profile of Randall (Randy) Johnson, MetroGIS Staff Coordinator,
Minneapolis–St. Paul, Minnesota . . . 139

Box 5.2   Victoria's Land Exchange . . . 152

Box 5.3   Profile of Bruce Thompson, Director, Spatial Information Infrastructure,
Strategic Policy and Projects, Department of Sustainability and
Environment . . . 155

Box 5.4   Profile of David Finley, Manager, Topographic Infrastructure,
Service New Brunswick, Fredericton, New Brunswick . . . 167

Box 6.1   An alternative regional SDI model : The Permanent Committee
on Geographic Information for Asia and the Pacific . . . 182

Box 6.2   Profile of Chukwudozie (Dozie) Ezigbalike, Senior Geographic
Information Systems Officer, United Nations Economic Commission
for Africa, Addis Ababa, Ethiopia . . . 184

Box 6.3   GI2000 . . . 194

Box 6.4   Profile of Anton Wolfkamp, Secretary General (1999–2002),
EUROGI, Apeldoorn, Netherlands . . . 195

Box 6.5   The reuse of public-sector information directive . . . 198

Box 6.6   The INfrastructure for SPatial InfoRmation in Europe (INSPIRE)
initiative . . . 199

Box 7.1   Profile of Santiago Borrero, Secretary General, Pan American Institute
for Geography and History, Mexico City, Mexico
(past president of GSDI, 2001–2002) . . . 234

Box 7.2   Profile of Mukund Rao, Deputy Director, Earth Observations System
Programme Office, Indian Space Research Organization (ISRO)
Headquarters, Bangalore, India (president of the GSDI Association,
2004–2005) . . . 235

List of figures

Figure 1.1   Information flows between data producers and data users
              in the Netherlands . . . 21

Figure 2.1   Innovativeness and adopter categories . . . 28

Figure 2.2   The eleven countries with national SDI initiatives . . . 31

Figure 2.3   Countries responding positively to the GSDI survey in 1998–2000 . . . 50

Figure 3.1   The state of play in Europe in spring 2003 . . . 61

Figure 3.2   Status of SDI in twenty-one countries in the Americas in 2000 . . . 67

Figure 3.3   Asia and Pacific countries responding to the regional fundamental data
              sets questionnaire in 2000 . . . 71

Figure 3.4   Partial list of SDI initiatives in Africa in 2003 . . . 76

Figure 4.1   The United Kingdom . . . 105

Figure 5.1   The United States (Alaska and Hawaii not shown) with case study
              area highlighted . . . 130

Figure 5.2   Twin Cities Metropolitan Areas MetroGIS location . . . 141

Figure 5.3   MetroGIS 2003 poster . . . 143

Figure 5.4   Australia with case study area highlighted . . . 144

Figure 5.5   CadLite: A seamless cadastral database for Australia . . . 148

Figure 5.6   Canada with case study areas highlighted . . . 157

Figure 5.7   A summary of Canadian data agencies . . . 163

Figure 5.8   The home page of Service New Brunswick . . . 165

Figure 6.1   National members of EUROGI . . . 201

Figure 7.1   The GSDI Board of Directors in July 2003 . . . 242

Figure 8.1   Geo One-Stop portal . . . 259

List of tables

Table 1.1   SDIs: Global to local . . . 15

Table 1.2   Some key players in the geographic information and spatial data
infrastructure field . . . 18

Table 2.1   The eleven innovators and early adopters . . . 30

Table 2.2   Some key indicators of the innovator and early adopter countries . . . 39

Table 3.1   SDI state of play in Europe in spring 2003 . . . 62

Table 3.2   Status of SDI in twenty-one countries in the Americas in 2000 . . . 68

Table 3.3   Asia and Pacific countries responding to the regional fundamental data
sets questionnaire in 2000 . . . 72

Table 3.4   Partial list of SDI initiatives in Africa in 2003 . . . 77

Table 3.5   Some key indicators for the case study countries . . . 81

Table 4.1   Population of the United Kingdom in 2001 . . . 105

Table 4.2   A comparative evaluation of UK SDIs . . . 122

Table 5.1   Examples of organizational structures created to facilitate
NSDI implementation . . . 174

Table 6.1   Some key indicators for the European countries . . . 186

Table 6.2   Some strengths and weaknesses of EUROGI as an organization . . . 203

Table 6.3   The establishment of national GI associations in Europe . . . 209

Table 6.4   National GI association names and combined membership . . . 212

Table 7.1   GSDI conferences . . . 224

Table 7.2   The evolution of GSDI . . . 227

Table 7.3   Officers and members of the Board of the GSDI Association
in June 2004 . . . 243

Table 8.1   Current trends in SDI development . . . 257

D r. Ian Masser's lifelong dedication to geography and his experience in the development of spatial data infrastructure (SDI) is unmatched. That he has been able to take time from his work worldwide to write *GIS Worlds* makes it possible for all of us to share his expertise and his understanding of the history of spatial data infrastructures.

The growth and adoption of geographic information systems (GIS) around the world has led to investments in geographic data and networked systems, developing them to their full advantage. Thus, we have the SDI phenomenon. Building a policy framework around GIS infrastructure enables good decision making that benefits citizens of each country with SDIs.

This GIS technology makes a difference in the world. In education, environmental management, disaster response, agriculture, health care, transportation planning, delivery of clean drinking water, the management of power delivery, land-records management, combating poverty, and defense and security, GIS is used every day by governments and their citizens. By making the most of GIS applications, SDIs are becoming an essential element of each country's information and communication technology (ICT) plan, fostered at all levels of government from local to national.

Foreword

Our work together is rooted in the conviction that geographic information and communication are indispensable elements of effective governance, including e-government and transparency in government, good science, and better decision making. Well-maintained SDIs empower people and the institutions that serve them. This is critical in the effort to realize the United Nation's Millennium Development Goals and build a better world in the twenty-first century.

Jack Dangermond
President, ESRI

This book is the product of a personal journey that has taken nearly twenty years. I first became involved as a computer literate urban planner with a human geography background in matters relating to geographic information (GI) policy and spatial data infrastructures (SDIs) during my time as the national coordinator of the United Kingdom Economic and Social Research Council's Regional Research Laboratory (RRL) initiative in the late 1980s. This coincided with the British government's publication of the *Chorley Report on Handling Geographic Information* in May 1987. This report was a milestone in the development of thinking about GI policy not only in the United Kingdom, but also throughout the world as a whole. Its message was both simple and very important: GIS technology has considerable potential for a very wide range of applications throughout both the public and private sectors, but this potential is unlikely to be realized until a number of institutional and organizational barriers have been overcome. Government, as the largest single supplier of GI, has a fundamental part to play in overcoming these barriers.

It was a short step from the publication of the Chorley report to the release of the revised Circular A–16 by the U.S. Office of Management and Budget in October 1990. This established a Federal Geographic Data Committee to coordinate the "development, use, sharing and dissemination of surveying, mapping and related spatial data." This circular marked the first step toward the creation of a National Spatial Data Infrastructure for the United States as promulgated by Executive Order 12906 signed by President Clinton in April 1994.

By this time I had moved on to become codirector of the European Science Foundation's GISDATA scientific program together with François Salge from Institut Géographique National (IGN) France. This program was funded by fifteen National Science Councils from fourteen European countries and also had strong links with the U.S. National Science Foundation through its National Centre for Geographic Information and Analysis. One of its three themes was data integration. For this reason three of its twelve specialist meetings were devoted to discussions of the factors governing the diffusion and take-up of GIS in different European countries, the development of strategies to make spatial data more widely available throughout Europe, and the creation of a European geographic information infrastructure.

During the lifetime of the GISDATA program (1993–1997), I was involved in a number of exciting GI developments that were taking place at the European level. The most important of these was the creation of an independent European Umbrella Organisation for Geographic Information (EUROGI) with help from the European Commission in November 1993, the series of debates hosted by the commission regarding the creation of a European Geographic Information Infrastructure (GI2000) between February 1995 and September 1998, and the organization of the first GSDI Conference in Bonn in September 1996. I was also fortunate in being able to take time out from my normal university duties during this period to carry out the comparative evaluation of national spatial data infrastructures in Australia, Britain, the Netherlands, and the United States that was published in *Governments and Geographic Information* in March 1998.

Between 1998 and 2002, I was associated with the International Institute for Geo-Information Science and Earth Observation (ITC) in the Netherlands. This gave me an opportunity to broaden my range of SDI experience through missions to places as far afield as China, Colombia, India, Peru, and Vietnam.

In March 1999, I was elected president of EUROGI. EUROGI collectively represents more than 6,500 organizations from both the public and private sectors that are members of its twenty-three member organizations. The most interesting developments during my time as president (1993–2003) were EUROGI's participation in the European-Commission-funded Geographic Information Networks in Europe (GINIE) project that provided lots of opportunities to explore various aspects of SDI development, and the organization of the sixth GSDI conference in Budapest in September 2002 on a global to local theme. At the end of this conference I took over the presidency of the emerging GSDI Association with a remit to make it operational and prepare a draft strategic plan in time for GSDI 7 in Bangalore in February 2004.

I have often been asked who were the most important influences on my own thinking about SDIs. I have discussed these matters with lots of people over the last twenty years but would nevertheless single out three individuals in this respect. These are my old RRL colleague Mike Blakemore, who first made me reflect on the role of government in relation to GI, David Rhind, who stimulated my research on the development of SDIs throughout the world, and Nancy Tosta, who, more than anyone else, made me realize that the successful implementation of SDIs is very much dependent on the degree to which they reflect the capabilities and aspirations of all the stakeholders involved.

The preparation of this book would not have been possible without the informed comments and suggestions that have been made by those directly involved in the development and implementation of SDIs. In particular I would like to thank Santiago Borrero, Mick Cory, Dozie Ezigbalike, David Finley, Randy Johnson, Mukund Rao, Gesche Schmid, and Anton Wolfkamp for providing the materials for their personal profiles at short notice. I would also like to acknowledge the valuable assistance that I have received from Bill Burgess, Lillian Cheung, David Coleman, Chris Corbin, Max Craglia, Joep Crompvoets, Lionel Elliott, Mike Goodchild, Don Grant, Ravi Gupta, Dora Ines Rey, Steve Jacoby, Judy Jerome, Rui Pedro Juliao, Paul Kelly, Jeff Labonte, Karen Levoleger, Mark Linehan, Angus MacDonald, Gareth McGrath, Bino Marchesini, Ron Matzner, Katie Medcalf, Adrian Moore, Zorica Nedovic–Budic, Eva Pauknerova, Abbas Rajabifard, Al Stevens, Bruce Thompson, and Ian Williamson. It goes without saying, however, that I alone am responsible for the interpretation of the comments and materials that they have given me.

I must also thank Jeanne Foust and David Maguire for encouraging me to start writing this book. Thanks go to Jack Dangermond, president of ESRI, and Christian Harder, publisher of ESRI Press, for supporting this book. I also thank the excellent team at ESRI Press: Judy Hawkins edited the book and helped sharpen up the arguments, Jennifer Galloway designed the book and improved the overall quality of its presentation, Tiffany Wilkerson copyedited the book, Suzanne Davis designed the cover, and Cliff Crabbe supervised print production. The final outcome owes a great deal to their helpful and constructive suggestions.

I also owe a great debt to my wife, Suzy, who has had to put up with me during the writing of this book. For this reason I dedicate it to her with much love and affection.

Taddington
November 2004

Acknowledgments

The author and publisher wish to thank the following individuals and organizations for granting permissions to publish materials in this book.

Canadian Institute of Geomatics, Ottawa, for the modified version of the table published in *Geomatica* 55, 221.

Max Craglia, University of Sheffield, for extracts from chapter 5 in M. Craglia et al., *Geographic information in Europe,* GINIE project deliverable 6.5.1, 2003.

Free Press (part of Simon and Schuster, New York), for the diagram published on p. 247 of E. M. Rogers, *Diffusion of innovations,* Fourth edition, 1983.

MetroGIS, St. Paul, Minnesota, for the poster displayed at URISA 2003.

Netherlands Council for Geographic Information (RAVI), Amersfoort, for the modified version of table published in *Structuurschets vastgoedinformatie voorziening, deel lll: inventarisatie en analyse,* 1992.

PSMA Australia Ltd, Griffith, ACT, for the CadLite map of Australia.

Service New Brunswick, Fredericton, New Brunswick, for the home page of SNB Web site.

Spatial Networks Pvt Ltd, Hyderabad, for the extracts from paper published in *Geospatial Today* 2, 5, 11–12, 2004.

Al Stevens, FGDC, Reston, Virginia, for the photograph taken at Cambridge in 2003.

Taylor and Francis Ltd., Abingdon, Oxon, for the extracts from paper published in *International Journal of Geographic Information Science* 13, 67–84, 1999.

CHAPTER I

An overview

In 1987, the British Government Committee of Enquiry on Handling Geographic Information, chaired by Lord Chorley, hailed the advent of geographical information systems (GIS) as "the biggest step forward in the handling of geographic information since the invention of the map" (Department of Environment 1987, para 1.7). They viewed GIS as "a system for capturing, storing, checking, integrating, manipulating, analysing, and displaying data which is spatially referenced to the Earth" (p. 132). This definition not only highlights the wide range of activities encompassed in this technology, but it also substantially expands the amount of information that can be treated as geographic information. This includes any kind of information linked to a geographic location through a coordinate reference or via its postal address or a reference to an administrative area. In this way the case of GIS illustrates the impact of recent developments in computer-based information technology on existing data management practices.

The impact of GIS on traditional map production and utilization practices is similar to that of the word processor on conventional typewriters and publishing practices. Word-processing technology made use of the typewriter keyboard, but it separated the processes of text input from text output. Inputted text could also be stored within the computer and retrieved if necessary at a later date. As a result, input text could be updated and modified over time, and the same input file could be output in a wide range of different formats and sizes for different purposes. Furthermore, sections of the file could be copied and incorporated in other documents without difficulty. In the process, the new technology massively changed the nature of text creation and completely transformed the whole publishing industry.

Similar developments occurred with GIS and traditional map production. GIS technology made use of conventional cartographic methods but separated the input of digital cartographic data from its output. Consequently, once a digital cartographic database was created, it could be output in a wide variety of formats to suit different purposes. It could also be updated over time to take account of developments such as new road construction and house-building projects. Sections of the map files could also be abstracted from the database and incorporated in other databases where necessary. In addition, the creation of geographic information systems made it easy to display statistical data in various map formats, as well as opening up new opportunities for spatial analysis.

The parallels between these developments and geographic information systems become evident in a report prepared by the U.S. Mapping Sciences Committee (MSC) entitled *Toward a Coordinated Infrastructure for the Nation.*

> Unlike maps, strings of geographic or spatially referenced digital data can be aggregated, transformed, and shared. Spatial data can now be more easily isolated and abstracted from the particular application in which it was developed and channelled into other settings and other GIS where it can be reused, enhanced, and routed to other potential user communities. The old "top down" model [especially appropriate for base data from (mapping agencies)] is inadequate to represent the multidirectional alternative information flows that are now theoretically feasible (National Research Council 1993, 8).

GIS is essentially an applications driven technology. Consequently, its nature and potential are best illustrated by reference to some typical applications. Much of its initial development was linked to the requirements of landscape architects and urban planners who wanted to bring together data from a variety of sources and overlay them on a standard topographic basemap to highlight sites that had potential for future urban expansion. GIS technologies proved to be a very effective tool for this purpose. They made it possible, for example, to superimpose map layers showing sites that were too steep for building operations, as well as sites where development was prohibited because of their scientific importance, together with sites that were within easy reach of the existing road network, onto an existing map base. The resultant "sieve" map provided them with a powerful analytical tool for policy formulation and design.

The same technologies also transformed many conventional administrative procedures in the public and private sectors. In many countries, for example, cadastral authorities pioneered the use of computers to manage the information contained in their land and property registers from the 1960s onwards. However, these registers contained only textual and statistical records, and separate files had to be maintained of the paper maps that showed the location and boundaries of each land parcel. The advent of GIS and the growing availability of digital map data from the mid-1980s onward made it possible to integrate textual, statistical, and map data within a single system. Such developments dramatically improved the administrative operations of these agencies and were also reflected in the quality of the services that they provided for the public as a whole.

WHY GIS IS VALUABLE

THE REPORT ALSO HIGHLIGHTS THE EXTENT to which GIS technology radically changes the potential value that is attached to geographic information. "Spatially referenced digital data can perhaps be thought of as molecules of water that in aggregate form a circulating fluid, flowing freely from application to application (or from system to system). Conceived of in this fashion, information can be seen to take on value and become a marketable commodity, quite apart from the context, need, or application for which it was originally developed" (National Research Council 1993, 8).

The extent of the value added by GIS technology is not easy to estimate with any precision, but two examples from Britain and the United States give some indication of its scale. A study for the British Ordnance Survey estimated that its products and services amounted to between 12 and 20 percent of the gross value added (GVA) and generated between £79 and £136 billion worth of GVA in 1996 (Oxford Economic Research Associates 1999). A similar study undertaken in the United States by the National Academy for Public Administration (NAPA) concluded that the spatial data products of twelve core federal functions facilitated national economic sectors from real estate and insurance to agriculture and defense worth more than $3.5 trillion (National Academy of Public Administration 1998, 12–3).

A new role for governments

However, these benefits cannot be realized without help from governments. To realize the potential of the technology on the scale quoted above, governments will have to regard geographic information as an asset that needs to be carefully managed in the national interest. The concept of asset management in this case is closely linked to the notion of an infrastructure. In this respect, national geographic information assets have much in common with other types of infrastructure such as national road and railway networks. In the process, governments will not only need to promote the diffusion of GIS technologies, but they will also have to take steps to overcome the institutional barriers that inhibit the potential use of GIS. These include a wide range of issues relating to restrictions on data availability and access.

The MSC suggests that this will require the U.S. government to create a national spatial data infrastructure (NSDI) for the nation as a whole. This is "the means to assemble geographic information that describes the arrangement and attributes of features and phenomena on the earth. The infrastructure includes the materials, technology, and people necessary to acquire, process, and distribute such information to meet a wide variety of needs" (National Research Council 1993, 16). The MSC also points out that NSDIs are already in existence in most parts of the world, but these are essentially *ad hoc* affairs arising out of the institutional arrangements that have been made for the discharge of responsibilities for cadastral, mapping, and statistical data.

NSDIs that facilitate the more effective use of national geographic information resources require governments to take a much more proactive role. This view is evident in the Executive Order signed by U.S. President Clinton entitled

"Coordinating Geographic Data Acquisition and Access: The National Spatial Data Infrastructure" (Executive Office of the President 1994). This gives a good overview of the driving forces that lay behind the U.S. government's thinking with respect to the need for an NSDI.

> Geographic information is critical to promote economic development, improve our stewardship of natural resources, and to protect the environment. Modern technology now permits improved acquisition, distribution, and utilization of geographic (or geospatial) data and mapping. The National Performance Review has recommended that the Executive Branch develop, in cooperation with state, local, and tribal governments and the private sector, a coordinated National Spatial Data Infrastructure to support public and private sector applications of geospatial data in such areas as transportation, community development, agriculture, emergency response, environmental management, and information technology (Executive Office of the President 1994).

Once a mechanism for coordinating a national spatial data infrastructure is in place, several tasks are identified in the Executive Order to guide the NSDI builders. Section 3 defines the concept of a national geospatial data clearinghouse as "a distributed network of geospatial producers, managers, and users linked electronically." This reflects the need to create various types of metadata service to increase user awareness of what data is available in each country. Section 4 sets out the procedures to be followed with respect to data standards, while section 5 describes the concept of a national digital geospatial data framework. The latter acknowledges that some core or framework data sets are common to a very wide range of applications and need to be made interoperable with one another during NSDI implementation.

The SDI phenomenon

Since the publication of the Executive Order in 1994, many countries throughout the world have taken steps to establish NSDIs. Although the words used vary from country to country, they have three elements in common. First, they are all explicitly national in nature. Second, they refer either to geographic information, spatial data, or geospatial data. Finally, they also use terms such as infrastructure, strategy, system, or framework, which imply the existence of some form of coordinating mechanism for policy formulation and implementation purposes. Given these common features, it can be argued that these initiatives should be regarded collectively as national spatial data infrastructures.

For example, Portugal's National System for Geographic Information, which was set up under the Decreto Lei No. 53/1990, even predates the U.S. Executive Order, while the Korean government's National Geographic Information System program began in 1995. In the same year, the Dutch Council for Real Estate Management (RAVI) published its National Geographic Information Infrastructure. The Canadian government started its Canadian Geospatial Data Infrastructure program in 1996, and Hungary's government published its National Spatial Data Strategy in 1997. Colombia's Infraestructura Colombiana de Datos Especiales dates back to 1999, and Ghana's National Framework for Geospatial Information Management to 2000. Similarly, India's NSDI program and Chile's Sistema Nacional de Informacion Territoriale both began in 2001.

Estimates vary as to the number of NSDI initiatives that have come into being. By the end of 1996, at least eleven NSDIs were already in operation in various parts of the world (Masser 1999). By 2000, about fifty countries in all parts of the world had responded to a survey to say that they were engaged in

SDI development *(www.spatial.maine.edu/~onsrud/GSDI.htm)*. Data collected by Crompvoets and Bregt (2003) suggests that by 2003 as many as 120 countries had considered projects of this kind.

Similar initiatives have also been emerging since the late 1980s at the subnational levels. This is particularly the case in countries with a federal system of government where the responsibilities for geographic information management have been devolved to the state or provincial levels. These are particularly well developed in countries such as Australia, Canada, Germany, Malaysia, Spain, and the United States. Examples of such initiatives include North Rhine Westphalia in Germany (Brueggemann 2004), Johor State in Malaysia (Fritz 2004), Catalonia in Spain (Guimet 2004), and Northern Ireland in the United Kingdom (Department of Culture, Arts, and Leisure 2002)

In addition to these initiatives, there have also been a number of transnational initiatives. These include the Environmental Information System Program for Sub Saharan Africa (EIS–Africa 2002), intergovernmental collaboration in the Tisza river basin in eastern Europe (Podolcsak and Jarolics 2003), the Blue Plan for the Mediterranean basin *(www.planbleu.org)*, and the European Commission's INfrastructure for SPatial InfoRmation in Europe (INSPIRE) initiative *(inspire.jrc.it)*.

Alongside these developments new institutions have come into being at the continental and global levels to promote SDI development. In 1993, the first of these continental bodies was set up in Europe. This was closely followed by the creation of a similar body for Asia and the Pacific (Masser et al. 2003). In September 1996, the first of what subsequently became a regular series of Global Spatial Data Infrastructure conferences was held at Bonn in Germany. In February 2004, this body became the GSDI Association (Holland and Borrero 2004).

Thus, there can be little doubt that the rapid diffusion of NSDIs throughout the world has given rise to an NSDI phenomenon. However, it is clear that while this phenomenon is particularly apparent at the national level, parallel developments are also taking place at the subnational and, to a lesser extent, at the transnational level. Consequently, it will be considered as an SDI rather than an NSDI phenomenon throughout the rest of this book.

THE OBJECTIVES OF THIS BOOK

THE MAIN OBJECTIVE OF THIS BOOK IS TO provide an overview of the developments that have taken place with respect to spatial data infrastructures (SDIs) over the last ten to fifteen years. It focuses on the new policy options and the institutional structures associated with the formulation and implementation of SDI initiatives. Note: technical issues are dealt with only briefly. The overall scope is worldwide, although particular attention is given to developments in four countries regarded as among the leaders in the field: Australia, Canada, the United Kingdom, and the United States.

Four main themes are explored in some detail:

- ⟡ Chapter 1: An overview
- ⟡ Chapters 2 and 3: *Diffusion* of SDIs
- ⟡ Chapter 4: *Evolution* of SDIs
- ⟡ Chapter 5: *Implementation* of SDIs
- ⟡ Chapters 6 and 7: *Institution building* for regional, continental, and global SDIs
- ⟡ Chapter 8: Conclusions

Chapters 2 and 3 consider the diffusion of SDIs throughout the world with particular reference to the diffusion of innovations model developed originally by Everett Rogers (1995). Chapter 2 draws upon earlier research by the author to explore some of the main features of the innovators and early adopters of SDIs as they appeared in 1998. Chapter 3 examines some of the characteristics of the early majority of adopters that have begun working on SDIs since 1998. The findings of chapter 2 are then compared to those of chapter 3 to highlight some of the most important differences between the strategies involved in each of the two periods.

Given that it may take many years or even decades before these SDIs become fully operational, and the institutional context in which they are developed may change substantially during this time, chapter 4 examines the evolution of thinking about SDIs with reference to the experiences of the United Kingdom over the last ten years. The United Kingdom case is especially interesting in view of the difficulties experienced by the National Geospatial Data Framework that led to its eventual take over by the Association for Geographic Information in 2001 and the extent to which the course of SDI development has subsequently been influenced by the devolution of powers to elected regional assemblies in Scotland, Wales, and Northern Ireland since 1998.

The next three chapters consider the multilevel implementation of SDIs and institution building for regional, continental, and global SDIs. These form a hierarchy *(table 1.1)*. The national level occupies a central position in this hierarchy as the critical link or hinge between the higher and the lower levels (Rajabifard et al. 2000). At this level, strategic initiatives are formulated and implemented by governments in most countries to manage their national geographic information assets. The term "national" in this context refers to a relative rather than an absolute sense. Consequently, it may refer in some countries to comprehensive and inclusive GI strategies from the standpoint of the stakeholders involved, whereas in others it may describe initiatives that are partial in their coverage and limited in stakeholder participation.

The main tasks associated with SDI development at the subnational level are closely linked to the operational needs of day-to-day decision making *(table 1.1)*. There is both a top-down and a bottom-up dimension to the relationships between the local and national levels. National SDI strategies drive local-level SDI strategies. However, as most of the detailed database maintenance and updating tasks are carried out at the local level, the input of local government also has a considerable influence on the process of SDI implementation at the national level.

Global and continental SDI bodies also have a strong interest in strategic issues and are actively engaged in promoting capacity building in their respective areas. They also play an important part in facilitating SDI development. However, in the absence of governmental bodies at these levels, the challenge facing those involved is to create the institutions that are needed to carry out these tasks.

With this in mind, chapter 5 examines the experiences of the United States, Australia, and Canada with respect to the multilevel implementation of NSDIs at the state and local levels. Chapters 6 and 7 consider institution building within a hierarchy of regional, continental, and global levels, respectively. The experiences of the oldest of these regional bodies, the European Umbrella Organisation for Geographic Information (EUROGI), are evaluated in chapter 6 while chapter 7 considers the development of the Global Spatial Data Infrastructure Association.

The final chapter of the book reflects the findings of the analysis as a whole and identifies some of the issues for future research that emerge from these findings.

Global and regional SDIs	Global and regional forums for collaboration and the exchange of ideas and experiences
National SDIs	Strategic initiatives concerned with the management of national information assets
Local SDIs	Municipal and provincial initiatives concerned with the operational needs of day-to-day decision making

Table 1.1
SDIs: Global to local.

SETTING THE SCENE

SDIs redefined

A more comprehensive definition of a spatial data infrastructure than the MSC's definition can be found on the Global Spatial Data Infrastructure Web site *(www.gsdi.org)*. It conveys some of the complexity of the issues involved:

> A . . . spatial data infrastructure supports *ready access to geographic information.* This is achieved through *the co-ordinated actions of nations and organizations* that promote awareness and implementation of complimentary policies, common standards and effective mechanisms for the development and availability of interoperable digital geographic data and technologies *to support decision making at all scales for multiple purposes.* These actions *encompass the policies, organizational remits, data, technologies, standards, delivery mechanisms, and financial and human resources* necessary to ensure that those working at the (national) and regional scale are not impeded in meeting their objectives. (Author's italics)

This definition shows that four key concepts underpin all SDIs:

1. The overriding objective of an SDI is to maximize the use of geographic information. This requires ready access to the geographic information assets held by a wide range of stakeholders in both the public and the private sector.

2. SDIs cannot be realized without coordinated action on the part of governments.

3. SDIs must be user driven. Their primary purpose is to support decision making for many different purposes.

4. SDI implementation involves a wide range of activities. These include not only technical matters such as data, technologies, standards, and delivery mechanisms, but also institutional matters related to organizational responsibilities and overall national information policies, as well as questions relating to the availability of the financial and human resources needed for this task.

Who are the main stakeholders in SDIs?

It is also important at the outset to identify some of the most important players or stakeholders with interests in geographic information and spatial data infrastructure matters. Rhind (2000, 42) offers a list of key players *(table 1.2)*. This indicates both the large numbers of players involved and their great diversity in terms of size and resources. It must also be recognized that the role and relative importance of these players may vary considerably from country to country as a result of the differing institutional contexts with which they operate.

The public sector, in the form of central and local government organizations, is both a major producer and consumer of geographic information products and services *(table 1.2)*. Key data producers within the public sector are typically surveying and mapping agencies, organizations concerned with land- and property-related matters such as the cadastre, and national

Table 1.2

Some key players in the geographic information and spatial data infrastructure field.

Central government organizations

Local government organizations

Commercial sector
    Information traders and publishers
    Hardware/software vendors
    Conglomerates

Not-for-profit/nongovernmental organizations

Academics

Individuals

Source: Rhind (2000, 42).

census and statistical bodies. Alongside these can often be found other data producers who are concerned with particular thematic interests such as environmental, geological, and hydrographical data.

Most central government ministries and local government departments are, in varying degrees of intensity, both producers and consumers of geographic information. In addition to these bodies, a wide range of other government bodies such as specialized research laboratories may also make extensive use of geographic information products and services. The number and diversity of these bodies is likely to vary from country to country. In highly developed countries such as the United Kingdom, for example, nearly one hundred separate public-sector agencies are members of the government's Intragovernmental Group for Geographic Information *(www.iggi. gov.uk)*.

In many countries, particularly those with federal systems of government, many key functions with respect to the collection and dissemination of geographic information may be devolved to the state or provincial levels. The powers given to local governments also vary considerably from country to country. In countries where powers are centralized, local government bodies may exercise relatively limited powers, whereas in others their range of administrative responsibilities and resources can be considerable.

The responsibility for utilities such as electricity, gas and water, and telecommunications and transport networks falls into the public sector in some countries, while in others it forms part of the private sector. These bodies tend to make extensive use of geographic products and services to manage their operations.

Three different types of private-sector organization are involved directly with geographic information *(table 1.2)*. These include companies that make their living primarily from producing and publishing value-added products from existing information sources. Then there are the hardware and software vendors who typically provide solutions to consumers often on an exclusive basis. Lastly, there are also a number of conglomerates that combine elements of the other two types often with the provision of a range of management consultancy services.

In addition to these companies, many other private-sector companies make use of geographic information products in the course of their activities. These include banks, insurance companies, retailing operations, and real estate companies.

The next category on Rhind's list are not-for-profit or nongovernmental organizations (NGOs). These include many different kinds of organization with many different demands for geographic information products and services. The range from international environmental bodies such Greenpeace and Friends of the Earth to groups concerned with particular neighborhoods at the local level. This type of organization is a particularly important feature of the landscape in many less-developed countries.

The last two categories are those sections of academia that have a professional interest in geographic information matters and individual citizens who wish to use GI to enhance their personal skills and knowledge development or to participate in decision making at the local or national levels.

Some of the interactions that take place between players in the Netherlands with particular reference to the property market highlight the key roles played by the national Cadastre, the national mapping agency (Topografische Dienst), and the national statistical agency in the provision of geographic information to both public- and private-sector users *(figure 1.1)*. At the same time, it also shows the extent to which the various directorates of the Ministry of Housing, Spatial

Planning, and the Environment, together with the two levels of local government occupy central positions as users of information from a wide variety of agencies. In contrast, the utility companies, the water boards, and the notaries are large users of geographic information, but these tend to draw upon a relatively limited number of sources. The diagram shows the extent to which individual households in the Netherlands are both receivers and creators of geographic information.

Figure 1.1
Information flows between data producers and data users in the Netherlands.

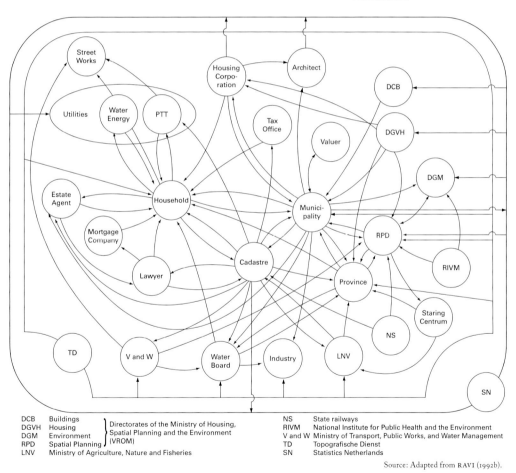

DCB Buildings
DGVH Housing
DGM Environment
RPD Spatial Planning
LNV Ministry of Agriculture, Nature and Fisheries

} Directorates of the Ministry of Housing, Spatial Planning and the Environment (VROM)

NS State railways
RIVM National Institute for Public Health and the Environment
V and W Ministry of Transport, Public Works, and Water Management
TD Topografische Dienst
SN Statistics Netherlands

Source: Adapted from RAVI (1992b).

SUMMARY

THIS CHAPTER HAS INTRODUCED THE concepts of GIS and SDI and has given some indication as to the driving forces behind the latter. In the process, attention has been drawn to the rapid diffusion of SDIs that has occurred over the last ten years, which has led to the emergence of the SDI phenomenon. The main objectives of this book have been outlined. The sequence of the arguments in the following chapters from the overall diffusion of SDIs to more detailed studies of their evolution and implementation within the context of a wider hierarchy has been explained. The final section of the chapter has considered in greater depth the main factors underlying the concept of an SDI and has identified some of the main players and stakeholders in the geographic information and spatial data infrastructure fields.

CHAPTER 2

The diffusion of national SDIs

Innovators and early adopters

One of the problems that those involved in diffusion research normally face is the lack of contemporary materials that describe the early stages of diffusion. However, the findings of an earlier study carried out by the author in 1998 (Masser 1999) review the experiences of the "first generation" of eleven SDIs that were in operation in 1996. This provides a starting point for a two-stage analysis of the SDI diffusion process.

This chapter is divided into four main sections:

1. The main features of the diffusion of innovations model that provides an overall framework for this analysis

2. Short profiles of the eleven innovators and early adopters as they were in 1998

3. A comparative evaluation of the nature of these initiatives with regard to the geographic, economic, and administrative circumstances of the countries involved, the driving forces behind the initiatives, and their main features

4. An evaluation of these findings with respect to the characteristics of the innovators and early adopters described in the diffusions of innovations model

THE DIFFUSION OF INNOVATIONS MODEL

THE DIFFUSION OF INNOVATIONS MODEL was originally developed more than half a century ago for the study of the diffusion of hybrid corn species in Iowa (Ryan and Gross 1943). Since that time it has been used to study thousands of different types of innovation in all parts of the world. There are four distinctive elements in the diffusion of innovations model developed by Everett Rogers. He defines diffusion as "the process by which (1) an innovation (2) is communicated through channels (3) over time (4) among the members of a social system" (Rogers 1995, 10). To understand the reasoning behind this definition, it is necessary to consider each of these elements in more detail.

The first element, the innovation, can be defined as "an idea, practice, or object that is perceived as new by an individual or unit of adoption" (Rogers 1995, 11). An SDI can be defined in these terms because the government agencies, or units of adoption, see it as a new concept. Innovations such as SDIs are dynamic innovations as they are likely to be re-invented during the diffusion process to meet the needs of different national circumstances.

The second element, the communication channel, refers to the means by which messages and information are sent from one group to another. Previous studies have shown that interpersonal channels are particularly important in the diffusion of innovations such as SDIs as most people rely on the subjective evaluations of the innovation that are conveyed to them by individuals like themselves who have some experience in the field.

The third element is time. Rogers regards the diffusion process as innovativeness or "the degree to which an individual or a unit of adoption is relatively earlier in adopting new ideas than other members of the system" (Rogers 1995, 22). With this in mind, he defines five adopter categories, each of which has its own distinctive features:

1. Innovators
2. Early adopters
3. Early majority
4. Late majority
5. Laggards

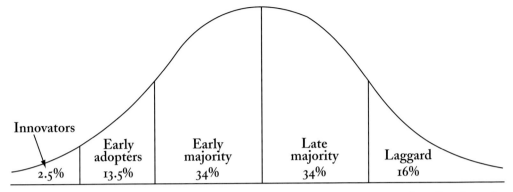

Innovators

Early adopters

Early majority

Late majority

Laggard

2.5%   13.5%   34%   34%   16%

Source: Rogers (1995, 247).

Figure 2.1
Innovativeness and adopter categories.

Rogers also suggests that the rate of adoption in most innovations follows a course similar to a bell-shaped curve *(figure 2.1)*. In the first instance, a relatively small number of innovators adopt the innovation. As the number of adoptions increases and reaches a critical mass, the slope of the curve becomes steeper during the early adopters and early majority periods. After this, the rate of adoption trails off during the late majority and laggard periods.

The last of the four elements concerns the social system in which the innovation takes place. Rogers defines this as "a set of interrelated units that are engaged in joint problem solving to accomplish a common goal" (Rogers 1995, 24). This shared objective is what binds the adopters together.

Each of the four elements raises interesting questions about the nature of the SDI diffusion process as a whole. In addition, Rogers' descriptions of the characteristics of the five user categories provides a good starting point for the evaluation of the experiences of the first three categories in this chapter and the next one. The descriptions also suggest some features of the fourth and fifth user categories that may be useful in the next stages of the diffusion process. For these reasons, they are described in more detail later.

Rogers also argues that innovators account for about 2.5 percent of the total population. Their interest in new ideas leads them out of their existing networks and into more cosmopolitan social relationships. Because of the risks involved, innovators must be able to cope with a high degree of uncertainty about an innovation at the time of adoption. Early adopters account for about 13.5 percent of the population. They tend to be a more integrated part of the existing system than the innovators. However, because early adopters are not too far ahead of the average, they provide an important role model for many other members of the social system. The early adopter also decreases uncertainty about a new idea by adopting it and plays a major part in conveying the subjective evaluations of the innovation to their peers through their interpersonal networks. As a result, they are instrumental in getting an innovation to the point of critical mass and hence in the successful diffusion of an innovation.

The size of the early majority is likely to be about one third of the total population. This is considerably greater than both the first two categories put together. This type adopts a new idea just ahead of the average members of the system. They provide much of the interconnectedness in the network through their frequent interactions with their peers but seldom hold positions of opinion leadership. Nevertheless, their unique position between the relatively early and the relatively late to adopt means that they have an important impact on the overall rate of adoption.

The other two categories are essentially followers rather than leaders. The late majority make up a third of the system and often approach an innovation with a skeptical and cautious air having bowed to increasing pressures from their peers. These critical qualities are likely to increase in the case of the laggards who make up the final sixth of the population.

INNOVATORS OR EARLY ADOPTERS

IF ROGERS' PROPORTIONS ARE TAKEN INTO account, the eleven first-generation SDIs include all the innovators and a sprinkling of the early adopters. In practice, however, it is not always easy to separate the two because some of these initiatives represent more a process of continuous development rather than a distinctly new innovation.

Table 2.1
The eleven innovators and early adopters.

COUNTRY	SDI
Australia	Australian Spatial Data Infrastructure
Canada	Canadian Geospatial Data Infrastructure
Indonesia	National Geographic Information Systems
Japan	National Spatial Data Infrastructure
Korea	National Geographic Information System
Malaysia	National Infrastructure for Land Information Systems
Netherlands	National Geographical Information Infrastructure
Portugal	National System for Geographic Information
Qatar	National Geographic Information System
United Kingdom	National Geospatial Data Framework
United States	National Spatial Data Infrastructure

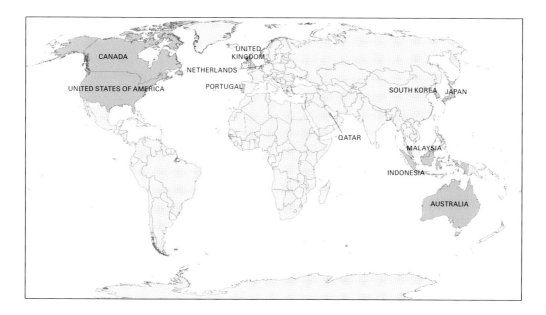

Figure 2.2
The eleven countries with national
SDI initiatives.

The eleven SDI initiatives that were reviewed in 1998 include two initiatives from North America, three from Europe, and six from the Asia and the Pacific regions *(table 2.1 and figure 2.2)*. No initiatives were listed from either Africa or South America. As noted in the previous chapter, the terms used to describe SDIs vary from country to country, but they have three elements in common:

1. They are explicitly national in nature

2. They refer either to geographic information, spatial data, geospatial data, or, in one case, to land information

3. They also refer to terms such as infrastructure, system, or framework, which imply the existence of some form of coordinating mechanism for policy formulation and implementation purposes

The following profiles were originally written in 1998 and represent the position at that time. They have not been updated to accommodate changes that have taken place since. However, further details about subsequent developments in the United Kingdom, the United States, Australia, and Canada can be found in chapters 4 and 5 of this book. Some of the main features of the SDIs in the eleven countries listed in table 2.1 are described in boxes 2.1 to 2.11 in chronological order.

Established in 1986 as a result of an agreement between the Australian prime minister and the heads of state governments, the Australian Land Information Council coordinates the collection and transfer of land-related information between the different levels of government. It also promotes the use of that information in decision making. In 1991, New Zealand became a full member of the council, which was renamed the Australia New Zealand Land Information Council (ANZLIC). In 1998, ANZLIC was based in the Spatial Data Infrastructure Program of the Australian Surveying and Land Information Group (AUSLIG). In 1988, 1990, 1994, and 1997, the council produced a number of major reports on the status of land information in Australia, as well as four versions of their national strategy for the management of land and geographic information. In 1996, ANZLIC produced a discussion paper setting out its vision of an Australian spatial data infrastructure. This argued that most of the components of this infrastructure already existed in some form, but there was nevertheless a need for the community to "more clearly define and describe the infrastructure as a coherent national identity." ANZLIC's role was "to lead the community in defining the components of the national spatial data infrastructure, the characteristics of those components, and provide a vehicle for the determination of national priorities and custodianship."

Box 2.1   The Australian Spatial Data Infrastructure (1998).
   Source: Australia New Zealand Land Information Council (1992 and 1996).

In the United States, an interagency Federal Geographic Data Committee (FGDC) was set up in 1990 as a result of a revised Circular A–16 issued by the Office of Management and Budget (OMB) to coordinate "the development, use, sharing, and dissemination of surveying, mapping, and related spatial data." President Clinton signed Executive Order 12906 entitled "Coordinating Geographic Data Acquisition and Access: The National Spatial Data Infrastructure" on April 11, 1994, "to strengthen and enhance the general policies described in OMB Circular A–16" four years after the establishment of the FGDC. In 1998, the FGDC was based in the National Mapping Division of the U.S. Geological Survey and chaired by the secretary of the Interior. Its members included representatives from all the major ministries with an interest in geographic information together with a variety of other public agencies concerned with its collection and management. The executive order set out in some detail the main tasks to be carried out and defined time limits for each of the initial stages of the National Spatial Data Infrastructure. Apart from the core task of interagency coordination through the FGDC, these included the establishment of a national geospatial data clearinghouse and the creation of a national digital geospatial data framework through a variety of partnerships between agencies at different levels of government and also between the public and private sectors.

Box 2.2   The U.S. National Spatial Data Infrastructure (1998).
   Sources: Executive Office of the President (1994), Office of Management and Budget (1990).

In 1988, the Qatar Minister of Municipal Affairs and Agriculture witnessed a demonstration of GIS technology in Canada and saw its potential to revolutionize the way information was managed in the small gulf state of Qatar. His vision led to a government-wide, user-needs study that recommended "that a digital mapping database be implemented for the entire country; that a comprehensive fully integrated nationwide GIS be created; and that a high-level national GIS steering committee be established to set standards and oversee the implementation and development of GIS in Qatar." As a result of these recommendations, a national steering committee was set up in 1990, and a national center for GIS was created to implement GIS in Qatar in an organized and systematic way. One of the first tasks of the center was to implement a high-resolution digital topographic database. In 1998, this was used by all sixteen national agencies involved in GIS through a single high-speed fiber-optic network. The citizens of Qatar could also access GIS data through this network.

Box 2.3   Qatar's National Geographic Information System (1998).
   Sources: Al Thani (1997), Tosta (1997a).

A National System for Geographic Information (SNIG) was created by the Portuguese government under the Decreto Lei No. 53/90 on February 13, 1990. Under the same law, the government set up a National Center for Geographic Information (CNIG) "to coordinate the integration of data at different levels of public administration and thus develop a National System of Geographic Information." In 1998, CNIG was a research center of the Ministry of Planning and Territorial Administration (MEPAT) and obtained part of its funding from national and international agencies. In addition to promoting the development of the GIS market in Portugal as a whole, CNIG supported the implementation of regional GIS nodes in the five regions of mainland Portugal. It also coordinated two major projects funded by the European Commission to develop local nodes at the municipality level with particular reference to the needs of land-use planning. The launch of the SNIG network on the Internet in May 1995 was a major step in the modernization of Portuguese public administration. As a result, Portugal can be regarded as "the first European country that has an operational national geographic information infrastructure, fully distributed, based on the most recent developments in information technology."

Box 2.4 Portugal's Sistema Nacionale de Informacao Geografica (1998).
  Sources: Arnaud et al. (1996), Gouveia et al. (1997), Henriques (1996).

The Dutch Council for Real Estate Information (RAVI) was set up originally as an independent nonprofit organization to advise the minister for Housing, Spatial Planning, and the Environment on matters relating to the operations of the cadastre. In 1992, it was reconfigured as the National Council for Geographic Information (also known as RAVI). The council believed that "the proper development of the National Geographic Information Infrastructure [would require] a well thought out policy, an adequate administrative organization, and the intensive coordination of all the involved parties." RAVI's view of the National Geographic Information Infrastructure made a basic distinction between core and thematic data. With this in mind, it played a leading role in the creation of digital core data sets for the Netherlands as a whole at the 1:10,000 scale and also at the larger scales required for the municipal administration and public utility management purposes. It also initiated a national geographic information clearinghouse project that built upon the experience of a number of metadata initiatives by various agencies in the Netherlands.

Box 2.5 The Netherlands National Geographic Information Infrastructure (1998).
  Source: Netherlands Council for Geographic Information (1992a, 1992b, and 1995).

In Indonesia, an interagency working group was established in 1993 to identify the primary land data users and producers with the objective of establishing a national geographic information system for planning purposes. This group was coordinated by the National Coordinating Agency for Surveying and Mapping (Bakosurtanal). In 1998, the group gave high priority to the creation of a national framework to ensure that the information produced by different agencies had the same geographic referencing frame. Given that only 62 percent of the land area of Indonesia was covered by topographic base maps, it was decided in 1993 to complete the coverage of the whole country using digital mapping methods. A national GIS arrangement law was also under preparation and a number of GIS projects were included in Indonesia's sixth Five Year Plan (REPELITA VI). These included GIS training and awareness raising activities, as well as technology transfer and digital database development.

Box 2.6   Indonesia's National Geographic Information System (1998).
Sources: Godfrey et al. (1997), Suharto (1995).

In the early 1970s, the Malaysian government recognized the need for an effective land information system to assist planning and development but did not take steps toward setting up a national infrastructure until 1994 when the Ministry of Land and Cooperative Development appointed Renong Berhad to carry out a feasibility study. This study produced a comprehensive set of proposals setting out a vision for the National Infrastructure for Land Information Systems that would "make it possible to access the entire range of information required for the planning and maintenance of expensive infrastructure systems and support the sustainable development of natural resources such as oil, gas, forests, water, and soil." Following the publication of this report, a task force developed proposals for implementation at both the federal and state levels. Work on a prototype began in the Kuala Lumpur area, and the prime minister's Department of the Federal Government issued its guidelines for the establishment of the National Infrastructure for Land Information System.

Box 2.7   Malaysia's National Land Information System (1998).
Sources: Government of Malaysia (1997), National Land Information System (1996), Renong Berhad (1995), Tamin (1997).

In 1995, the Korean government set up the National Geographic Information System (NGIS) to stimulate the development of digital spatial databases and the standardization of geographic information. A steering committee of representatives from eleven ministries chaired by the vice-minister of the Ministry of Construction and Transportation oversaw the implementation of this program. The budget allocated to NGIS was $360 million over a five-year period. The government expected that about 64 percent of these costs would be met by central and local government and that the remainder would come from the private sector. In 1998, it was envisaged that phase one of this program would last from 1995 to 2002. Phase one was primarily concerned with the creation of a digital topographic map base for the country as a whole at scales ranging from 1:1,000 in urban areas to 1:25,000 in mountain regions, although special attention was also given to the digital mapping of underground facilities. From the outset, the Korean initiative was seen by the government as a joint venture as it was assumed that, "although the development of databases, including geographic information, is largely controlled by the Korean government, the application of GIS will be carried out by private sectors and research institutes."

Box 2.8   The Korean National Geographic Information System (1998).
  Source: MOCT (1995).

The starting point for the Japanese National Spatial Data Infrastructure initiative was the government's reaction to the Kobe earthquake of January 1995. This led to a major review of emergency management services and their related data needs. A Liaison Committee of Ministries and Agencies concerned with GIS was set up as part of these developments in September 1995 under the supervision of the cabinet. This included representatives from twenty-one government agencies including the Ministry of International Trade and Industry (MITI). The Cabinet Councillors Office of the Cabinet Secretariat serviced the committee with assistance from the National Mapping Agency and the National Land Agency. In December 1996, the Liaison Committee published its plan of action up to the beginning of the twenty-first century. They envisaged that the first phase of this plan would last until 1999 and include the standardization of metadata, clarifying the roles of government, local governments, and the private sector and promoting the establishment of the NSDI. A separate NSDI Promotion Association with a membership of more than eighty private-sector companies was also set up to support these activities.

Box 2.9   The Japanese National Spatial Data Infrastructure (1998).
  Sources: Godfrey et al. (1997), Yamaura (1996).

In 1995, the Canadian Council on Geomatics, which represents the provincial geomatics agencies, asked Geoplan to prepare proposals for an integrated spatial data model for Canada as a whole and to make recommendations on its implementation. Geoplan's report made a case for "a cooperative development which builds on Canadian strengths and recognizes the current restrictions under which Canadian public sector geomatics agencies must operate." As a result, in December 1996, the Canadian Council on Geomatics asked the federal Inter-Agency Committee on Geomatics to take a leading role in guiding federal and provincial governments and the private sector to create a Canadian Geospatial Data Infrastructure. The latter was chaired by the Assistant Deputy Minister of the Earth Science Sector in Natural Resources Canada. The Canadian Geospatial Data Infrastructure identified five basic themes: (1) to foster geospatial data access, (2) to provide a foundation of framework data, (3) to foster the harmonization of geospatial standards, (4) to encourage the establishment of data sharing partnerships, and (5) to create a supportive policy environment that facilitates the wider use of geospatial data.

Box 2.10   The Canadian Geospatial Data Infrastructure (1998).
Sources: Corey (1998), Geoplan Consultants (1996).

In 1987, the recommendation of the Committee of Enquiry into the Handling of Geographic Information, headed by Lord Chorley, to set up an independent national center for geographic information was rejected by the UK government of the day. Consequently, the British National Geospatial Data Framework was the most recent of the "first generation" of national SDIs. It dates from late 1996 when the first meeting of the NGDF Board took place. The board consisted of data producers from both the public and private sectors and was chaired by the director general and chief executive of Ordnance Survey Great Britain. To facilitate these activities, the Association for Geographic Information set up an advisory council consisting mainly of data users. Both the board and the advisory council were independent bodies who worked closely with the government.

Box 2.11   The United Kingdom's National Geospatial Data Framework (1998).
Sources: Department of the Environment (1987), Nanson and Rhind (1998).

COMPARATIVE EVALUATION

THESE BRIEF NATIONAL PROFILES HIGHLIGHT
the diversity of the eleven national SDIs. The profiles refer to
some recent initiatives that had little to show other than good
intentions in 1998, as well as some more established initiatives
that had already achieved a great deal. They also juxtaposed
small with large countries, wealthy with poor, as well as countries with and without federal systems of government.

Key indicators include population, land area, gross national
product (GNP), and economic status *(table 2.2)*. There are massive differences between these countries, both in terms of area
and population. The United States, for example, covers an area
that is nearly a thousand times that of Qatar and has nearly
five hundred times the population. Even if Qatar is discarded
on the grounds that it is essentially a city–state, the differences
remain considerable with both the Netherlands and Portugal
being smaller in both area and population than most American states.

Most of these countries had a relatively high GNP per capita
in 2001 according to the World Bank's ranking system. The
list includes only one low-income country, Indonesia, whose
per capita income was less than one-fifth of the two wealthiest countries, Japan and the United States. Only one other
country falls below the high-income category. This is Malaysia, which is ranked as an upper-middle-income country in the
World Bank system. However, it should be noted that the high-
income category covers a wide band of incomes. For example,
Korea and Portugal fall into this category even though their
respective per capita incomes were only a third of those of the
two richest countries.

Five of these countries have some form of federal system of
government (Australia, Canada, Indonesia, Malaysia, and

	2001 POP. (MILLIONS)	LAND AREA IN SQ.KMS (THOUSANDS)	GNP IN $ PER CAP 2001	STATUS
Australia	19	7,741	19,900	HI
Canada	31	9,971	21,930	HI
Indonesia	209	1,905	690	LI
Japan	127	378	35,610	HI
Korea	47	99	9,460	HI
Malaysia	24	330	3,330	UMI
Netherlands	16	42	24,330	HI
Portugal	10	92	10,900	HI
Qatar*				HI
United Kingdom	59	243	25,120	HI
United States	285	9,629	34,280	HI

GNP refers to gross national product per capita.

* Countries with less the one million population.

The last column of the table indicates the status of each country according to the ranking system of the World Bank: HI refers to high-income countries with GNP per capita incomes of more than $9,206; UMI to upper-middle-income countries with GNP per capita incomes of $2,975–$9,206; LMI to lower-middle-income countries with GNP per capita incomes of $746–$2,975; and LI to lower-income countries with GNP per capita incomes of less than $746.

Source: World Bank 2003, table 1.1, 14–17.

Table 2.2

Some key indicators of the innovator and early adopter countries.

the United States), although the extent to which powers are devolved to state and local government agencies varies considerably. At one end of the spectrum is the United States where a wide range of responsibilities relating to geographic information have been delegated to over eighty thousand separate state and local government agencies (Tosta 1997a). At the other end come Indonesia and Malaysia, which retain a considerable degree of federal control over land-related matters. In contrast, in the six countries with nonfederal systems of government, most of the responsibilities for geographic information are handled centrally.

Driving forces

The driving forces behind most SDI development can be summarized in similar terms to those set out in President Clinton's Executive Order quoted in the introduction: "to promote economic development, improve our stewardship of natural resources, and to protect the environment." These shared objectives generally support Rogers' claims that innovations such as SDIs can be regarded as a social system bound together by a common goal.

In the eyes of the Korean government, the need for government intervention to exploit the potential of digital geographic information technology was particularly important:

> The National Geographic Information System (NGIS) is recognized as one of the most fundamental infrastructures required in promoting national competitiveness and productivity. This enormous task is a national project that is led by the government since a substantial funding is required, and based on the fact that the usage of GIS [is] mainly for the public sectors. Furthermore, since the geographical factors as well as the attribute information are the basic assets of our country, construction or development of the relevant databases has been recognized as a national project. Accordingly, the Korean government is exerting significant efforts to develop and improve NGIS (Ministry of Construction and Transportation 1995, 10).

ANZLIC highlights the parallels between geographic information and other types of infrastructure:

> ANZLIC views land and geographic information as an infrastructure, with the same rationale and characteristics as roads, communications and other infrastructure. As the peak coordinating body for the management of land and geographic information, ANZLIC believes that Australia and New Zealand should have the spatial data infrastructure needed to support their economic growth and their social and environmental interests, backed by national standards, guidelines and policies on community access to the data (ANZLIC 1997, 1).

However, the notion of better government was interpreted in several different ways. In many countries it meant better planning and development. This was particularly the case in developing countries such as Indonesia and Malaysia. Planning, in the sense of a better state of readiness to deal with emergencies, brought about by natural hazards was also an important driving force in the establishment of the Japanese National Spatial Data Infrastructure, while in Portugal the National Geographic Information System was seen as an instrument for modernizing central, regional, and local administration.

On the other hand, better government was also interpreted in terms of more open government as a result of better access to information. The importance of access was particularly apparent in the mission statement of the British National Geospatial Data Framework which sought "to provide a framework to unlock geospatial information for the benefit of the citizen, business growth and good government through enabling viable, comprehensive, demand-led and easily accessed services" (National Geospatial Data Framework 1998, 4).

Key features

STATUS

These eleven countries fall into two broad categories with respect to the status of their SDIs: those that are the result of a formal mandate from government and those that have largely grown out of existing geographic information coordination activities.

The first category included Portugal, where the National Geographic Information System was created by the Decreto Lei of 53/90 *(box 2.4)*, and the United States *(box 2.2)*, where the National Spatial Data Infrastructure was the subject of an Executive Order of the President in April 1994. There was also clear evidence of strong government involvement in the establishment of the Japanese SDI *(box 2.9)* and the Korean NGIS *(box 2.8)*, as well as the NGIS in Qatar *(box 2.3)*. The Indonesian NGIS *(box 2.6)* was built into the country's sixth Five Year Plan, and a GIS arrangement law was currently under consideration. Similarly, the prime mover of the Malaysian National Land Information System was the Ministry of Land and Cooperative Development *(box 2.7)*.

The second category consisted of countries where SDI initiatives had largely grown out of existing coordination activities. This was clearly the case in Australia *(box 2.1)* where the discussions regarding spatial data infrastructure were essentially an expansion of earlier discussions regarding national land information strategies. Similarly, the reconstitution of the Dutch Council for Real Estate Information in 1992 as the National Council for Geographic Information marked a significant step toward the development of a national geographic information infrastructure *(box 2.5)*. Canada also fell into this category as the Federal Inter-Agency Committee on Geomatics was asked by the Canadian Council on Geomatics in 1996 to take a leading role in creating a Canadian Geographic Information

Infrastructure *(box 2.10)*. The U.S. Federal Geographic Data Committee was also an outgrowth from the previous Federal Inter-Agency Committee on Digital Cartography.

The British National Geospatial Data Framework *(box 2.11)* fell into a category of its own in that it had no direct mandate from government, nor was it in any real sense a direct product of any existing governmental coordination activities, although it was strongly supported by professional bodies such as the Association of Geographic Information and government agencies such as the Ordnance Survey of Great Britain. Nevertheless, its formal status *vis-a-vis* government remained unclear in 1998.

SCOPE

Scope can also be looked at from two different standpoints: the range of substantive geographic information interests that was represented in the different coordinating bodies and the extent to which the main stakeholders were directly involved.

With respect to the former, the membership of the U.S. Federal Geographic Data Committee covered a very wide range of substantive interests. These included the Departments of Agriculture, Commerce, Defense, Energy, Housing and Urban Development, Interior, State, and Transportation, as well as the Federal Emergency Management Agency, the Environmental Protection Agency, the National Aeronautics and Space Administration, the Library of Congress, and the National Archives and Records Administration. The Canadian Inter-Agency Committee on Geomatics also included representatives from a wide range of federal agencies, but unlike the FGDC, it also had a representative from the Geomatics Industry Association of Canada that represented the private sector.

The Portuguese and Qatar National Geographic Information Systems also involved a wide range of central government agencies. In contrast, the Indonesian and Malaysian National Geographic Information Systems tended to be focused mainly on surveying and mapping activities associated with land management. The initial stages of the Korean National Geographic Information System and the Japanese National Spatial Data Infrastructure were also primarily focused around central government surveying and mapping activities. However, in the case of the latter, an NSDI Promotion Association was also set up to complement these activities. This was chaired by a representative of the Mitsubishi Corporation.

The Australian coordinating body was concerned primarily with the collection and transfer of land-related information between different levels of government. Each of the ten members of ANZLIC represented a coordinating body within their jurisdiction (i.e., the Commonwealth Spatial Data Committee, the respective coordinating bodies at the eight state and territory levels and Land Information New Zealand). These members had the responsibility for both expressing that jurisdiction's views at the council and also for promoting ANZLIC's activities within their jurisdiction (Masser 1998, 64).

The Dutch and British initiatives were dependent on voluntary rather than mandatory participation. Nevertheless, the board of the RAVI consisted of most of the data providers and users in the Netherlands. These included the Cadastre, the Topografische Dienst (national mapping agency), and Statistics Netherlands, together with representatives from various groups within the Ministry of Housing, Spatial Planning, and the Environment (VROM), the survey department of the Ministry of Transport, Public Works, and Water Management (V&W), the National Institute for Public Health and Environment (RIVM), and the Center for Land Development and Soil Mapping (Staring Center), as well as representatives from the Association of Provincial Agencies (IPO), the consultative group of the Public Utilities Companies, the Royal

Association of Civil Law Notaries, and the Association of Water Boards. Another major stakeholder, the Association of Dutch Municipalities (VNG) also supported RAVI by contributing to the costs of some of its projects but was not a member of its board (Masser 1998, 47).

There were important differences between the national SDIs, particularly in terms of the extent to which the main stakeholders were involved in the management of them. Most of these initiatives were primarily public sector in scope and most were largely concerned with central or federal government activities. Although essentially public sector in scope, ANZLIC was unusual in that it was centrally concerned with the interface between the different levels of government.

The exceptions to this general rule were the British and Dutch initiatives whose coordinating bodies were not a formal part of government and also included private sector and user representation. This was particularly well developed in the case of RAVI where a separate business platform consisting of representatives from the main geographic information service providers had been established to complement the activities of its council. By comparison, representation on the British National Geospatial Data Framework bodies was more of a hit and miss affair, particularly with respect to the Advisory Council whose members were elected on an individual rather than an institutional basis.

IMPLEMENTATION

Only two out of the eleven countries had set up specialist centers to implement their national spatial data infrastructures. These were the National Center for Geographic Information Systems in Qatar and the National Center for Geographic Information (CNIG) in Portugal. Although in both cases their work program was overseen by government ministries, both these centers had a considerable degree of autonomy regarding the planning and implementation of particular projects.

The Portuguese case is especially interesting in that its activities included more general geographic information research and development activities, as well as national geographic information system implementation. Part of its funding was also derived from projects funded by the European Community and other agencies.

Feasibility studies were commissioned in Malaysia and Canada to explore the options for a national geographic information strategy. In the case of Malaysia, these included the controversial option of privatization where the consultants recommended that "in the long term, the implementation of NaLIS should be privatized in order to transfer the burden of funding from the government to private sector and accelerate implementation" (Renong Berhad 1995, para 6.2). The Canadian study reviewed some of the other national spatial data infrastructures described above and recommended a cooperative approach toward implementation, which took account of circumstances specific to Canada as opposed to the U.S. National Spatial Data Infrastructure model, which has "tried to accommodate the prevailing fragmented conditions, arrangements and the underlying culture defining geographic information management in the U.S. at this time" (Geoplan Consultants 1996, 43).

Only in the case of Australia had there been any attempt to quantify the benefits associated with the implementation of a national land and geographic data infrastructure. ANZLIC commissioned Price Waterhouse to carry out a study of the economic benefits arising from the acquisition and maintenance of land and geographic information at the national level in 1994. The findings of this study suggested a benefit–cost ratio for data usage on the order of 4:1. They also showed that

> The existing infrastructure for supplying data had provided information to users at a cost far lower than alternative methods. If this infrastructure had not been in place, and users had been forced to meet their data requirements from other sources, their costs would have been approximately six times higher. Over the past five years alone, an established infrastructure has saved users 5 billion Australian dollars, much of which has been reinvested to generate additional economic activity (Price Waterhouse 1995, 1).

RESOURCES

Resource information on the eleven national SDIs was both difficult to obtain and interpret. Nevertheless, it was clear that the task of coordination was relatively inexpensive in relation to the overall expenditure on geographic information, whereas the task of core digital database development was relatively expensive. For example, the U.S. Office of Management and Budget estimated that federal agencies alone spent $4 billion annually to collect and manage domestic geospatial data (Federal Geographic Data Committee 1994, 2). This sum is of a very different order to the $25 million spent by the USGS up till 1996 to support the FGDC and its work (Tosta 1997b, 4). Developing a core digital database took up most of Korea's NGIS budget. Digital topographic, thematic, and underground facility mapping accounted for $288.5 million out of its $360 million budget (Ministry of Construction and Transportation 1995, 8). Similarly, in Malaysia, the development costs of the initial NaLIS prototype in Wilayah Persekutuan Kuala Lumpur amounted to nearly $50 million (National Land Information System 1996). Even in Qatar, building the database sets cost $5 million (Tosta 1997a).

CHARACTERISTICS OF THE INNOVATORS/EARLY ADOPTERS

THE FINDINGS OF THIS ANALYSIS GENERALLY support the descriptions of the innovators and early adopters outlined by Rogers (1995). If it assumed that there are two hundred nations in the world and that 2.5 percent of these, as suggested by him, fall into the innovators category, the first five of these nations to develop an SDI should be classified in this way.

The first two adopters in chronological order, Australia and the United States, are both wealthy countries who were in a position to cope with the uncertainties involved in such an innovation. From the outset, the U.S. NSDI was also seen as a high-profile initiative internationally reflecting that country's status as an opinion leader in the field. The inclusion of Qatar as an innovator is less predictable, although it is also a wealthy country. In this case, particular importance must be attached to the communication channels with Canada that resulted in the early adoption of GIS technology for the country as a whole. The case of Portugal is also an interesting one, as Portugal comes toward the bottom of the category of high-income countries ranked by the World Bank. Two factors probably played a key role in this case. As in Qatar, communications channels played an important part in persuading Portugal to become an innovator. The model that particularly influenced the Portuguese government was the concept of an independent national GI center that had been advocated in the report brought forth by the Committee of Enquiry into the Handling of Geographic Information (the Chorley Report) to the British government (Henriques 1992). The other driving force behind these developments in Portugal was to take advantage of the special opportunities for funding that existed as a result of the European Union's regional policies.

The fifth country, the Netherlands, probably falls somewhere between the innovator and early adopter category in terms of its SDI initiative. It is a relatively wealthy country that has been a longstanding opinion leader and innovator in the international surveying and cadastral field, and its national body, the RAVI, was set up as far back as 1984. It 1992, this body restructured itself as the National Council for Geographic Information, but its National Geographic Information Infrastructure document was not released until 1995, that is, after Indonesia and Malaysia and about the same time as Japan and Korea.

According to Rogers, 13.5 percent or twenty-seven countries are likely to fall into the early adopters category. Even if the Netherlands is included in this group, the other seven cases reviewed would account for only a quarter of these countries. Nevertheless, the cases reviewed probably give a good indication of the likely eventual composition of this group. They include a greater diversity of countries than the innovators group. For example, two out of the seven are not high-income countries. There are also signs that some of these countries are followers rather than leaders in the innovation process. This is particularly the case of Japan where the primary driving force for infrastructure was the need to improve emergency services to avoid the problems that arose as a result of the Kobe earthquake. The development of a national SDI must be seen in this case as part of the solution to an existing problem rather than an innovation in itself. This can also be seen in developing countries like Indonesia and Malaysia where infrastructure development was seen as a means of facilitating government planning and resource development.

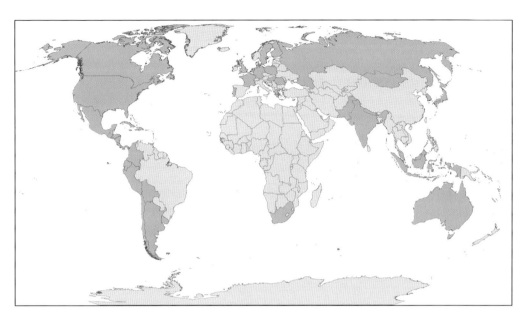

Figure 2.3
Countries responding positively to
the GSDI survey in 1998–2000.

Argentina	Greece	Nicaragua
Australia	Guatemala	Pakistan
Bermuda	Honduras	Panama
Bolivia	Hungary	Peru
Canada	India	Poland
Chile	Indonesia	Portugal
Colombia	Japan	Romania
Costa Rica	Jamaica	Russia
Cuba	Kiribati	South Africa
Cyprus	Macau	South Korea
Dominican Republic	Malaysia	Sweden
Ecuador	Mexico	Trinidad and Tobago
El Salvador	Mongolia	Tuvalu
Finland	Nepal	United Kingdom
France	Netherlands	United States
Germany	New Zealand	Uruguay

It is not easy to identify the other twenty countries that made up the early adopter category if the proportions suggested by Rogers are used in this case. However, some indication of the rest of this group, together with the initial members of the early majority group that will be considered in the next chapter, is given in the findings of the survey conducted by Harlan Onsrud for the GSDI between 1998 and 2000 *(www.spatial. maine.edu/~onsrud/GSDI.htm)*. This shows that fifty-four countries responded positively to his questionnaire between 1998 and 2000. When the five projects are taken out of this total, twenty-one of these came from the Americas, fourteen from Europe, thirteen from Asia and the Pacific, and one from Africa *(figure 2.3)*.

There is also some evidence to suggest that several countries in the early adopters category as a whole played an important role in promoting SDIs in their specific regions. This is particularly the case with respect to the Colombian Infraestructura Colombiana de Datos Espaciales *(box 2.12)* (Borrero 1998, Instituto Geographico Agustin Codazzi 1999). This also featured prominently as the only national case study in the first edition of the GSDI cookbook (Nebert 2000). The South African National Spatial Information Framework played a key role in Africa in fostering SDI development *(box 2.13)*, while Hungary *(box 2.14)* occupies a similar position with respect to the central and eastern European countries that have recently joined the European Union (see, for example, Remetey–Fulopp 1998).

With these considerations in mind it can be concluded that the early adopters of SDIs quite closely resemble the characteristics described by Rogers. These countries tended to be more integrated in existing regional systems than the innovators. Their experiences reduced the uncertainties about adoption. Consequently, they provided a role model for subsequent adoptions and, in the process, created the critical mass that spawned the subsequent SDI phenomenon.

The development of the NSDI in Colombia (Infraestructura Colombiana de Datos Espaciales or ICDE) is a joint venture between various agencies, including the national surveying and mapping agency (IGAC), the national statistical agency (DANE), the national geology agency (Ingeominas), and the national oil company (Ecopetrol). Colombia's ICDE can be described as "the set of policies, standards, organizations, and technology working together to produce, share, and use geographic information about Colombia in order to support national sustainable development." It builds upon American and European concepts, but it retains a distinct Colombian flavor given that the nation is rich in biodiversity, mineral resources, natural hazards, and socio-economic problems. The initiative's empirical approach has broken down inter-organizational barriers and demonstrated the practical benefits of data sharing. It has achieved a great deal without a formal mandate from the government, but its future development requires high-level support from the government in the form of either a presidential decree or a ministerial council order.

Box 2.12   Infraestructura Colombiana de Datos Espaciales (ICDE).
Sources: Instituto Geografico Agustin Codazzi (1999), Nebert (2000).

In 1997, the South African Department of Land Affairs began work on the National Spatial Information Framework. Its objective is "to produce the parameters for a coherent SDI characterized by the availability of relevant, reliable spatial information for planning, delivering services and the optimal allocation of resources." This involves the sharing and reuse of spatial information without unnecessary and costly duplication of effort. A spatial information bill to promote the use of spatial information to support decision making is currently being considered by the South African Parliament. This bill provides for the creation of a committee for spatial information to promote cooperation within the public and private sectors in the development and implementation of a South Africa Spatial Information Infrastructure (SASDI). Three subcommittees dealing with technical, liaison, and policy matters respectively will support the work of the Committee for Spatial Information.

Box 2.13   South Africa's National Spatial Information Framework
Source: www.nsif.org.za.

Hungary's National Informatics Strategy was set up from 1995 to 1996. Discussions regarding the development of a NSDI proceeded alongside these developments. Consequently, in 1997, National Spatial Data Strategy (NSDS) was produced by a working group consisting of representatives of the prime minister's office, several ministries, national institutions, and the HUNGIS Foundation. These NSDS activities were initially carried out within the prime minister's office but were transferred to the Ministry of Informatics and Communication in 2002. The most important executive player in the NSDS is the Institute of Geodesy, Cartography, and Remote Sensing (FOMI) within the Ministry for Agriculture and Regional Development. There is a high level of cooperation between the different data producers and users within Hungary. Most of the building blocks for implementing this strategy are in place as a result of a large number of projects that have been supported by the European Commission to facilitate Hungary's accession to the European Union. These include major initiatives in the field of land registration administered by 136 district and county land offices. As a result, the Leuven study concludes that a NSDI exists in Hungary, although it is at the early stages of development.

Box 2.14   Hungary's National Spatial Data Strategy
Sources: Remety–Fulopp (1998), Spatial Applications Division, Catholic University of Leuven (2003e).

SUMMARY

SOME OF THE CHARACTERISTICS OF THE innovators and early adopters who were involved in the diffusion of NSDIs have been considered with particular reference to the findings of a comparative evaluation undertaken in 1998. It has been shown that these NSDIs came in all shapes and sizes. All but two of these initiatives are located in high-income countries, and the driving forces behind most of them are the desire to promote economic development, better government, and environmental sustainability.

The status of these SDIs differs considerably from those that had a formal mandate from their governments to SDIs that are essentially outgrowths from existing national GI coordination arrangements. There are also important differences between them in scope. Some SDIs are essentially central government initiatives whereas others involve all levels if government as well as the private sector and academia.

The group of innovators include two of the longstanding leaders in the field (Australia and the United States), who are also wealthy countries that were in a position to handle the uncertainties associated with innovations of this kind. The other two members of this group (Portugal and Qatar) became involved at this early stage largely because of parallel developments in Canada and the United Kingdom. Most of the early adopters came from Europe, North America, the Far East, and Australia. Several countries in the early adopters category also took on the role of innovators within their regions. These include Colombia, with respect to Latin America, Hungary, in connection with central and eastern Europe, and South Africa, with reference to sub-Saharan Africa.

CHAPTER 3

The diffusion of national SDIs

The early majority

T his chapter forms the second part of the discussion of the diffusion of national SDIs that began in the previous chapter. The focus of the discussion in this chapter is the characteristics of the early majority that, according to Rogers (1995), account for a third of all the potential adopters of SDI. When applied to the total number of countries in the world, this implies that at least sixty countries could fall into the early majority category. Taken together with the innovators and early adopters, this suggests somewhere in the region of one hundred SDI adopters. This number is broadly in line with Crompvoets and Bregt's (2003) estimate that as many as 120 countries may be considering SDI projects.

The presentation in the chapter is divided into three sections:

1. Profiles of the current position in the four main regions of the world: Europe, the Americas, Asia and the Pacific, and Africa

2. A comparative evaluation using similar criteria to those used in the previous chapter with respect to the geographic, economic, and administrative circumstances of the involved countries, the driving forces behind the initiatives, and their main features

3. The characteristics of the early majority that were described in the diffusion of innovations model

PROFILES OF EUROPE, THE AMERICAS, ASIA AND THE PACIFIC, AND AFRICA

DUE TO THE LARGE NUMBER OF ADOPTERS involved, each of these profiles begins with an overview of the state of the art in SDI development in the whole region and then highlights some of their distinctive features with reference to short profiles of selected countries.

Europe

The development of SDIs has been studied extensively in Europe over the last five years. This is partly due to the interest of the European Commission in such activities expressed initially in the GI2000 initiative and more recently in the INfrastructure for SPatial InfoRmation in Europe (INSPIRE) program *(box 6.6)*. In the process, the commission has also funded a number of important studies in this field. These include the Methods for Access to Data and Metadata in Europe (MADAME) project (Blakemore et al. 1999) and the Geographic Information Network in Europe (GINIE) project (Craglia et al. 2002, Craglia et al. 2003). More recently, two of the three European Commission directorate generals responsible for the INSPIRE program commissioned separate studies of the state of play of SDI activities in all the European countries from the Catholic University of Leuven in Belgium *(inspire.jrc. it/state_of_play.cfm)*. The findings of these studies constitute a major resource for SDI research not only in Europe but also for the rest of the world.

The findings of the Leuven studies suggest that only a handful of European countries have anything like a full-blown SDI either planned or in place at the present time. Even countries like the Netherlands and Portugal, which were discussed in the previous chapter, do not meet all of their criteria for a complete SDI as "in neither case, all components of a theoretical SDI are in place or even planned" (Spatial Applications Division, Catholic University of Leuven 2003a, 9). As a result, the authors claim that most of these "NSDI initiatives can therefore better be described as SDI-like or SDI-supporting initiatives."

The authors of the Leuven studies subsequently developed a typology of SDIs. The typology primarily distinguishes between countries that are national data producer led and those that are not. Within the countries that are led by national data producers, the typology further distinguishes between initiatives that involve users and those that do not. Within the countries that are not national data producer led, the typology further distinguishes between initiatives that are based on a formal government mandate and those initiatives for which there was no formal government mandate *(figure 3.1 and table 3.1)*. With this typology, each of the European countries can be classified according to these criteria as a result of these studies.

Figure 3.1
The state of play in Europe in
spring 2003.

NATIONAL DATA PRODUCER LED	
Users involved	
Operational	Denmark, Finland, Hungary, Iceland, Norway, Sweden
Partially operational	Austria, Czech Republic, Poland
Not operational	Greece, Luxembourg
Users not involved	
Operational	Slovenia
Partially operational	Lithuania
Not operational	Estonia, Latvia, Malta, Slovakia

NOT NATIONAL DATA PRODUCER LED	
Formal mandate	
Operational	Belgium (Flanders), Germany, Portugal, Switzerland
Partially operational	Ireland, Italy
Not operational	None
No formal mandate	
Operational	Netherlands, United Kingdom
Partially operational	Belgium (Wallonia)
Not operational	Spain, France

Cyprus, Romania, and Turkey are not included in this table because the Spatial Applications Division was unable to get any feedback from these countries on their preliminary survey findings, and Bulgaria was not classified as "it was not clear at all whether there is coordination."

Source: Spatial Applications Division, Catholic University of Leuven (2003a, 24).

Table 3.1
SDI state of play in Europe in
spring 2003.

Thus, more than half of the SDI initiatives are led by national data producers. This is particularly the case in the central and eastern European countries that have recently become members of the European Union (EU), as well as the Nordic countries. All the Nordic countries explicitly include data users in the coordination process, whereas only a minority of former accession countries make provision for user involvement. However, it should be noted that not all these SDI initiatives are operational. This is the case in Greece and Luxembourg, as well as several of the former accession countries.

The remaining countries have made other arrangements for the coordination of their national SDI activities. In two countries (Germany and Portugal), a government interdepartmental body has been formally mandated to create a national SDI that is now operational. In the Netherlands, as noted in the previous chapter, a national GI association has been encouraged by the government to take the lead, and it has succeeded in developing an operational national SDI. Belgium presents a special case as two different agencies have come into being to coordinate SDI activities in Flemish speaking Flanders and French speaking Wallonia. However, only the former has been given a formal mandate to carry out this task. France, the authors note, is a special case where coordination is in the hands of an advisory body "that has yet to mobilize the national GI sector as a cooperative undertaking" (Spatial Applications Division, Catholic University of Leuven 2003a, 25).

The issue of accession to the EU has been a major driving force for SDI development in most of the central and eastern European countries. This has been seen as a unique historic opportunity to further the integration of the continent by peaceful means and extend the zone of stability and prosperity to new members (Commission of the European Communities 2000). Ten of these countries joined the EU on May 1, 2004: Cyprus, the Czech Republic, Estonia, Hungary, Latvia, Lithuania, Malta, Poland, the Slovak Republic, and Slovenia. Bulgaria and Romania hope to do so by 2007.

The EU has been assisting these countries in taking on EU laws. It has also provided a range of financial incentives to improve their infrastructures and economies. The process of enlargement can be seen as both a carrot and a stick for SDI development in this case. The carrot is the need to develop an effective means of monitoring the spatial impacts of a wide range of social, economic, and environmental policies that are associated with EU accession, while the stick is the need to take steps to modernize public administration in these countries to make this possible (Craglia and Masser 2002).

Boxes 3.1 and 3.2, profiles of the Czech Republic and Finland, give some indication of the diversity of European countries. Both countries were classified in table 3.1 as data producer led SDIs that involved users. Finland is one of the Nordic countries, and the Czech Republic became a member of the EU in May 2004.

A clear framework has been created for the Czech national SDI. Within the country's broader national information infrastructure and well-developed mechanisms for coordination, core data integration and metadata services have also come in to being. There are three main players: the Czech Office for Surveying, Mapping, and Cadastre; the Czech Association for Geographic Information; and Nemoforum. Nemoforum was set up in 1999 to promote cooperation in the GI field within the framework of an EU funded Phare project led by the Dutch Cadastre. It consists of a public and a private platform. The public platform includes most of the key players from central and local government, while the private platform brings together representatives from the main professional bodies with an interest in GI and the utilities. Nemoforum has produced a plan for the development of the Czech National Geoinformation Infrastructure from 2001 to 2005. The Czech Government's Council accepted this plan as background material for State Information Policy in September 2001. The plan identifies ten main priority areas for action. These include formalizing the status of the initiative, developing the MIDAS metadata service as a subproject of the public metadata information system, and capacity building to enable the wider public to exploit the opportunities opened up by increased access to the country's geographic information resources. Work is still in progress on these actions. Consequently, the Leuven study classifies the Czech SDI as partially rather than fully operational.

Box 3.1 The National SDI of the Czech Republic.
Sources: Nemoforum (2001), Spatial Applications Division, Catholic University of Leuven (2003c).

The *de facto* leader of SDI developments at the national level in Finland is the National Land Survey (Maanmittauslaitos). Since the 1980s, the National Land Survey (NLS) has been active in this field, but the term "SDI" has only recently been used in Finland. Prior to that, it was customary to refer to the "shared or joint use of geographic information." The NLS produced a vision paper on a national geographic infrastructure for Finland in 1996, but it was not until 2001 that the Council of State established the Finnish Council for Geographic Information to oversee SDI activities. This is a high-level body that has a formal mandate to develop strategies for SDI implementation. Its seventeen members include all the key stakeholders in central and local government, and the private sector. The Finnish national GI association and the Finnish Environmental Institute (SYKE) have strong links with this body. It is envisaged that the NLS and other data producers will work within this framework with reference to the maintenance and updating of the national base registers, the national topographical and land-information systems, and the various local data sets.

Box 3.2 The Finnish National Spatial Data Infrastructure.
Sources: National Land Survey (1996), Spatial Applications Division, Catholic University of Leuven (2003b).

The Americas

Given that the initial American and Canadian SDI experiences were described in the previous chapter, the following discussion focuses on developments in Central and South America. The findings of a survey of twenty-one countries in the Americas carried out in 2000 give a useful overview of the state of SDI development (Hyman and Lance 2000). The survey creates an overall impression that in 2000 countries in Central and South America were becoming more aware of NSDI concepts and approaches. They also began to recognize that the main obstacles to be overcome were institutional rather than technical in nature (Borrero 1998). They are also concerned about the question of the resources that would be required for effective SDI implementation.

The findings of the survey highlight the range of different kinds of SDI initiatives that existed at that time. Formal mandates for the development and implementation of SDIs existed in only six out of the twenty-one countries *(table 3.2 and figure 3.2)*. In the majority of cases, a single institute, normally the national mapping agency, or in some countries such as Mexico, the national mapping and statistical agency, was the lead organization in these initiatives. In some other countries, the Ministries of the Environment, Science and Technology, and Transportation and Public Works acted as focal points. Generally these initiatives were restricted to the central government sector, although the utilities were involved in several countries together with the private sector. An interesting example of the latter is the Uruguay clearinghouse, which is managed by a private company under contract to the Ministry of Works. In most countries, the basic data with reference to topography, transport, hydrology, land cover, and administrative boundaries was available in digital form, but there was often a lack of standardization and harmonization.

CANADA

UNITED STATES OF AMERICA

MEXICO

CUBA

DOMINICAN REPUBLIC

JAMAICA

GUATEMALA
HONDURAS
EL SALVADOR
NICARAGUA
COSTA RICA
PANAMA

VENEZUELA

COLOMBIA

ECUADOR

PERU

BRAZIL

BOLIVIA

CHILE

URUGUAY

ARGENTINA

FORMAL MANDATE
NO FORMAL MANDATE

Figure 3.2
Status of SDI in twenty-one
countries in the Americas in 2000.

COUNTRIES WITH FORMAL MANDATE	COUNTRIES WITHOUT FORMAL MANDATE
Argentina	Brazil
Cuba	Bolivia
Guatemala	Canada
Mexico	Chile
Dominican Republic	Colombia
United States of America	Costa Rica
	Ecuador
	El Salvador
	Honduras
	Jamaica
	Nicaragua
	Panama
	Peru
	Uruguay
	Venezuela

Table 3.2

Status of SDI in twenty-one countries in the Americas in 2000.

Source: Hyman and Lance (2000).

The two examples contained in boxes 3.3 and 3.4 illustrate the diversity of SDI initiatives in Central and South America. Chile enacted a presidential decree in 2001, establishing a formal mandate for SDI development. Mexico's national mapping and statistical agency has a longstanding interest in the development of a national geographic information system but only recently expanded its activities to coordinate the national SDI initiative.

A presidential decree in September 2001 set out the guidelines for the establishment of a Sistema Nacional de Informacion Territorial (SNIT) in Chile. This document also assigns the overall management tasks to a technical and executive secretariat based in the Ministry of National Assets and Resources. The objective underlying the decree was to modernize the way that territorial information is handled by state agencies and to create a cooperative and collaborative scheme for its future management. It is envisaged that such a scheme will result in "a qualitative jump in relation to the availability and access to land information for government authorities as well as common citizens." The whole project is based on three technological foundations: the accurate location of spatial data, their management in an online environment, and the use of GIS. The SNIT is under the political control of the Committee of Urban and Territorial Ministers. Seven thematic areas have been identified within the SNIT. These are social issues, infrastructure, cultural heritage, territorial planning, property, natural resources, and basic territorial information. The latter is concerned with managing the standardization process for the fundamental data needed for a wide range of activities. This group produced a document entitled *Basis for a state policy for territorial information management—National Territorial Information System,* which was approved by the Committee of Urban and Territorial Ministers in December 2003. When approved by the president and congress, it will provide the legal foundation for the SNIT.

Box 3.3 Chile's Sistema Nacionale de Informacion Territoriale.
Source: Barriga Vargas (2004).

The lead agency for SDI development in Mexico is the National Institute for Statistics, Geography, and Informatics (INEGI). As its title suggests, this agency is unusual in that it has responsibilities for both statistical and geographic information under the Statistical and Geographic Information law of 1980. INEGI has been developing a national geographic information system for some time, but it was not until relatively recently that a Mexican SDI (IDEMEX) came into being to "facilitate compilation, access, distribution, management and use of geographic information in the national context." INEGI is the coordinating body for the IDEMEX initiative and operates in conjunction with the Technical Advisory Committee that was set up in February 2003 to oversee the national program of GI development. This committee brings together high-level representatives from both the federal and state governments. There are also close links between the IDEMEX initiative and the implementation of Mexico's National Development Plan for 2001–2006. This is built around three courses of action: human and social development, growth with quality, and order and respect.

Box 3.4 Mexico's IDEMEX.
Source: Hanson–Albites (2004).

Asia and the Pacific

The Asia and Pacific region is both the largest and the most diverse region in the world. Its fifty-five countries contain 60 percent of the world's population. They include some of the largest countries in the world, as well as many small island countries in the Pacific with tiny populations. They also include countries from the Middle East and the Indian sub-continent, as well as southeast and eastern Asia, Australia, and New Zealand. This diversity is reflected in the national SDIs that have come into being in the region. It is worth noting that six of the eleven first-generation SDI countries came from this region. Of these, Australia, Japan, Korea, and Qatar are relatively wealthy countries, while Malaysia and Indonesia fell into the upper-middle-income and the lower-income categories, respectively.

This diversity may also be the reason for the relative lack of regional studies of SDI diffusion of the kind described above for Europe and the Americas. Nevertheless, Rajabifard and Williamson (2003) estimate that somewhere between 20 and 30 percent of countries in the Asia and the Pacific region are developing or have plans to develop national SDIs. This broadly confirms the findings of their earlier survey of regional fundamental data sets (Rajabifard and Williamson 2000) when seventeen out of the fifty-fve members of the Permanent Committee for GI in Asia and the Pacific, or just under a third of the members, responded to their questionnaire *(table 3.3 and figure 3.3)*. These were essentially national mapping agencies.

Figure 3.3

Asia and Pacific countries responding to the regional fundamental data sets questionnaire in 2000.

Australia	Australian Surveying and Land Information Group
Hong Kong	Survey and Mapping Office, Land Department
Islamic Republic of Iran	National Cartographic Centre
Japan	Geographic Survey Institute
Kiribati	Land Management Division
Laos	National Geographic Department
Macau	Direcao dos servicos da Cartografia e Cadastre
Malaysia	Department of Survey and Mapping
Maldives	Ministry of Construction and Public Works
Mongolia	State Administration of Geodesy and Cartography
Nepal	Survey Department
New Zealand	Land Information New Zealand (LINZ)
Republic of Palau	Bureau of Lands and Surveys
Peoples Republic of China	State Bureau of Surveying and Mapping
Singapore	Survey Department
Solomon Islands	Survey and Mapping Department
Tuvalu	Lands and Survey Department

Source: Rajabifard and Williamson (2000, 9).

Table 3.3
Asia and Pacific countries
responding to the regional
fundamental data sets
questionnaire in 2000.

In this region, an obvious distinction can be made between developed and developing countries in terms of their needs and aspirations. Within the developing countries category, a further distinction can be made between countries in the process of transition from a less developed to a more developed state, countries at an early stage of economic development, and the Pacific island nations. It can also be argued that developing countries face different challenges from those of developed countries. "The main limitations are a lack of appreciation of what SDI can and cannot do, lack of resources and trained personnel, inefficient bureaucratic processes, lack of data, and lack of infrastructure" (Rajabifard and Williamson 2003, 34).

Boxes 3.5 and 3.6 illustrate the diffusion of SDIs within the region. India has been chosen as it is one of the largest countries in the world, as well as a country that has a longstanding interest in matters relating to geographic information. Nepal is a relatively small and poor developing country that is taking its first steps toward an NSDI.

India's Department of Science and Technology set up a task force to prepare proposals for an Indian National Spatial Data Infrastructure in 2000. Its proposals are contained in the NSDI Strategy and Action Plan that was approved by the Indian Government in December 2002. This sets out a vision of a national infrastructure that promotes access to organized spatial data and facilitates the use of this infrastructure at the local, state, regional, and national levels for sustained economic growth. It provides an overall framework for a decentralized NSDI that takes account of the need to maintain standard digital collections of spatial data; the importance of developing common solutions for the discovery, access, and use of such data to meet the requirements of diverse user groups; and the need to build relationships among the organizations involved to support its continuing development. With this in mind, particular attention is devoted to metadata standards and provision, and the creation of an organizational framework that is inclusive of all the stakeholders. To achieve these objectives, the government drafted a National Spatial Data Infrastructure Bill in 2002 that lays down guidelines for the commitment of the key players. The NSDI is seen as a national endeavor toward greater transparency and e-governance. It comes under the overall direction of a high-level National Spatial Data Commission chaired by the Minister of Science and Technology. The nodal agency for the NSDI is the Survey of India, and a secretariat has been set up in New Delhi to support its implementation.

Box 3.5   The Indian National Spatial Data Infrastructure.
Sources: Department of Science and Technology (2004), *www.nsdiindia.org*

The Government of Nepal began the pilot phase of its National Geographic Information Infrastructure Program (NGIIP) in 2002. This involves six government departments: Survey, Statistics, Local Development, Agriculture, Health, and Population and Environment. The main objective of the program is to strengthen planning and resource management. During the pilot phase, an NGII platform is being developed to facilitate data sharing between the two main departments with holdings of digital data (the Survey Department and the Central Bureau for Statistics) and the other participating user agencies. This platform is being used for the dissemination of the results of the 2001 Population and Housing Census. Although the program is still in its infancy, it has already been useful in building up operational experience among the participants and raising awareness of the potential of such an infrastructure within government. It has also stimulated strategic thinking about the medium-term objectives of such a program given the relatively limited amount of digital data that is currently available in Nepal and the need for capacity building in the geographic information technology field.

Box 3.6   Nepal's National Geographic Information Infrastructure Program.
Source: Budhathoki and Chhatkuli (2004).

Africa

The World Summit on Sustainable Development that took place in Johannesburg in September 2002 stimulated several Africa-wide studies on SDI related topics. These included *Geographic Information for Sustainable Development* published by the Open GIS Consortium *(www.opengis.org/gisd)* and a report entitled *Down to Earth: Geographic Information for Sustainable Development in Africa* prepared by the Committee on the Geographic Foundation for Agenda 21 of the U.S. National Research Council (2002). The latter is particularly interesting in that it directly covers most of the key components of an SDI, and it highlights a particularly African problem. "African countries are at various points in development of their SDIs. SDIs and telecommunications are intimately linked. To realize the full potential of a SDI requires a telecommunications infrastructure that facilitates access, use, and sharing of geographic data and information. Although telecommunications infrastructures are improving in Africa, they currently limit transmission of vital data and information for Agenda 21 issues" (National Research Council 2002, 50).

In many respects, these studies build upon earlier work in the environmental field in Africa. A good example of this is the Environmental Information System Program for Sub Saharan Africa (EIS) that has played an important role in harmonizing standards for data capture and exchange, coordinating data collection and maintenance, and promoting the use of common data sets by the different agencies involved (EIS-Africa 2002).

Kate Lance (2003) gives a good overview of the current state of the art in SDI development in Africa. This highlights the diversity of SDI initiatives that have come into being in Africa over the last ten years and the role that international agencies of all kinds have played in facilitating the development of SDIs. This is particularly evident in the publication of an African version of the GSDI cookbook (United Nations Economic Commission for Africa 2003) based on the efforts of GSDI, EIS–Africa, the UN Economic Commission for Africa, and the International Institute for Geoinformation Science and Earth Observation (ITC) in the Netherlands.

Figure 3.4
Partial list of SDI initiatives in Africa in 2003.

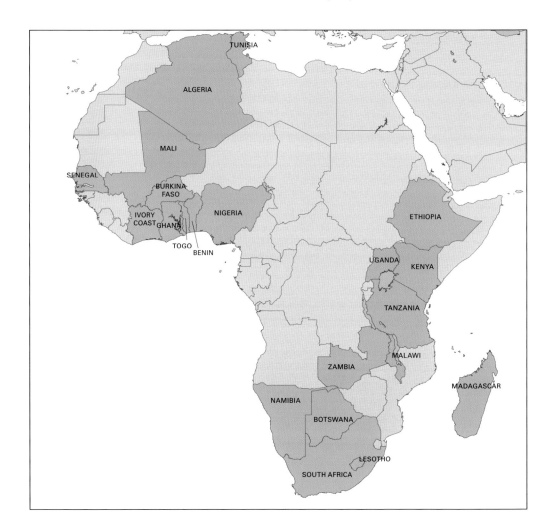

Algeria	National Council for Geographic Information
Benin	Environmental Information and Monitoring System
Botswana	National GIS Coordination Committee
Burkina Faso	Programme National de Gestion de L'Information sur le Milieu
Ethiopia	Ethiopian Spatial Data Infrastructure
Ghana	National Framework for Geospatial Information in Ghana
Ivory Coast	National Committee for Remote Sensing and Geographic Information
Kenya	National Spatial Data Infrastructure
Lesotho	Committee on Environmental Data Management
Madagascar	Association Réseau Système d'Information sur l'Environnement
Malawi	Malawi Geographical Information Council
Mali	Le Conseil interministériel d'information géographique
Namibia	Environmental Monitoring and Indicators Network
Nigeria	National Geospatial Information Infrastructure
Senegal	Groupe de Travail Inter-institutionnel
South Africa	National Spatial Information Framework
Tanzania	National GIS Interim Steering Committee
Togo	Togo Geodata
Tunisia	Schéma national de géomatique
Uganda	Uganda Spatial Data Infrastructure
Zambia	Environmental Information Network and Monitoring System/ Zambian Association for GIS

Source: Lance (2003, 40).

Table 3.4

Partial list of SDI initiatives in Africa in 2003.

Lance also lists twenty-one national SDI initiatives that are currently under way in all parts of Africa *(table 3.4)*. These include countries from both anglophone and francophone Africa *(figure 3.4)*. Her review also identifies some of the main problems facing SDI development on this continent. One of the most important of these is the question of political support as very few of the initiatives *(table 3.3)* have a legal status or enabling legislation to support their efforts. There are only a few countries where SDIs have achieved the status of funded activities with a budget from central government. Another particularly African problem is that of leadership. While the national mapping agencies are a key contributor to SDI development, it is quite common in Africa to find that other entities have the political influence (and funding) that drives the initiatives.

Boxes 3.7 and 3.8 illustrate some of the main features of the diffusion of national SDIs in Africa. The experience of Ghana draws attention to the advantages and the disadvantages of making use of donor agency assistance to get an SDI initiative under way, while Kenya is a relatively rare example in Africa of an SDI that has been incorporated into the National Development Plan for the country.

Ghana's NSDI began life as a World Bank funded "Country at a Glance" project that was carried out for the Environmental Protection Agency (EPA) as part of the Ghana Environmental Resource Management Project between 1993 and 1998. The main objective of this project was to create "a synoptic, interoperable, and user friendly geographic database designed to assist national level environmental management and planning." This provided the starting point for the launch of the National Framework for Geographic Information Management (NAFGIM) initiative by the Natural Resources Management Group of the Ministry of Land and Forests in April 2000. This is an interdisciplinary and an interagency SDI that is intended to embrace all the institutions that produce or use geographic information in Ghana. Its Steering Committee is appointed by the Ministry of Environment, Science, and Technology, acting through the Environmental Protection Agency. The latter also houses its coordinator, technical, and administrative staff. It operates to a large extent through its workgroups on base cartographic data, biophysical data, socio-economic data, and applications.

Box 3.7   Ghana's National Framework for Geographic Information Management.
Sources: Ghana Environmental Protection Agency and World Bank (1999), National Framework for Geographic Information Management (2001).

The government of Kenya is in the process of establishing an initiative for the efficient management of geospatial data in the country through its National Development Plan for 2002–2008. As a result, the Ministry of Lands and Settlements has a mandate to invest staff time and resources into SDI activities. The starting point for the Kenyan SDI was a workshop organized by the Survey of Kenya and the Ministry of Lands and Settlements in collaboration with the Japan International Cooperation Agency in November 2001. The main objective of this workshop was to raise awareness of the potential benefits of an NSDI among key stakeholders from government, education, the private sector, and also international organizations. As a result of the workshop, it was agreed that the Survey of Kenya should provide the secretarial resources to support this initiative. Another workshop was held in April 2002 to consider possible structures for an NSDI. As a result of this workshop, it was agreed that a national steering committee should be established and that four working groups should be created to deal with matters relating to standards, legal issues, education, and dissemination, respectively. The Survey of Kenya agreed to convene these working groups in the first place until they were in a position to elect convenors from the agencies most involved.

Box 3.8   The Kenyan National Spatial Data Infrastructure.
Source: Mbaria (2002).

COMPARATIVE EVALUATION

LIKE THE CASES DESCRIBED IN THE previous chapter, these eight short profiles of NSDI initiatives *(boxes 3.1 to 3.8)* show the extent to which these initiatives come in all shapes and sizes with respect to population size, land area, level of economic development, and distribution of administrative responsibilities. They include India, which is the second largest population in the world with over one billion inhabitants, to relatively small countries such as Finland with a population of only five million *(table 3.5)*. However, there is a marked difference between these eight countries and those described in the previous chapter with respect to income levels. All but two of the eleven countries that were classified as innovators or early adopters were high-income countries, whereas only one of the eight countries *(table 3.5)* fell into this category. Overall income levels in the early majority are much lower than in the innovators, and half of them are classified as low-income countries where the gross domestic product per capita in 2001 was less than five hundred U.S. dollars. It should also be noted that there is a difference within the group between Europe and the Americas on the one hand and Asia and the Pacific and Africa on the other. All four cases in Europe and the Americas were classified as either upper-middle or high income while all four in the Asia and the Pacific and Africa were low-income countries. These differences reflect the considerable gap that exists between these two parts of the world with respect to wealth and also, to a large extent, the resources that are likely to be available to implement SDI initiatives.

	2001 POP. (MILLIONS)	LAND AREA SQ. KMS (THOUSANDS)	GNP IN $ PER CAP 2001	STATUS
Europe				
Czech Republic	10	79	5,310	UMI
Finland	5	338	23,780	HI
The Americas				
Chile	15	757	4,590	UMI
Mexico	99	1,958	5,530	UMI
Asia and the Pacific				
India	1,032	3,287	460	LI
Nepal	24	147	250	LI
Africa				
Ghana	20	239	290	LI
Kenya	31	580	350	LI

GNP refers to gross national product per capita.

The last column of the table indicates the status of each country according to the ranking system of the World Bank: HI refers to high-income countries with GNP per capita incomes of more than $9,206; UMI to upper-middle-income countries with GNP per capita incomes of $2,975–$9,206; LMI to lower-middle-income countries with GNP per capita incomes of $746–$2,975; and LI to lower-income countries with GNP per capita incomes of less than $746.

Source: World Bank 2003, table 1.1, 14–17.

Table 3.5

Some key indicators for the case study countries.

The question of administrative responsibilities appears to be less significant in this case than in some of the cases discussed in the previous chapter. Although some form of federal government exists, for example, in both India and Mexico, the devolution of responsibilities with respect to the collection of geographic information in these countries is more limited than was the case with countries such as Australia and Canada.

Driving forces

In many respects, the driving forces behind the initiatives of the early majority are similar to those behind the innovators and the early adopters: promoting economic development, stimulating better government, and fostering environmental sustainability. This can be seen, for example, in India's NSDI, which sets out its objectives as follows: "The NSDI must aim to promote and establish, at the national level for the availability of organized spatial (and nonspatial) data and multilevel networking to contribute to local, national, and global needs of sustained economic growth, environmental quality and stability, and social progress" (Department of Science and Technology 2002, para 8.0).

Other driving forces featured in the previous chapter include modernization and environmental management. One of the main objectives of the Chile SNIT is to modernize the way that territorial information is handled by government agencies and to create a collaborative scheme for its future management. Environmental concerns feature prominently in Africa, and the starting point for the Ghana NAFGIM was a World Bank funded project carried out for the EPA as part of the Ghana Resource Management Project.

It is also worth noting that eGovernment has emerged as an important driving force since the initial survey was carried out in 1998. This features prominently in the Czech SDI that is linked closely to that country's overall national information infrastructure program. Specific factors in certain regions may also act as a strong driving force in SDI development. This is particularly the case in the accession countries in central and eastern Europe. This is reflected not only in the nature of the Czech SDI, but also in the fact that the initial development of Nemoforum was directly funded by the European Union through the Phare program that was set up specifically to help these countries meet the requirements for EU accession. International donors such as the World Bank also played an important role in SDI development in three out of the other seven case-study countries: Ghana, Kenya, and Nepal.

Key features

STATUS

The typology used a refinement of the distinction made in the previous chapter between SDIs with a formal mandate and those that have largely grown out of existing structures *(table 3.1).* SDIs led by national data producers fall into the latter category, whereas those led by councils of ministries or partnerships of data users fall into the former. A formal mandate is particularly important where interagency bodies are involved as it defines their position and their status with respect to government; but some of these bodies enjoy *de facto* recognition without the need for a formal mandate. This is the case with respect to RAVI, which was discussed in the previous chapter.

These differences are reflected in the arrangements described in the eight case studies. In Finland, Kenya, and Mexico, the development of NSDIs has been largely a process of evolution within well-established national data producers. In Chile, however, it was necessary to enact a presidential decree in September 2001 to set up its Sistema Nacional de Informacion Territorial, which comes under the political control of the Committee of Urban and Territorial Ministers. Participating agencies in the Indian NSDI include the Survey of India, the Natural Resource Data Management System, the Geological Survey of India, the Office of the Registrar General for India, and the Forest Survey. The Indian Government is also considering a National Spatial Data Infrastructure Bill that sets out the formal arrangements for its implementation and ensures the commitment of the participating agencies. The Czech national SDI is an interesting case that was classified as national data producer led in table 3.1, even though a partnership body, Nemoforum, is playing a leading role in its implementation. Given these circumstances, it is not surprising to find that one of the top ten priority actions contained in its plan is to formalize the status of this initiative.

In both Ghana and Nepal interdepartmental bodies are leading the NSDI initiatives. Consequently, they come somewhere between the implicit mandates of the national data producer led initiatives and the need for a formal or *de facto* status that characterizes the non-national data producer led ones.

SCOPE

The two different standpoints outlined in the previous chapter with respect to the range of substantive interests represented in the coordinating bodies and the extent to which stakeholders are directly involved can also be used for the examination of the experiences described in the eight case studies in this chapter.

Both the Finnish Council of Geographic Information and the Czech Nemoforum include a very wide range of substantive interests from all levels of government and the private sectors. This is reinforced by the participation of the respective national GI associations in these bodies. The steering committee of Ghana's National Framework for Geospatial Information Management also includes a diversity of substantive interests from eleven different government departments, the National Association of Local Authorities, and several universities. Similarly, the proposed National Spatial Data Commission for India has a senior cabinet minister as its chair, senior representatives from all the involved ministries, and representatives from different stakeholder groups. On the other hand, Nepal's National Geographic

Information Infrastructure Program must be seen as a limited effort involving several government departments to build up operational experience in connection with multi-agency geographic information management.

Most of the stakeholders are directly involved in the Finnish SDI and the Czech Republic's Nemoforum. This is also the case in the various working groups set up as part of the Kenyan SDI. Substantial stakeholder involvement is also one of the goals of the Indian NSDI but this may be very difficult to achieve given the size of the country and the large number of organizations involved.

In contrast, the NSDIs in Chile, Ghana, Mexico, and Nepal are essentially governmental in nature, and there is only limited scope for the participation of stakeholders from outside the public sector.

IMPLEMENTATION

SDI feasibility studies have been undertaken for Canada and Malaysia (as described in chapter 2). These studies are not mentioned in any of the eight case studies or reviews of experiences in different parts of the world. This is probably symptomatic of the extent to which the early majority has built upon the experience of its predecessors. Nor is there any reference to specialized centers being set up to lead the national effort, as was the case in Portugal and Qatar; although India is considering the creation of a center of excellence to create awareness and to meet the needs of the user community with respect to the skilled personnel that will be needed in the geographic information field (Masser 2001).

Despite the fact that half the case-study countries are low-income countries, questions of funding and resources do not feature very prominently in their discussion of SDI development. A notable exception to this is the Indian NSDI which devotes a complete section of its strategy document to this matter. To get its NSDI off the ground, the government of India has committed one hundred crore rupees (about $19 million) to set up the Geospatial Infrastructure Development Fund. The Spatial Data Infrastructure Commission will manage this fund. It is envisaged that it "will be solely utilized for generation of data which is not available, technology management, research and to support the Government's policy directives in poverty alleviation etc" (Department of Science and Technology 2002, para 74.0). At the same time, the government is exploring various options for attracting private capital to the NSDI. These include public–private partnerships, donor funding, and a levy for a fixed term on new projects initiated by the utility companies (Sarma 2003).

Where national data producers are involved as the lead agencies in SDI development, it is likely that some of the costs will come from their own budgets. In Kenya, for example, the Survey of Kenya was able to insert the Kenyan SDI into the National Development Plan for 2002–2008. This means that the Ministry of Lands and Settlements has a mandate to invest staff time and resources into this initiative.

Other possibilities include international funding through World Bank and similar projects. Projects of this kind played an important role in setting up Ghana's National Framework for Geospatial Information Management and creating Nemoforum in the Czech Republic. Similarly, the Japan International Cooperation Agency was involved in the workshop that led to the creation of the Kenyan SDI. However, projects such as these generally have a limited life span, whereas SDI development requires sustained efforts over a long period of time. This is one of the reasons why Kate Lance sees SDIs as difficult in regions such as Africa. "SDI is a hard sell. It is a 'beast' of an initiative since it requires inter-institutional, cross sector, long term coordination—something that defies the administrative and budgetary structures in Africa, as well as the donor agencies' funding cycles" (Lance 2003, 36).

Giff and Coleman (2002) are also skeptical about the prospects of funding SDI development through government funding in emerging nations. "The models [of funding] presented so far relied heavily on the assumption that the economies and government structures of the implementation environments are vibrant and stable. However, this is not the case in most emerging nations as these nations tend to have very weak, if stagnant, economies with unstable governments. Therefore, it is hardly likely that the struggling economies of emerging nations will be capable of financially sustaining the implementation of a SDI through government funding" (Giff and Coleman 2002, 10).

Their solution is to encourage more donor agencies to become involved. They argue that some of the problems associated with the limited life span of donor-funded projects can be resolved by the development of operational business plans that identify possible topics for this kind of funding.

Funding difficulties of this kind imply that it will be necessary to adopt a pragmatic approach to SDI development in many African countries. Consequently, the most appropriate answer to the question of how to develop SDIs in Africa may be, in the words of Dozie Ezigbalike from the United Nations Economic Commission for Africa, "the same way as one eats an elephant—one bite at a time" (quoted in Lance 2002, 41).

CHARACTERISTICS OF THE EARLY MAJORITY

THE SHEER SIZE OF THE EARLY MAJORITY group makes it difficult to generalize about its characteristics with any degree of certainty. According to Rogers (1995), this is the group that adopts the idea just ahead of the average member of the social system. Because of its size, it is also the group that provides much of the interconnectedness in the network through the interactions that take place between peers. This is reflected in the growing number of opportunities that have come into being for interaction on SDI matters at the regional and global levels as a result of the efforts of bodies such as EUROGI and the GSDI Association (see chapters 6 and 7). It can also be seen in the emergence of comparative studies of SDI experiences at these levels. These have made possible the generalizations about developments in the different regions of the world that have accompanied the case studies in this chapter.

There is a marked contrast between the relative wealth of most of the innovator and early adopter countries and the relative poverty of many of the early majority countries. This highlights the extent to which the take up of SDIs has shifted from countries with the resources to take risks and cope with the uncertainties associated with innovation to countries that have to wait until these risks and uncertainties are substantially reduced. Thus, unlike some of the innovators and early adopters, there was no evidence from among this group of the need to undertake feasibility studies to explore the issues involved before committing a country to SDI development or the need for specialized centers to be set up to lead SDI development.

The overall impact of these developments has been substantial. As a result, the overall rate of adoption has accelerated considerably over the last few years. Whether the late majority and the laggards will sustain this rate over the next few years is, however, open to question given the discussion on funding in the previous sections.

SUMMARY

THIS CHAPTER HAS CONSIDERED SOME OF the main features of the large number of countries that form the early majority of national SDI initiatives throughout the world. Many of these have been carried out in low- and lower-middle-income countries in Asia and Africa where both the human skills and the financial resources required for SDI development are likely to be limited. Generally the driving forces behind these initiatives have been similar to those of the innovators and early adopters, although eGovernment has given a new dimension to some SDIs. The early majority of adopters also has provided much of the interconnectedness in the interactions that take place between similar countries. This has been reflected in the rapid increase in the rate of adoptions since 1998.

National SDIs have recently been the subject of a number of comparative evaluations in Europe and a useful typology has been developed as a result of these efforts. This is based on the nature of the bodies that have emerged to coordinate SDIs in different countries, as this is seen as an important success factor in SDI development. This distinguishes between national data producer led initiatives on the one hand and non-national data producer led initiatives on the other. Because of the economic and political circumstances of many African and Asian countries, projects funded by donor agencies such as the World Bank have played an important role in the early stages of the development of their NSDI initiatives. But it must be recognized that these projects have a limited life span, whereas SDIs will require sustained commitment over longer time periods. Given these circumstances, many of these countries have had to adopt a pragmatic approach to SDI development.

CHAPTER 4

The evolution of SDIs in the United Kingdom

The old adage that Rome wasn't built in a day applies equally to SDIs. The creation of SDIs, a long-term task, may take years or even decades in some cases before they are fully operational. This SDI growth process evolves, reflecting the extent to which the organizations involved also change over time. As a result, major changes in the form and content of SDIs can be expected over time as they "reinvent" themselves.

With this in mind, this chapter examines the evolution of thinking about spatial data infrastructures and geographic information strategies in the United Kingdom since the publication of the Chorley Report (Department of the Environment 1987). The United Kingdom case is particularly interesting as an example of SDI evolution because of the changes that have taken place with respect to the UK SDI, the National Geospatial Data Framework, since its launch in 1996. Alongside these national developments, regional SDIs have recently emerged within the United Kingdom. These regional developments were stimulated by the transfer of some powers to elected regional assemblies in Scotland, Wales, and Northern Ireland.

The chapter is divided into four sections:

1. The evolution of strategic thinking about geographic information in the United Kingdom from the publication of the Chorley report in 1987 up to the establishment of the National Geospatial Data Framework (NGDF) in 1996

2. The evolution of the NGDF up to 2001

3. The recent emergence of regional SDIs following the devolution of some powers to elected regional assemblies in Scotland, Wales, and Northern Ireland

4. Some the general lessons for SDI development in other parts of the world that can be learned from this experience

The chapter ends with box 4.4 that summarizes what has happened to the other ten NSDI initiatives reviewed in chapter 1.

THE IMPACT OF THE CHORLEY
REPORT

THE DISCUSSION ABOUT SPATIAL DATA infrastructures in the United Kingdom begins with a publication called Handling Geographic Information: Report to the Secretary of State for the Environment of the Committee of Enquiry into the Handling of Geographic Information (Department of Environment 1987), also referred to as "the Chorley Report." The Chorley Report built on the findings of two earlier committees: the Ordnance Survey Review Committee chaired by Sir David Serpell that reported in 1979 (Serpell 1979) and the survey of remote sensing and digital mapping undertaken by the House of Lords Select Committee on Science and Technology (1983).

The Chorley Report set the scene for the subsequent discussion about SDIs in the United Kingdom. It reflects the committee's enthusiasm for the new GIS technology as "the biggest step forward in the handling of geographic information since the invention of the map" (para 1.7), and also their concern that information technology in itself must be regarded as "a necessary, though not sufficient, condition for the take up of geographic information systems to increase rapidly" (para 1.22). To facilitate the rapid take up of GIS, the committee recommended overcoming two important barriers that users face: (1) users need to become more aware of GIS technology, and (2) they also need more digital data for particular applications.

Given this context, the committee recommended three important changes. One, with respect to digital topographic mapping, it recommended accelerating the program of digital data conversion using a simplified specification for conversion. This is now largely a matter of historic interest, given the completion of the national digital topographic database by Ordnance Survey in May 1995 (Rhind 1997a).

Two, in contrast, the committee's recommendations on data availability are still of considerable relevance (see, for example, Heywood 1997). They stressed the importance of giving users greater access to data held by government and other public-sector agencies. They also argued that the agencies involved should take the necessary steps to make their data available to users, preferably in a disaggregated form, except where this is prevented by the questions of confidentiality. The committee also pointed out that the main benefits of introducing GIS depend to a large extent on linking data sets together, and that government and public-sector agencies must develop standard forms of geographic description to facilitate linkage based either on the coordinates of the National Grid, or in the case of socio-economic data, on postal geographies such as those used by the Royal Mail.

Third, underlying their whole line of reasoning, the committee argued that government must clearly lead the way and play a central role in the future development of the geographic information field. With this in mind, the committee recommended that the government establish an independent national Centre for Geographic Information with strong links to government to promote the use of geographic information technology and provide a forum for wider debate. The government's response was generally negative with respect to this proposal. It argued that it was better to encourage existing organizations to expand their range of activities rather than set up a new organization. Nevertheless, a new organization, the Association for Geographic Information (AGI) was set up in January 1989 with some help from the government. In 2004, the AGI had over one thousand members from central and local government, the private sector, the utilities, and academia. It is a major player in the geographic information debate within the United Kingdom. The AGI sees its mission as "to maximize the use of geographic information for the benefit of the citizen, good governance, and commerce" *(www.agi.org.uk)*.

An official working group was also established to follow up the recommendations of the Chorley Committee that required cooperation between government departments (Oliver 1996, 26). In 1993, this working group was relaunched as the Interdepartmental Group on Geographic Information (IGGI). In 1998, renamed the Intra-governmental Group on Geographic Information, this group regularly brings together representatives from nearly one hundred central government agencies covering a great diversity of applications *(www.iggi.gov.uk)*. The chairman and secretariat of the IGGI are currently based in the Office of the Deputy Prime Minister.

Similar developments have taken place at the local government level. The Local Government Management Board played an active role in the development of the geographic information field in the mid 1990s, and the local government Improvement and Development Agency (I&DeA) has played a similar role in recent years. Its subsidiary, Information House, is currently working in partnership with the local government community on a number of national infrastructure projects that enable councils to deliver local services more effectively. These include the National Land Information Service (NLIS) and the National Land and Property Gazetteer (NLPG) *(www.idea. gov.uk)*. The latter has developed a considerable momentum in its own right as a bottom up SDI initiative. Over half the local authority respondents to a recent survey claimed that they updated their files daily or weekly at the end of 2003, and all of them expressed an interest in actively creating a local land and property gazetteer (Whitefield 2003).

THE NATIONAL GEOSPATIAL DATA FRAMEWORK

THE PRINCIPLES UNDERLYING THE NATIONAL Geospatial Data Framework (NGDF) as it appeared in 1998 have already been described in chapter 2. This section considers the context within which the NGDF came into being in more detail and outlines the circumstances that led to its transfer to the AGI in 2001.

The basic concepts underlying what eventually became Britain's NGDF were set out in a paper written by three Ordnance Survey staff (Nanson et al. 1996). At the 1995 Conference of the Association for Geographic Information, they presented their paper and argued that "throughout the world, people are increasingly aware of the potential for using advances in technology to bring together the many data sets that contain geospatial references" to create a National Geospatial Database (NGD). To support their arguments, they cited parallel developments in the United States following President Clinton's 1994 Executive Order establishing a National Spatial Data Infrastructure linked together by common standards, clearinghouses to show users where to find the data, and freedom of access to federal government information. They recognized, however, that there were important cultural differences between the United Kingdom and the United States, particularly in the autonomy granted to government departments and the pressures exerted by the Treasury to reduce direct costs and generate income from tradeable information.

The authors saw the NGD as a virtual database that brings together "many of the data sets collected and held by many different organizations." To qualify for inclusion, a data set must conform to agreed standards. It must also be accessible on defined and published terms, and it must also be capable of being linked to other data sets through the Ordnance Survey's National Geospatial Framework.

Subsequently renamed the National Geospatial Data Framework (NGDF), the project got under way in late 1996 serviced by a small team of seconded Ordnance Survey staff. These reported to a management board chaired by the head of Ordnance Survey at that time, David Rhind. Its members included the Office for National Statistics, Ordnance Survey, and HM Land Registry together with their Scottish and Northern Irish equivalents in the public sector, and Landmark and Property Intelligence in the private sector, as well as representatives from the Information Management Advisory Group of the Local Government Management Board and the Natural Environment Research Council. The AGI also set up an advisory council with an even wider remit. Its members were drawn from government departments such as the Environment Agency, the Public Records Office, as well as ESRI (UK), and MVA Systematica in the private sector, academia, and bodies such as Friends of the Earth.

The main objective of the NGDF was to unlock geospatial information (National Geospatial Data Framework 1998, 1). Its strategy was built around three "pillars":

1. Collaborating through identifying key players, sharing experiences, and encouraging new partnerships

2. Using business driven standards to promote interoperability

3. Facilitating access to geospatial data (Rhind 1997b)

Its work program was managed by a taskforce that reported to its board. The board set up working groups on various priority areas including metadata, accreditation, and research.

The driving forces behind the NGDF were the data producers, particularly Ordnance Survey. There was a strong project/product emphasis in its activities, which was also reflected in its strategic plan (National Geospatial Data Framework 1998). By the beginning of 1999, the work of the NGDF staff largely revolved around two projects (Payne 1999): the UK Standard Geographic Base (UKSGB) project that was originally commissioned by IGGI in the mid 1990s, and the development of a distributed national metadata service, which emerged in 2000 under the heading of askGIraffe (Elliot 2000). From April 1999, both these projects were primarily funded by Ordnance Survey under its National Interest Mapping Services Agreement (NIMSA) with the government (Oliver and Havercroft 2000).

During the latter part of 2000, the NGDF board asked for a strategic review of NGDF. As a result of this review, the board decided that the NGDF should cease to exist as an entity during 2001 (Hadley and Elliott 2001). It was agreed that

+ the objectives of AGI and NGDF would converge,

+ the AGI would take over all the NGDF existing operations such as askGIraffe, and

+ a strategic alliance would be formed to deliver NGDF's "joined up geography" objectives.

This resulted in contracts for the initial secondment of NGDF staff from Ordnance Survey to the AGI from September 2001 and for the continued funding of NGDF-related activities through the NIMSA agreement between Ordnance Survey and the government. Full responsibility for the askGIraffe service was transferred to the AGI in April 2002. The AGI set up a new team to develop this service and rebranded it as GIgateway *(www.GIgateway.org)*. GIgateway is a service for metadata discovery and ultimately access to complex geospatial data sets.

THE CURRENT STATE OF SDI
DEVELOPMENT IN THE
UNITED KINGDOM

IN THE LAST FEW YEARS, A CRITICAL
factor in SDI development in the United Kingdom has been the
devolution of powers from Westminster to Scotland, Wales,
and Northern Ireland *(figure 4.1)*. The three Acts of Parliament dealing with devolution—the Scotland Act of 1998, the
Government of Wales Act of 1998, and the Northern Ireland
Act of 1998—define the functions of the UK government and
the devolved administrations in different ways. The Scottish
Parliament and the Northern Ireland Assembly have a general
competence over all matters not specifically kept by Westminster, although these are expressed rather differently. In contrast,
the National Assembly for Wales has only secondary legislative and executive responsibility for a list of powers devolved
from Westminster and must get Parliamentary approval for
any changes in primary laws (Keating 2002). These differences reflect the situation prior to devolution in which Wales
was much more closely tied to Westminster than either Scotland or Northern Ireland.

Notwithstanding the differences in powers devolved to them,
an important impact of devolution in all of them was an upsurge
of interest in regional as opposed to national UK issues. One
outcome of this is the emergence of SDIs or regional GI strategies in all three regions. England, in contrast, did not pursue
its own strategy until relatively recently. It should also be noted
that the decision of the AGI to establish regional branches in
Northern Ireland, Scotland, and Wales in 1999 was an important contributory factor to these developments.

There are also considerable differences in size between the four
component parts of the United Kingdom. Table 4.1 shows that
83.6 percent of the UK population live in England, while Scotland, Wales, and Northern Ireland account for 8.6, 4.9, and
2.9 percent, respectively.

Figure 4.1
The United Kingdom.

	NUMBER (THOUSANDS)	PERCENTAGE UK POPULATION
England	49,139	83.6
Scotland	5,062	8.6
Wales	2,903	4.9
Northern Ireland	1,685	2.9
Total	58,789	100.0

Table 4.1
Population of the United Kingdom
in 2001.

Source: Censuses of population for England and Wales, Scotland, and Northern Ireland
(www.statistics.gov.uk).

Geographical information strategy action plan for Wales

Wales was the first region in the United Kingdom to start formulating a geographic information strategy. This reflects the strong links that have been built up with the Welsh Assembly since the establishment of AGI Cymru along with the regional groups for Scotland and Northern Ireland in 1999. In 2001, the eMinister for Wales, Andrew Davies, addressed the AGI Cymru Conference and challenged the participants to identify how Wales could make the best use of its geographic information assets.

As a result of this challenge, AGI Cymru carried out a wide ranging consultation of 106 organizations throughout Wales. The findings of this study were published the following year in a consultation paper on a national strategy for Wales (AGI 2002). Subsequently, they were substantially embodied in the Geographic Information Plan prepared by AGI Cymru with sponsorship from the Welsh Assembly Government (AGI Cymru 2003). This sets out its vision for geographic information in Wales, "the opportunities and drivers and the simple action points that the GI community need to progress in the next year to move the initiative forward" (p. 5). This vision can be achieved through the following actions for AGI Cymru, the Welsh Assembly, and Welsh local government:

- ✦ the adoption and use of common data standards
- ✦ the adoption and use of common metadata standards
- ✦ promoting a "collect once use many times" philosophy
- ✦ providing strong leadership
- ✦ joint working
- ✦ communication and promotion of best practice

In his foreword to the Action Plan, the eMinister for Wales expresses his support for the initiative. "This Action Plan is an important step on the way to realizing the benefits of GI for Wales, and I hope that you will join us in implementing it effectively and successfully."

A geographic information strategy for Northern Ireland

One of the most distinctive features of the strategy that has emerged in Northern Ireland is the innovative process used to build up collective ownership of the geographic information strategy among the key stakeholders. Because of this, it is worth describing the initial stages of the process in some detail.

Ordnance Survey of Northern Ireland and its parent ministry, the Department of Culture, Arts, and Leisure, decided that a new approach was required to develop and implement geographic information policy in Northern Ireland. They decided to make use of the Future Search method to develop an initial GI policy agenda for the province *(box 4.1)*. This method had already been successfully used to develop the Sustainable Northern Ireland program.

According to its inventors, Future Search is "a unique planning meeting that is used worldwide by hundreds of communities and organizations. It meets two goals at the same time: (1) helping large diverse groups discover values, purposes and projects they hold in common, and (2) enabling people to create a desired future together and start working towards it right away." Typically a Future Search involves a group of sixty to seventy people, which is large enough to contain different perspectives, but small enough to engage in a dialogue at every stage in the process. The optimal length for a Future Search meeting is two and a half days with a minimum of four half-day sessions.

The Future Search process itself involves five main stages. The first of these establishes the common history of the participants, while the second maps the world trends affecting the whole group. In the third stage, each of the stakeholder groups is asked to evaluate what they are doing, while the fourth considers some ideal future scenarios. The group as a whole then identifies the common ground themes that appear in each scenario and confirms their common future. In the last stage, group members sign up to work together on their desired action plans.

Future Search avoids conflicts and focuses attention on the evolution of a shared agenda. This is done by treating "problems and conflicts as information rather than action items while searching for common ground and desirable futures." In essence, it is a highly structured process that enables diverse groups of stakeholders to work alongside each to find common ground. Implicit in the process is the extent to which those involved feel that they have created the desirable futures and have had the opportunity to commit themselves and their organizations to participate in the action plans that concern them most. Under such circumstances it is axiomatic that the process as a whole is facilitated by someone with no direct involvement in the issues being discussed.

Box 4.1   The Future Search method.
Source: Weissbord and Janoff (2002).

Mick Cory studied surveying at the University of Newcastle upon Tyne in England. After his graduation, he joined the Directorate of Overseas Surveys and spent six years working in Liberia, Malawi, and Yemen. On his return to Britain, he worked for Ordnance Survey Great Britain for eight years before moving to Dublin where he had responsibility for the overall management of production and the technical development of Ordnance Survey Ireland. Mick was appointed Chief Executive of Ordnance Survey Northern Ireland in 1999. In this capacity, he is responsible to Parliament through the Minister of Culture, Arts, and Leisure for the management, direction, and operation of this agency within the Northern Ireland Civil Service. Mick's twenty-five years experience in leading, facilitating, and coordinating national, pan-national, and public–private sector collaborative ventures is reflected in the important contribution that he has made to the development of the Northern Ireland GI Strategy, Mosaic.

Mick Cory's view of the key success factors in Northern Ireland:

> We worked hard to ensure that all stakeholders were involved in developing a shared vision, a shared understanding, and therefore shared ownership for the Northern Ireland spatial data infrastructure, now called "Mosaic: Information on Location." We began by involving stakeholders at a unique three-day retreat on Lusty Beg Island, Lower Lough Erne in County Fermanagh, Northern Ireland. Original participants still proudly declare they were there. Today the involvement, participation, and ownership of all stakeholders remain crucial to the future of Mosaic.

Box 4.2　Profile of Mick Cory, Chief Executive, Ordnance Survey Northern Ireland, Belfast.

The department invited more than fifty people and organizations to participate in a GI policy Future Search on the island of Lusty Beg in Fermanagh in February 2002. The group consisted of representatives from all the main stakeholders in Northern Ireland together with a number of invited participants from British and European organizations. It was divided into six more or less equal groups: GI industry (technical), GI industry (systems and data), culture arts leisure and tourism, agriculture and environment, emergency services, health and transport, and land property and networks.

The Future Search process worked well at the Lusty Beg meeting. The participants collectively created a mind map with thirty-two main trends and an even larger numbers of sub-trends within these trends. Each of the participants was then given the opportunity to identify and vote (privately) for their main priorities within this mind map. From this it emerged that the already complete digital topographic data coverage of Northern Ireland was the key factor, in this case closely followed by the need to take account of the growing pressures on public funding. Other factors that rated highly include the recognition that GI is an economic resource, the need to promote environmentally sustainable development, and concerns about the lack of standardization.

During subsequent discussions the following issues emerged as key elements for common ground and future growth:

- the importance of creating an overall GI strategy for Northern Ireland

- the importance of facilitating access

- the importance of promoting awareness

- the importance of building partnerships to achieve these objectives

The impact of the debates that took place at Lusty Beg can be seen in the consultation paper subsequently published by Ordnance Survey Northern Ireland (OSNI) (Ordnance Survey Northern Ireland 2002). This paper proposed steering groups for each key sector interested in better coordinating their efforts. These steering groups cover sectors such as public safety and emergency services, land and property, transport, environment, utilities and networks, statistics, and key data sets. All these sectors were involved in the Lusty Beg meeting. A feedback workshop for Lusty Beg participants was also organized by the department in March 2003 to review progress. As a result of these developments, OSNI proposed that "a suitably robust and high-level strategic framework" should be set up to manage and coordinate the successful implementation of the GI strategy. This should be chaired at the Deputy Secretary level within the Department of Culture, Arts, and Leisure.

Following the feedback workshop, OSNI prepared an implementation plan. The GI strategy was subsequently approved by the Minister of Culture, Arts, and Leisure, and the eGovernment board. A small GI support office with two and a half staff positions has been set up to support the activities of the Implementation Project Board and to provide a focal point for geographic information coordination in Northern Ireland.

AGI Northern Ireland (AGINI) has been closely involved in these developments, and its chair and three of its committee members are members of the Implementation Project Board. AGINI together with the University of Ulster and Ordnance Survey Northern Ireland also organized a major conference in Belfast in May 2004. At this conference, the Parliamentary Under Secretary of State for Northern Ireland, Angela Smith, launched the Mosaic program for implementing the Northern Ireland GI strategy. The Mosaic program's vision is

> to provide the strategic leadership required for a practical, coordinated, and inclusive approach to improving the collection, funding, dissemination, and use of geographic information, in order to maximize the social, economic, and educational potential of this crucial component of the national information infrastructure resource.

A geographic information strategy for Scotland

Developments in Wales and Northern Ireland prompted AGI Scotland to organize a seminar in November 2002 where they considered how to move Scotland towards a national GI strategy. AGI Scotland concluded that

> ↬ "the GI community have identified broad ranging requirements for a GI strategy which needs to fundamentally address issues concerning policy, data, and the roles of different organizations involved in the collection and utilization of GI

> ↬ the Scottish Executive is one of the key stakeholders in the creation and implementation of a Scottish GI strategy

> ↬ other stakeholders include data providers from central and local government, citizens, technology providers, and the education community

> ↬ some of the components of a strategy are already in place, or are currently being developed at a local, organizational, or sectoral level

> ↬ some of the key gaps to be addressed are the creation of leadership and vision, coordination of existing initiatives (many of which are fragmented along traditional, i.e., vested interest lines), institutional barriers, and clear identification of current shortcomings (AGI Scotland 2003, 6)"

As a result of this seminar, AGI Scotland published a consultation paper outlining its own GI strategy for Scotland in July 2003 (AGI Scotland 2003). This paper sets out its vision of a Scottish GI strategy to "ensure the effective and consistent provision, management, and utilization of geographic information to support and sustain the needs of the citizen, business, and governance in 21st century Scotland." The main message of this document is that, while many of the building blocks are already in place, not much more can be done without the direct involvement of the Scottish Executive. Consequently, AGI Scotland formally invited the Scottish Executive "to assume ownership of the process for creating and championing a Scottish Geographic Information Strategy" (p. 18).

In September 2004, the Scottish Executive published its response to AGI Scotland (Scottish Executive 2004). This took the form of a paper entitled *One Scotland—One Geography: A Geographic Information Strategy for Scotland.* The Executive plans to discuss the contents of this paper with all interested parties so that an amended strategy can be adopted by all of them by March 2005. The Minister for Finance and Public Services, Andy Kerr, sets out his expectations from the strategy in his foreword to this paper, "This draft strategy is intended to help deliver better and more cost-effective support through geographical information for the whole range of public services in Scotland. The vision of the strategy is 'One Scotland—One Geography' and this reflects our commitment to a joined up approach to our policy development and to our service delivery" (Scottish Executive 2004, 4).

These are the five objectives of the strategy:

1. Provide strategic vision and leadership to ensure an inclusive, coordinated, and pragmatic approach to information about Scotland's geography

2. Ensure that everyone can use the most up-to-date and accurate information about Scotland that can be delivered with best use of resources

3. Develop and promote the means whereby geographic information can be shared, within the practical limits of best value, so as to give high quality and knowledge "return" from each set of data

4. Promote the benefits of geographic information across the public, private, community, and voluntary sectors, taking account of international activities and ensuring that Scotland's successes are celebrated and communicated to an international audience

5. Promote the appropriate technical and professional standards for efficient and effective use of geographic information in Scotland

The Scottish Executive views the strategy as an enabling document that commits the Executive to work with partners to address the issues, rather than as a detailed prescriptive strategy document.

A geographic information strategy for England

The last piece of the UK jigsaw fell into place when the local government sector saw the need for a special interest group within the AGI to provide standardized data sets and services to help join up their services with respect to eGovernment. In June 2003, the AGI local government Special Interest Group in collaboration with IGGI and I&DeA organized a seminar to address the need for a joined up GI framework initiative that had not been resolved by the NGDF initiative or through other means.

The seminar participants wanted to establish a case for a geographic information framework so that the English government could promote effective management and enable various agencies to share geographic information (Schmid and Keith 2003).

As was the case in Scotland, the participants at the seminar agreed that many component parts of a GI framework currently existed and that there had been a number of significant achievements in the last decade that would help in creating an overarching framework for geographic information. The issue is not to begin again in establishing a GI framework for England (or for the United Kingdom as a whole), but to make better use of existing organizations and initiatives that currently use geographic information in a way that is beneficial to the GI community as a whole. With this in mind, the participants agreed that those involved should work toward the following vision: "to be able to access and share up-to-date and accurate geographic information between all government departments and national organizations according to a common reference framework with the overall aim to facilitate joined up e-service delivery to the citizens" (Schmid and Keith 2003).

Dr. Gesche Schmid was born and raised in Germany and has a Ph.D. in digital terrain modeling from the University of Alberta, Canada. She started her professional career in Britain in 1993 as lecturer in GIS at the University of Greenwich where she is still a visiting research fellow. She moved to local government in 1998 to lead the development and implementation of GIS in Medway Council for which Medway won the AGI Local Government best practice award in 2000. In 2001, Gesche was promoted to ICT and information manager responsible for coordinating e-service delivery initiatives and managing information for development and environmental services at Medway Council.

Gesche has taken the lead in sponsoring and developing a GI strategy for England through the Association for Geographic Information (AGI). Since 1998, she has been actively involved in the AGI as a member of various committees, as a council member from 2000 to 2003, and most recently as chair of the GI strategy for England action group. Gesche was the founder, chair, and recently deputy chair of the local government special interest group that raises awareness of the benefits of geographical information and promotes its appropriate use and good management in local government. She is also a local government representative on the Intra-government Group for Geographic Information (IGGI), a member of Central-Local Government Information Partnership and the Local Government GI Committee (LOGGIC) in which she promotes the use and sharing of geographic information within the government sector.

Gesche Schmid has a keen interest in providing easy access to seamless, accurate, and up-to-date information as part of e-service delivery. She sees in the development and implementation of a GI strategy for England a way to facilitate sharing of geographic information between local and central government and commercial organizations to the benefit of citizens, good governance, and commerce.

Box 4.3   Profile of Gesche Schmid, ICT and Information Manager, Medway District Council, Chatham, Kent.

Following this seminar, the AGI set up an action working group to develop a GI strategy for England. This group, which includes representatives from central and local government as well as the private sector, produced a consultation document in April 2004 (Association for Geographic Information 2004). One of the most challenging tasks for the action working group has been to identify the nature of government commitment and leadership in connection with the proposed GI strategy for England, as the political and administrative situation in England is not as clearly defined as that in the devolved regions.

With this in mind, the group's mission is set out in the consultation paper in the following terms. "The Geographic Information Strategy for England will establish a viable and user-acceptable GI framework based on nationally—and ultimately internationally—recognized standards. It will permit the accurate and simple linking of people, organizations, and services to specific geographic locations. It will do this in the interests of delivering better quality information, better use of available information, improved services, improved access to those services, increased service efficiency, and improved interoperability to the benefit of citizens, government, and business organizations" (Association for Geographic Information 2004, 16).

SOME GENERAL LESSONS
FROM THE UNITED KINGDOM
EXPERIENCE

SDI EVOLUTION IN THE UNITED KINGDOM shows that process of evolution is not always straightforward. The transfer of NGDF activities to the AGI and the subsequent emergence of SDIs in each of the different members of the United Kingdom reflect far reaching institutional changes in geographic information policy in the United Kingdom. In particular, the devolution of powers to Scotland, Wales, and Northern Ireland led to an upsurge of interest in regional as opposed to national UK issues. These regional issues were exploited by the newly established regional branches of the AGI. It should be noted in this respect that England does not have its own AGI regional branch.

Another important contributory factor to these developments was the impact of the European Commission's INfrastructure for SPatial InfoRmation in Europe (INSPIRE) initiative that got under way in late 2001 (see chapter 6). This substantially raised the profile of SDI development in Europe as a whole and stimulated people and organizations in many European countries to start thinking more substantively about GI strategies at all levels of government.

The terminology used in these initiatives is also revealing. All of the initiatives avoid the term "infrastructure" and refer instead to "strategy." This reflects the distinction made by EUROGI in their consultation paper on a GI strategy for Europe. EUROGI prefer the term "strategy" over "infrastructure" because the former "includes awareness raising, promoting greater usage, and capacity building as well as the more limited set of activities listed [under the heading of infrastructure]. It also assumes that the main problems to be tackled are primarily political and institutional rather than technical in nature" (European Umbrella Organisation for Geographic Information 2000).

There are also some useful lessons to be learned from the methodologies used for SDI development in Northern Ireland. The Future Search procedure appears to have considerable potential for assisting in coalition formation at an early stage of SDI development in relatively small countries where the number of stakeholders is limited. Obviously, it would need to be modified for applications in large countries or countries in the later stages of SDI development.

	NGDF	WALES	NORTHERN IRELAND	SCOTLAND	ENGLAND
Predominant approach	Product	Process	Process	Process	Process
Driving force	Ordnance Survey	AGI Cymru	DCAL NI	AGI Scotland	IGGI/AGI/ I&DeA
Role of government	Passive	Facilitator	Facilitator	Facilitator	Passive
Role of AGI body	Advisory Council*	GI strategy preparation	Important participant	Pressure group	GI strategy

* The AGI was also a member of the NGDF Board

Table 4.2
A comparative evaluation of UK SDIs.

It must also be recognized that each of the recent GI strategy initiatives described above are still evolving in themselves, and that each of them will require sustained commitment over time to realize their objectives. The main features of each of these GI strategies as they stand at the present time are summarized in table 4.2. From this it can be seen that there is a sharp contrast in approach between the recent initiatives and the NGDF. This reflects the shift from the first to the second generation of national SDIs over the last ten years that has been described by Rajabifard et al. (2003). They argue that the distinctive feature of the second generation of NSDIs is the change from the product model that characterized most of the first generation to a process model. The shift from the product to the process model is essentially a change in emphasis from the concerns of data producers to those of data users *(table 4.2)*.

The analysis also raises questions about the changing role of government with respect to SDI development. The study of the United Kingdom carried out for the INSPIRE initiative by the Spatial Applications Division (SAD) of the Catholic University of Leuven concluded that, "there is no single high profile central government led initiative to coordinate the provision and dissemination of GI at the national level. In Britain, central government does not see this as its business, even though some of its core policies such as partnerships between government agencies in delivering services at the local level would clearly benefit from a coordinated GI framework as the basis for sharing information" (Spatial Applications Division, Catholic University of Leuven 2003d, 7).

In the absence of a formal mandate, the role of government with respect to the NGDF was passive. This was also the case to some extent in Scotland prior to the publication of the Scottish Executive's response to AGI Scotland. In contrast, the role of government in Northern Ireland and Wales has been essentially as a facilitator. However, Northern Ireland is the only one of these initiatives that has a formal mandate from government to begin implementing its geographic information strategy. AGI regional bodies have played a more central role in initial GI strategy formulation in Wales and Scotland than in the NGDF or Northern Ireland. Because of the lack of an appropriate regional body for England, the local government special interest group of the AGI became the driving force in the development of thinking about a GI strategy for England.

In this way, the findings of the UK case study raise some interesting general questions regarding the role that national GI associations can play in SDI development. The activities of the AGI and its regional branches demonstrate the benefits that the Chorley Committee had in mind when they recommended the establishment of an independent national center for geographic information with strong links to government. They wanted to promote the use of geographic information technology and to provide a forum for wider debate. One of the reasons for the transfer of activities from the NGDF to the AGI was the degree of overlap between the basic objectives of the two organizations. The differing roles that the regional branches have recently played in SDI development are also very interesting. In Wales, AGI Cymru was challenged by the minister to develop a GI strategy for Wales that could be implemented by the Welsh Assembly Government. In Northern Ireland, AGINI played a less central role but nevertheless made an important input to the development of the Northern Ireland GI strategy. AGI Scotland acted more as a pressure group to provoke a response from the Scottish Executive, while developments in the rest of the United Kingdom have stimulated the AGI local government SIG to work together with the main central and local governmental bodies and the private sector to develop a GI framework for England.

Notwithstanding these developments, it must be borne in mind that while national GI associations can both support and stimulate government to develop and implement SDIs, they can never replace governments in this respect. SDI development cannot take place in isolation as it ultimately requires the resources and powers that are at the disposal of governments. It also requires that governments recognize the importance of making the maximum use of their national geographic information assets, as well as bringing benefits to their citizens through the delivery of e-services.

The changes that have taken place in the last ten years in the United Kingdom inevitably prompt the question as to what has happened in the other ten countries that were reviewed in chapter 2. The majority of them have experienced important changes during this period although none of these have been as dramatic as those in the United Kingdom *(box 4.4)*.

In some cases, the underlying framework governing these initiatives has not substantially changed since 1998. This is essentially the case in Australia and the United States, as will be seen in the next chapter. It is also the case in Qatar and Japan. However, important changes have taken place since 1998 with respect to some of the other initiatives that highlight the extent to which they must be seen as evolving processes. In Malaysia, for example, a special center, the Malaysian Center for Geospatial Data Infrastructure has been established to facilitate the implementation of the NaLIS initiative. In Portugal, on the other hand, the previously independent National Center for Geographic Information has been merged with the national mapping and cadastral agency, the Instituto Geografico Portuguese.

During this period, Korea enacted legislation to promote the construction and use of the NGIS in 2000 and moved on to its second NGIS master plan, which envisages a considerable expansion of the basis for the national GIS to create a Digital National Land. In Indonesia, the position of Bakosurtanal was changed by Presidential Decree 87/1998. This decree stated that Indonesia's position is "to promote a reliable SDI as a base of existing natural resources and environmental information for development." In Canada, the government has funded a new agency, GeoConnections, to implement the GCDI, as will be seen in the next chapter. And, finally, in the Netherlands, the RAVI has restructured its activities yet again and formed a consortium of ten universities, twenty research institutes, sixty companies, forty government bodies, and thirty data producers to promote GI knowledge transfer in its Space for Geoinformation program. This has a total budget of more than 68 million Euros (about 83.5 million U.S. dollars) from 2003 to 2006 from a mixture of public- and private-sector sources.

Box 4.4   What happened to the other ten national SDIs surveyed in 1998?
Sources: Ministry of Construction and Transportation (2003), Netherlands Council for Geographic Information (2002), Tarigi and Al Malki (2003), *www.bakosurtanal.go.id, www.gsi.go.jp, www.igeo.pt, www.nalis.gov.my.*

SUMMARY

THIS CHAPTER HAS EXAMINED THE NOTION of SDI evolution with particular reference to events in the United Kingdom since the publication of the Chorley Report in 1987. The underlying message of this report was that governments must take a central role in the development of the geographic information field in order to exploit the potential opportunities opened up by new technologies. Its proposal to set up a national center for GI was rejected by the government of the day and, as a result, Britain's national SDI initiative did not get under way until 1996. Although the National Geospatial Data Framework had many positive features at the outset, including the involvement of all sectors of the GI community, by 1999 the work of the NGDF team largely revolved around only two projects. Consequently it was agreed in 2001 that it should cease to exist as an entity and that the Association for Geographic Information should take over its existing operations. These developments coincided with an upsurge of interest in regional as opposed to national GI strategies following the devolution of powers to Northern Ireland, Scotland, and Wales in 1998. The regional branches of the AGI have played an important role in facilitating the emergence of GI strategies for these three regions. However, the largest region, England, has lagged behind the others because of the absence of an appropriate regional body.

CHAPTER 5

Implementing multilevel SDIs in the United States, Australia, and Canada

The Australian Land Information Council came into being in 1986, and the Federal Geographic Data Committee (FGDC) was set up to coordinate SDI activities in the United States in 1990. Work on the Canadian Geospatial Data Infrastructure (CGDI) began later than in Australia and the United States, but a considerable body of operational experience has nevertheless been built up in Canada. This chapter considers what has happened since the descriptions of the three initiatives were compiled for chapter 2 and explores the way in which each of these countries has been going about the task of implementing their NSDIs in a multilevel environment.

The chapter is divided into four main sections:

1. What has happened in the United States

2. What has happened in Australia

3. What has happened in Canada

4. A comparative evaluation

In each case, the national case studies consist of four sections:

⟶ an introduction

⟶ an update

⟶ implementation issues

⟶ SDI implementation issues at the state and local levels

In each case study the state and local level section includes one or more case studies of statewide and local initiatives.

Before going any further, it is important to note that these three countries are all large and wealthy countries with federal systems of administration. Consequently, although their administrative structures highlight some of the issues involved in multilevel SDI implementation, some measure of caution may be required in translating the lessons of this experience into actions for small or poor countries with or without more centralized systems of government.

THE UNITED STATES

ONE OF THE MOST DISTINCTIVE FEATURES of the United States is the large number of agencies involved in creating geographic information *(figure 5.1)*. As might be expected given the federal structure of the U.S. government, many important responsibilities for geographic information are dealt with at the state and local government level, and there are wide variations between states in the way that these responsibilities are carried out. Particularly important from this standpoint are land titles registration and land taxation matters that rest with local governments in each state. As a result, over eighty thousand agencies, including fifty states, more than three thousand counties, and seven thousand cities, are involved in some way with geographic information creation (Tosta 1997a).

Figure 5.1
The United States (Alaska and Hawaii not shown) with case study area highlighted.

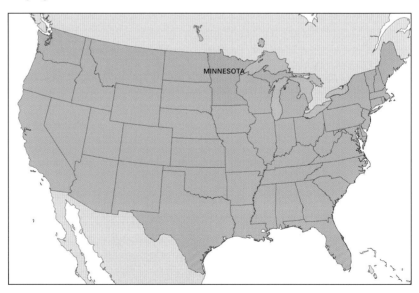

The U.S. NSDI: An update

The U.S. Office of Management and Budget (OMB) Circular A–16 on Coordination of Geographic Information and Related Spatial Data Activities was revised in 2002 (Office of Management and Budget 2002). This official circular has been sent to all heads of executive departments and establishments setting out the case for an NSDI, as well as defining its scope and the role of the FGDC. The NSDI vision this circular presents has several objectives: "to assure that spatial data from multiple sources (federal, state, and local governments, academia, and the private sector) are widely available and easily integrated to enhance knowledge and understanding of our physical and cultural world. The NSDI shall honor several key public values in its development and administration."

These public values include

> * privacy, security, and accuracy of citizens' personal data
> * access for all citizens to spatial data, information, and interpretive products
> * protection of proprietary interests related to licensed information and data
> * interoperability of federal information systems to enable the drawing of resources from multiple federal agencies and their partners

The lead agency responsible for facilitating Circular A–16 related activities and the implementation of the NSDI is the Department of the Interior through the FGDC. This is an interagency committee whose membership represents nineteen federal agencies with responsibilities for geographic information.

The NSDI is federally driven, and other public-sector stake-holders at the state, county, and city levels have only a sub-sidiary role in its management structure, as does the private sector. This led a panel, made up of academy fellows and lead-ing geographic information experts set up by the U.S. National Academy of Public Administration (NAPA), to recommend the establishment of a broadly representative National Spatial Data Council to complement the FGDC in providing national leadership and coordination for the NSDI.

> While the FGDC has been instrumental in much of the progress achieved over the past few years, the panel is convinced that an organization is needed which provides full participation by all the major parties and interests engaged in developing and maintaining the NSDI. Without such participation, the NSDI is likely to be seen as a federal program run from Washington of limited value to state and local governments. Without stronger private sector participation, there will likely be less cooperation and continued efforts in Congress to limit or abolish federal capabilities needed to realize the full NSDI. In addition, some of the functions now being performed by government would benefit by the conduct of them in a more businesslike manner (National Academy of Public Administration 1998, 74–75).

The U.S. federal government did not act upon this recommen-dation. However, in 1999, FGDC commissioned a design study team to look into ways of improving federal agency geospatial coordination (Federal Geographic Data Committee 2000).

Implementation issues

The FGDC secretariat is located within the Geographic Information Office of the United States Geological Survey of the Federal Department of the Interior in Reston, Virginia. It is a relatively small operation with twenty-four staff members (Stevens 2004). Its budget covers the costs of the FGDC secretariat, some interagency projects, basic infrastructure maintenance, and the costs of the GSDI secretariat. In contrast to the amount of funding required for NSDI coordination, the financial support needed for NSDI implementation is in the billions of dollars. The FGDC only requires millions. Consequently, a recurrent theme of U.S. NSDI implementation is the search for partners to leverage funding mechanisms to support this task.

In 2000, the FGDC commissioned a report on funding the NSDI from Urban Logic (2000). This report considers a wide range of potential opportunities to align or leverage resources and investments for spatial data activities in support of the NSDI. It argues that spatial data has multiple communities who share the same region, industry, or thematic issues. With this in mind, SDIs can be seen as multisector spatial data communities who are seeking to make spatial data accessible within the context of the digital economy. Under these circumstances, there is a need for a national capital financing initiative to support the creation and growth of regional, industry, and thematic interest group consortia.

Another study commissioned by the FGDC addressed the issue of increasing private-sector awareness of and enthusiastic participation in the NSDI. The Spatial Technologies Industry Association (STIA) carried out this study. STIA is a group of private-sector companies set up in 1996 to foster public-sector policies conducive to the industry achieving its full potential in private sector, public sector, and global markets. The starting point for this study was the recognition that the NSDI has not attracted the level of private-sector participation that was expected when the NSDI was created in 1994. The report of the first phase of this study (Spatial Technologies Industry Association 2001) concluded that the private sector is an important stakeholder in the NSDI initiative, but it recommended that the FGDC must take account of how spatial technology markets have developed over the last five years if the FGDC is to attract greater private-sector support and participation. One reason for this apparent lack of support is the extent to which many federal programs operate independently from the NSDI.

Similar criticisms were made in the Mapping Sciences Committee's (MSC) report on FGDC's Partnership programs (National Research Council 2001). This report pointed out that "FGDC provided only a minuscule proportion of the total resources available nationally to support geospatial partnerships" (p. 4) and that future programs initiated by them should be designed to augment and leverage these investments.

The testimony of the Government Audit Office (GAO) (2003) Director of Information Management Services, Linda D. Koontz, to the Congressional Subcommittee on Technology, Information Policy, Intergovernmental Relations, and the Census also claimed that many federal GIS activities overlap and that "although efforts to build the NSDI are progressing, achieving the vision of a nationwide GIS network remains a formidable challenge" (p. 9). The GAO subsequently recommended that "the OMB Director and Secretary of the Interior devise a current comprehensive strategic plan for coordinating federal geospatial assets" (GAO 2004).

These and other similar criticisms have prompted the FGDC to clarify its position with respect to other federal government initiatives such as Geospatial One Stop and also to consider its future directions. In a paper co-authored by colleagues from Geospatial One Stop and the U. S. Geological Survey

National Map program, senior staff at the FGDC (Ryan et al. 2004) addressed the confusion that exists in the geospatial community's mind about the interrelationship between these initiatives and the perceived duplication of effort that arises as a result. They argue that the NSDI is "a work in progress" and its implementation will require a concerted effort on the part of all the stakeholders. They see the role of the federal agencies as being a critical one that accomplishes the following:

→ provides leadership

→ promotes best practices to ensure consistency of data

→ fosters meaningful partnerships with state and local governments as well as the private and nonprofit sectors

The FGDC has also set up its own Future Directions Project "to craft a strategy and implementation plan to further the development of the NSDI." Following consultations with many of the stakeholders involved, it has produced a document (Federal Geographic Data Committee 2004) that identifies three overarching themes that will provide the context for its future target goals and strategies:

1. "Forging partnerships with purpose: A governance structure that includes representatives of all stakeholder groups guides the development of the NSDI

2. Making framework real: Nationally coordinated programs that include collection, documentation, access, and utilization of data are in place for generating framework data themes

3. Communicating the message: The NSDI is recognized across the nation as the primary mechanism for assuring access to reliable geospatial data" (Federal Geographic Data Committee 2004, 1)

The first of these themes is of particular interest. The initial target goals and actions relating to this theme suggest that the FGDC is considering a radical departure from its previous practices:

+ "By 2005, agreements are in place to facilitate participation of the private sector and utility industry in building the NSDI

+ By 2005, options for restructuring the FGDC to make it more effective and inclusive are identified, evaluated and acted upon

+ By 2006, a governance model that includes representatives of all stakeholder groups will guide the NSDI

+ By 2006, fifty state/territory coordinating councils are in place and routinely contributing to the governance of the NSDI

+ By 2006, twenty tribes are engaged and contributing to the development of the NSDI

+ By 2007, ten non-geospatial national organizations are engaged in and contributing to the NSDI" (Federal Geographic Data Committee 2004, 7)

SDI implementation at the state and local levels

During its lifetime the FGDC, together with other federal agencies, has made repeated efforts to promote and encourage partnerships and collaborative efforts at the state and local levels. Two of the most interesting of these have been the establishment of the national GeoData Alliance in November 2000 to "foster trusted and inclusive processes to enable the creation, effective and equitable flow, and beneficial use of geographic information" and the Implementation Team (I-Team) initiative that was also set up in 2000 to tackle the problems of upgrading and maintaining the seven framework data layers defined by the FGDC.

The GeoData Alliance *(www.geoall.net)* is based on the principles of chaordic self organization, a system that is simultaneously chaotic and ordered around a common purpose. This system is

- open and inclusive
- member driven and member governed
- minimally structured
- multicentric and distributive
- self organizing and emergent
- highly interconnected and fluid
- innovative and adaptive
- strongly grounded in purpose and principles

In September 2001, the GeoData Alliance produced a guidebook to organizing and sustaining geodata collaboratives (Johnson et al. 2001). The main section of this report is devoted to contributions from six "successful" GeoData collaboratives describing their experiences. On the basis of this material, seventeen key practices to successfully creating and sustaining these initiatives were identified. Six practices were common to all the cases:

1. Offering broad support for vision and expectations

2. Championing individuals or community support

3. Supporting knowledgeable, respected participants

4. Maintaining frequent contact with national (higher order) organizations

5. Developing proactive, open, and inclusive processes/ procedures to enable minimum participation/diverse perspectives

6. Improving understanding or outreach

The I-Team initiative addresses the institutional and financial barriers to development of the NSDI by helping the community come together to produce and maintain portions of America's framework and other geographic data assets. It is a joint project of the OMB, the FGDC, and other partners *(www. fgdc.gov/I-Team)*.

Like the GeoData Alliance, the I-Team initiative tries to promote the creation of self-organizing and self-authorizing geographic information consortia at the subnational level. In essence, then, I-Teams are "voluntary, open, flexible, and adaptive collaborations for shared capital planning, building, using, and financing spatial data. They optimize and align the interdependencies, allowing institutions and citizens to rely on and share quality data from other trusted sources."

According to the FGDC Web site, some forty-nine states and regions had taken up the I-Team idea by late 2003. Most of these are state-based, but there are also several regional I-Teams that nest within their states, and several other I-Team areas go across state boundaries. These include the Colorado Plateau initiative, which consists of five I-Team states.

THE CASE OF MetroGIS

MetroGIS *(figure 5.3)* was one of the case studies featured in the GeoData Alliance report previously described. It is also a regional I-Team initiative within the state of Minnesota. MetroGIS is "a multi participant, geodata collaborative" that serves the seven county, three-thousand square mile Twin City Metropolitan Area based on Minneapolis–St. Paul. It was set up in 1996 "to provide an ongoing, stakeholder-governed, metro-wide mechanism through which participants easily and equitably share geographically referenced graphic and associated attribute data that are accurate, current, secure, of common benefit, and readily usable" (Johnson and Arbeit 2002, 3).

 Randy Johnson has served as MetroGIS's Staff Coordinator since MetroGIS's launch in 1995 by the Metropolitan Council to foster intergovernmental collaboration in developing and sharing geospatial data. He holds a master's degree in urban geography and served as a city planner for over twenty years prior to joining MetroGIS. In the course of building a modest GIS capability to support his municipal planning responsibilities, he encountered substantial barriers to acquiring and using geospatial data produced by other government interests. This experience kindled his interest in improving government efficiencies through ready access and use of geospatial data produced by others.

A driving force behind MetroGIS's success is the Metropolitan Council's need for trusted, compatible geospatial data across the entire seven-county, Minneapolis–St. Paul (Minnesota) metropolitan area to support its transportation, wastewater management, and growth management responsibilities. MetroGIS's unprecedented organizational structure is also a key to its success, providing the ability to raise issues to a level of public policy debate among elected officials who represent all core stakeholder interests. Current challenges include a continual need to nurture champions at the management and policy levels, and establishing an effective mechanism to integrate locally produced geospatial data into state and national programs.

Box 5.1   Profile of Randall (Randy) Johnson, MetroGIS Staff Coordinator, Minneapolis–St. Paul, Minnesota.

From its inception, MetroGIS has supported the NSDI initiative. Its success owes a great deal to its organizational structure, its active membership, and the financial support that it has received from the Metropolitan Council. Its organization structure is based on a policy board consisting of twelve elected officials from core stakeholders and stakeholder communities, a coordinating committee of more than twenty managers and administrators, and a small technical advisory team.

MetroGIS has no legal standing but relies on an informal structure where participants collaboratively develop and implement regional solutions to common geographic information needs. Three principles guide its decision making:

- "encourage a consensus decision making process involving all Policy Board members for matters fundamental to the long term success of MetroGIS

- seek the powers and resources needed to develop and sustain MetroGIS through a voluntary, collaborative and cooperative process

- require a super majority of 75 percent of Coordinating Committee members for recommendations to the Policy Board and, if not a unanimous, forward dissenting opinions with the recommendation" (Johnson and Arbeit 2002, 5)

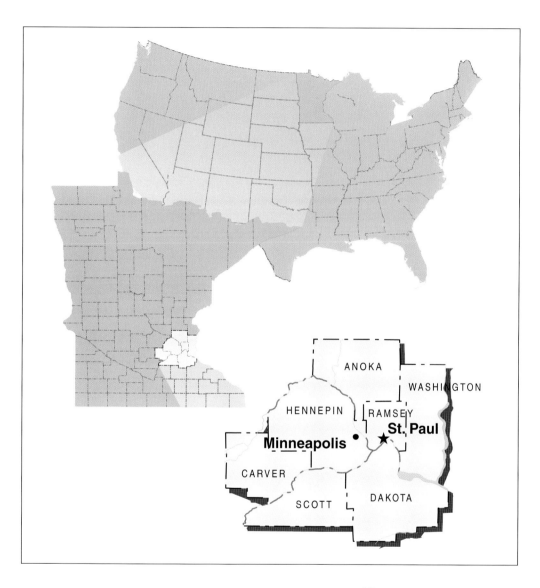

Figure 5.2
Twin Cities Metropolitan Area
MetroGIS location.

The key to its operational success is the data custodian, especially as it has no legal standing and no technical staff.

Some of the recent accomplishments of MetroGIS are set out in its business plan for 2003–2005 (MetroGIS 2002). These include

> * improved decision support through more accessible data that meets user needs
> * a state-of-the-art Internet-enabled geodata discovery and distribution mechanism (DataFinder) that is a registered node of the National Geospatial Clearinghouse
> * national professional recognition through the award of one of the Urban and Regional Information Systems Association's Exemplary Systems in Government award in 2002

A poster exhibited at the 2003 Urban and Regional Information Systems Association (URISA) conference acts as a showcase for MetroGIS's activities *(figure 5.3)*.

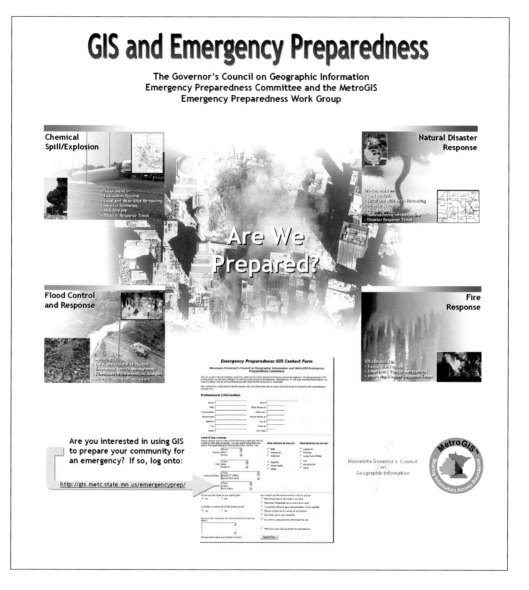

Figure 5.3
MetroGIS 2003 poster.

AUSTRALIA

LAND ADMINISTRATION IN AUSTRALIA IS the responsibility of the six states and the two territories that make up the Commonwealth of Australia *(figure 5.4)*. Consequently, eight separate systems for registering land titles and eight separate systems for surveying and mapping exist, though there are many similarities between them (Masser, 1998). An important consequence of the way in which land administration systems have developed in Australia is the high degree of centralization that exists at the state and territory level with respect to the handling of cadastral records. Given the parallel development of surveying and mapping, it is not surprising to find that a great deal of effort has already been devoted to the computerization of these activities and that all the states have already established digital cadastral databases.

Figure 5.4
Australia with case study
area highlighted.

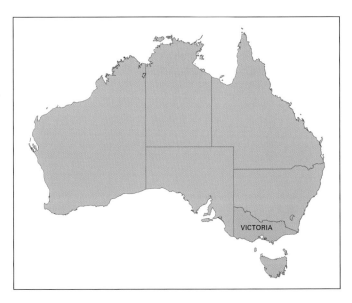

VICTORIA

The Australian Spatial Data Infrastructure: An update

The precursor of the Australia New Zealand Land Information Council (ANZLIC) was set up in 1986. ANZLIC is a result of an agreement between the Australian prime minister and the heads of the state governments who wanted to coordinate the collection and transfer of land-related information between the different levels of government. They also wanted to promote the use of that information in decision making. Each of the members of ANZLIC represents a coordinating body within their jurisdiction (i.e., the Commonwealth Office for Spatial Data Management, the relevant coordination bodies at the state and territory levels, and Land Information New Zealand).

ANZLIC's responsibilities are not restricted to cadastral and mapping matters but cover all types of land information, including socio-economic data, natural resource information, environmental data, and utilities and infrastructure information. During its lifetime, the council has produced a number of major reports on the status of land information in Australia as well as five versions of its national strategic plan for the management of land geographic information. ANZLIC's vision is that "Australia and New Zealand's economic growth, and social and environmental interests are underpinned by quality spatially referenced information" (Australia New Zealand Land Information Council 2003, 2).

In essence, ANZLIC has been developing some elements of an Australian Spatial Data Infrastructure (ASDI) since 1986. The constitutional structure of Australia means that the development of an ASDI can only take place through intergovernmental cooperation, and ANZLIC is the vehicle for this cooperative approach (Clarke 2001, 2).

The conceptual model for the ASDI was set out in 1996 in an ANZLIC discussion paper. This remains formal ANZLIC policy, although it is currently under review. Its primary objective is "to ensure that users of land and geographic data who require a national coverage will be able to acquire complete and consistent data sets meeting their requirements, even though the data is collected and maintained by different jurisdictions. The issue, therefore, is to determine what is required of jurisdictions and their data sets, to enable them to meet national needs" (Australia New Zealand Land Information Council 1996, 5)

For this purpose ANZLIC envisages the creation of "a distributed network of databases, linked by common standards and protocols to ensure compatibility, each managed by custodians with the expertise and incentive to maintain the database to the standards required by the community and committed to the principles of custodianship." Custodianship plays an important role in the thinking behind the ASDI. The notion of a custodian is defined in the following terms:

> A **custodian** of a fundamental data set, or a component of that data set, is an agency recognized by ANZLIC as having the responsibility to ensure that a fundamental data set is collected and maintained according to specifications and priorities determined by consultation with the user community, and made available to the community under conditions and in a format that conform with standards and policies established for the national spatial data infrastructure (Australia New Zealand Land Information Council 1996, 7).

Implementation issues

ANZLIC has always had very limited resources at its disposal. Until 2001 it was serviced by a part-time executive officer provided by the commonwealth government. Its members paid a modest annual subscription to support the administrative cost and also jointly funded specific projects such as consultancies, publications, and workshops. The position changed in 2001 when it was agreed that a national office should be established with a full-time executive director and two project officers to support its ASDI and industry objectives.

Notwithstanding these developments, the ANZLIC structure has its limitations with respect to ASDI implementation. It is a consensus building agency. It can develop models, standards, and protocols, but has no powers to make their implementation mandatory. It also has no funding capacity and must rely on its members who also have to take account of their own jurisdictions when committing resources (Clarke 2001).

Despite these limitations, there has been a considerable degree of cooperation between ANZLIC's members. One of the most interesting outcomes of this can be found in the formation of an interjurisdictional Public Sector Mapping Agencies (PSMA) consortium to create an integrated national digital basemap for the 1996 Census. The success of this project subsequently led to a resolution passed by ANZLIC in June 1996 "that the PSMA expand its role to make the PSMA data set available to users under conditions to be determined by the Board of Management and that PSMA has a role in establishing a mechanism for enhancing the database with other appropriate national data sets" (Grant and Hedberg 2001). Since then, PSMA has developed a number of national data products. One of the most interesting products was launched in October 2001. CadLite is a seamless cadastral database containing details of more than ten million separate land parcels. It is designed to meet the needs of organizations that require a graphical representation of land parcel boundaries on a broad scale to integrate with other data servicing their business needs *(figure 5.5)*.

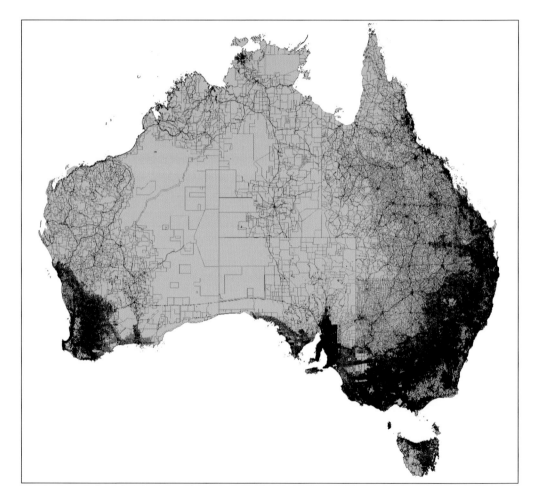

Figure 5.5
CadLite: A seamless cadastral
database for Australia.

The impact of these developments has been considerable, and PSMA became a government-owned company in 2001. Its vision is "the return of economic benefits to the nation through the coordination, assembly, and delivery of standards compliant, client specific national data sets from fundamental databases held by member agencies" *(www.psma.com.au)*. It regards itself as a clearinghouse within the ANZLIC model of the Australian SDI and sees its activities as essentially complementary to those of the private sector.

A further boost to ASDI implementation came in May 2000 when the Minister of Industry, Science, and Resources announced that a Spatial Information Industry Action Agenda would be prepared as one of twenty-seven industry-specific action agendas that the government plans to use in its Investing for Growth strategy. The preparation of an action agenda for this industry with a current annual turnover in excess of one billion Australian dollars was seen from the outset as requiring a joint effort from all the key stakeholders in business, research, and all levels of government. The Action Agenda itself identifies five strategic goals as being essential to the future success of the industry (Ministry of Industry, Science, and Resources 2001):

1. Develop a mutually beneficial relationship between business and government

2. Maximize the creation, utility, and use of publicly funded data products and services

3. Create an innovative, strong industry that focuses on value adding

4. Build and maintain a highly skilled and innovative work force

5. Develop overseas export opportunities and boost the industry's international competitiveness

An early outcome of this initiative was the formation of an Australian Spatial Industry Business Association (ASIBA) in July 2001 to act as the single point of contact for government and the key stakeholders. ASIBA represents the interests of the commercial sector of the spatial information industry. These include businesses that provide surveying, mapping, remote sensing, GIS, and related products and services such as hardware and software development. They also supply data brokerage as well as management and training. The ASIBA (n.d.) has produced a policy brief that has been widely circulated to politicians and decision makers in Australia. This brief argues that the private sector must have an ongoing and meaningful input into national spatial information policy.

In addition to the establishment of the ASIBA, a number of other new institutions developed over the last few years will play an important role in the implementation of Australia's SDI:

* the Spatial Sciences Institute, which brings together the professional disciplines of surveying, mapping, engineering and mining, surveying, remote sensing, photogrammetry, and spatial information

* the Cooperative Research Centre for Spatial Information headed by the University of Melbourne that has been set up to develop the concept of a Virtual Australia

* the Australian Spatial Information Education and Research Association

As a result of these developments, ANZLIC (2004) has concluded that the institution building phase of the original Action Agenda is nearly complete. It is now time to move beyond the data-provider focus inherent in the original agenda to more user-oriented activities. These activities include a greater emphasis on capacity building across the industry to remove the remaining barriers to the access and use of geographic information in the context of the ASDI. With this in mind, ANZLIC produced an action plan in 2003 to implement the ASDI in this new institutional context. This plan identified five key priority areas:

1. ASDI governance

2. Data access

3. Data quality

4. Interoperability

5. Intergratability

Under the heading of ASDI governance, the action plan suggests that the institutional arrangements supporting the ASDI need to be improved. The current cooperative approach depends largely on personal relationships, and this can present problems when personnel changes occur. Consequently, there is a need to develop "enduring underpinning structures." There is also a need for new governance arrangements that take into account "the balance between public and private sectors, data sources and data users" (Australia New Zealand Land Information Council 2003, 5).

The term "intergratability" refers to the ability to integrate data to improve its usability.

SDI implementation at the state and local levels

Each of the eight states and two territories in Australia have their own mechanisms for state-level SDI development and implementation. They have been working together for many years within the ANZLIC framework on the ASDI *(figure 5.4)*. The State of Victoria's ANZLIC member is the Department of Sustainability and Environment (DSE). Within the DSE, Spatial Information Infrastructure (formerly known as Land Information Group–Land Victoria) is the lead agency for spatial data management. Land Victoria was set up in 1996 when a number of disparate state government entities with responsibilities for various aspects of land administration were merged to create a coordinated land administration agency for the state (Thompson et al. 2003). Spatial Information Infrastructure acts as the facilitator for the state's Spatial Information Strategy.

According to the *Victoria Property Gazette* of February 2004, "Victoria is building the world's first online system for property settlement and development approvals." When the system is fully operational, most of the 400,000 conveyancing transactions undertaken each year will be made online. This could amount to savings in terms of time and paper on the order of $100 million per annum. At the same time, the Exchange will also provide additional benefits. First, planning, building, and subdivision applications will be lodged online. Second, the way Crown land is identified and its status in terms of ownership and boundaries will be overhauled. The system will be implemented in stages. The first stage will be a pilot to lodge and track subdivision applications online. This should be completed by the middle of 2004. The next stage will involve a limited pilot with financial institutions. It is anticipated that full electronic financial settlements will be available in early 2005.

Box 5.2   Victoria's Land Exchange.
   Source: *www.landexchange.vic.gov.au*

The Victorian Spatial Information Strategy for 2004–2007 is the fourth in a series of strategies that have shaped the spatial information environment in the state since 1991. This strategy differs from earlier strategies in that, while the development and maintenance of Vicmap (the state's suite of eight integrated spatial information products) will continue, the overall priority has shifted toward more comprehensive "whole of industry" approach to acquiring spatial information. As a result, the current document stresses the need for a high-level coordination body to

 » oversee the implementation of the Victorian Spatial Information Strategy within government

 » engage with the private and academic sectors to ensure their full participation in realizing its objectives

Two examples illustrate the nature of the work these strategies support. First, the Land Exchange program, set up in 2002, is highly innovative *(box 5.2)*. It is currently running alongside existing arrangements for the exchange of land-related information and the conduct of land transactions. There are two main projects within this 24 million dollar (Australian) program. First is the Electronic Conveyancing (EC) project, which is an Internet-based system that enables online processing for the settlement and lodgement of land dealings. The Streamlined Planning through Electronic Applications and Referrals (SPEAR) project aims to streamline the planning, building, and subdivision process by allowing applications to be lodged and tracked online and referred electronically to stakeholders for comment.

Second, the Property Information Project (PIP) seeks "to establish a common geospatial infrastructure between local and state government based around the digital cadastral map base." (Jacoby et al. 2002). This reflects the state's need for information about proposed property developments that are taking place in its seventy-eight local government agencies (LGAs). Although the state maintains the cadastral map base, there is often little or no commonality between the LGA data and its database. To deal with these problems, the state obtained funding to match or reconcile each LGA database with that of the state. It was agreed that each LGA would be allowed free use of the state's database and would be periodically supplied with updates. In return, they had to agree to adopt the state's version and advise them of all proposed plans and subdivisions in their areas. The state also found that there was a great degree of uncertainty among many LGAs as to the best way to introduce GIS. PIP provided a well-structured approach that was independent of vendors, as well as a low-risk path to GIS implementation. Given these circumstances, it is not surprising to find that all seventy-eight LGAs have signed up to the scheme, and, as a result, Victoria has been able to drastically reduce the amount of duplicative maintenance work that is taking place within the state.

Bruce Thompson is Director of the Spatial Information Infrastructure, Strategic Policy and Projects, (formerly known as Land Information Group, Land Victoria), Department of Sustainability and Environment, which has responsibility for Victorian spatial information strategy and policies, and for the management of Vicmap, the Victoria's spatial information infrastructure.

Bruce's primary responsibility is for the development and implementation of Victoria's whole of government spatial information policy and strategy, mostly through the Victorian Spatial Information Strategy 2004–2007 (VSIS). He is also involved with the development of national spatial policy, and national spatial information industry development through Victoria's participation in ANZLIC.

Prior to joining the Spatial Information Infrastructure in 1999, Bruce worked in Strategic Planning and Economic Services in Victoria's Department of Infrastructure, and in the Planning Division of the Queensland Department of Housing, Local Government, and Planning.

Box 5.3   Profile of Bruce Thompson, Director, Spatial Information Infrastructure, Strategic Policy and Projects, Department of Sustainability and Environment.

CANADA

IN MANY RESPECTS, CANADA IS MORE LIKE Australia than the United States. Land administration in Canada is also a provincial responsibility, and there is some measure of centralization within each province in the handling of cadastral records. As a result, there is a long tradition of the creation and management of large computerized databases at the provincial level. However, there are much greater differences between the Canadian provinces than is the case with the Australian states in terms of history, language, and culture *(figure 5.6)*. Unlike either Australia or the United States, the private sector has played an important role in the formulation of the CGDI through the work of the Geomatics Industry Association of Canada.

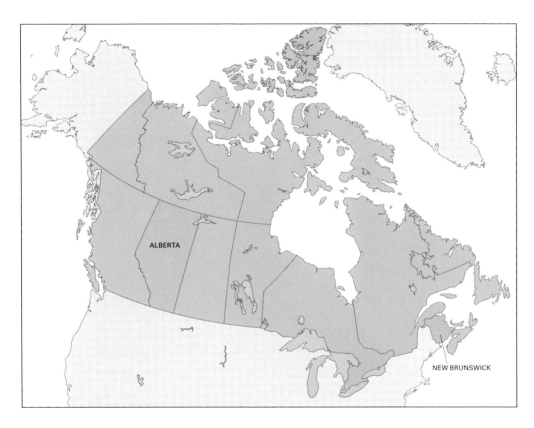

Figure 5.6
Canada with case study areas
highlighted.

The Canadian Geospatial Data Infrastructure: An update

The early stages of the CGDI were described in chapter 2. In early 1998, Labonte et al. (1998) reported that "Over the last several years, the Inter-Agency Committee on Geomatics, with the Canadian Council on Geomatics, and the Geomatics Industry Association of Canada, has been developing the Canadian Geospatial Data Infrastructure. Development of CGDI has taken the form of a host of different projects, partnerships, and co-operative activities—all working collectively towards a national infrastructure for access to geospatial information in Canada."

The target vision underlying the CGDI, according to its architecture working group (Canadian Geospatial Data Infrastructure 2001) is "a Canadian geospatial data infrastructure that is accessible to all communities, pervasive throughout our country, ubiquitous for its users, and self sustaining, to support the protection and betterment of Canada's health, social, cultural, economic, and natural resources heritage and future."

To realize this vision, the Canadian government set up and funded GeoConnections in 1999. GeoConnections brings together all levels of government, the private sector, and academia to work toward the establishment and implementation of the CGDI. Five key policy thrusts underlie the work of Geo-Connections:

1. "Access data: Making geospatial data accessible on the Internet so that businesses, governments and Canadians can download geospatial information on demand, 24 hours per day, 365 days per year

2. Framework data: Establishing a framework of data that will make it easier to integrate information to speed decision making and develop new information products

3. Geospatial standards: Ensuring that information matches international standards, so that Canada can share information with other nations, and Canadian businesses can sell geospatial information technology and services in the global marketplace

4. Partnerships: Collaborating in partnership with various levels of government, the private sector and the academic community to capitalize on their collective expertise and to ensure the seamless delivery of information

5. Supportive policy: Developing supportive policy at all levels of government to accelerate private sector commercialization of geospatial information, and to develop e-commerce, integrated technologies and services" *(www.geoconnections.org)*

The lead agency for GeoConnections is Natural Resources Canada. Its work is guided by a management board consisting of senior government officials from the federal agencies represented on the Inter-Agency Committee for Geomatics, and provincial and territorial representatives from the Canadian Council on Geomatics, as well as representatives from academia and industry. It is chaired by the Assistant Deputy Minister of the Earth Resources Sector of Natural Resources Canada.

Implementation issues

GeoConnections has been allocated $60 million (Canadian) spread over six years by the Canadian government out of its 1999 budget to implement the CGDI. Much of its work revolves around the creation of partnerships and the promotion of data sharing activities through its GeoPartners program. This includes a wide range of activities from coordination and communication to policy and research. GeoPartners is seen as a catalyst for success. "When teams and organizations are committed to working in the same direction, great things can happen. That's what GeoPartners is all about: helping GeoConnections fulfill its potential. By co-ordinating, communicating, facilitating, and managing, the secretariat serves as a springboard for GeoConnections' achievements, both present and future" *(www.geoconnections.org).*

There are strong links between this work and that of the Geomatics Industry Association of Canada (GIAC). The GIAC has been in existence for more than forty years. Its predecessor, the Canadian Association of Aerial Surveyors was formed by a small group of aerial surveying and mapping service companies in 1961. They lobbied the federal government to contract out air survey and photogrammetric work to the private sector. The organization evolved and took on an international business development role before changing its name to the Geomatics Industry Association of Canada in 1987. Since then its membership has grown from thirty to ninety companies involved in surveying, mapping, remote sensing, and GIS activities (Kennedy 2002).

A Program Advisory Network supports the work of GeoConnections. At the present time this consists of twelve committees or nodes whose open national membership enables them to leverage experience and contributions from stakeholders. The twelve nodes consist of five funded, three policy support, and four application area nodes. The five funded nodes deal with access, core data, sustainable communities, geomatics skills, and the Atlas of Canada. The three policy support nodes deal with technical matters, standards, and broader policy issues such as pricing and data sharing, while the four application area nodes cover resource management, ground transportation, disaster management, and marine issues, respectively. Given the emphasis given to the creation of a supportive policy environment for the CGDI, the activities of the policy advisory node are of particular interest, although it is worth noting that capacity building also features in the list in the geomatic skills policy node. In December 2003, the policy advisory node was co-chaired by representatives from Natural Resources Canada and ESRI Canada. There was a project manager from Stats Canada and a secretary from Natural Resources Canada. Its membership consisted of five representatives from federal government agencies, six from provinces, two from municipalities, five from the private sector, and three academics.

The Policy Node, currently working to develop and recommend implementation of policies that accomplish several goals, works to

- ⇥ "foster increased access to and use of geospatial data in the public and private sectors

- ⇥ resolve licensing and distribution issues in support of data sharing and use

- ⇥ facilitate inter-agency geospatial data-sharing arrangements

- ⇥ expand partnerships, and

- ⇥ reduce the cost of the collection, maintenance and distribution of geospatial data" *(www.geoconnections.org)*.

SDI implementation at the province and local levels

In 2000, the Policy Advisory node of GeoConnections commissioned the management consultants KPMG to carry out a geospatial data policy study to help define a policy for the CGDI (Spears 2001). This study gives a comprehensive picture of the state of the art with respect to SDI implementation in Canada. It includes a major review of data producers at the federal, provincial, and municipal levels, and a survey of users in the public, private, academic, and nonprofit sectors. The findings of this survey suggest that most of the sample agencies at all levels of government had a strong focus on either core or thematic data *(figure 5.7)*. At the same time, many of the provincial agencies have developed transaction-based data organizations to manage and distribute their cadastral and valuation data. Some of these, like AltaLis in Alberta and Teranet in Ontario, are self-financing organizations that charge their commercial and individual clients market prices for their data, whereas others such as the Manitoba Department of Conservation and Service Nova Scotia and Municipal Affairs operate a free-data policy directed primarily toward their own and other government departments. To highlight these differences, the approaches adopted in Alberta and New Brunswick are described in the following sections.

Figure 5.7
A summary of Canadian data
agencies.

	Type	ACTIVITIES				CLIENTS					PRICING POLICY					
		Framework	Statistical	Transactional	Thematic	Own department	Other govt. dept.	Commercial	Individuals	Other levels of govt.	Free	Data exchange group	Cost of provision	Self financing	Value added fees	Market price
Agriculture Canada	F				●	●	●	●	●	●	●					
Canada Post-GIS	F				●	●	●		○				●			○
Elections Canada–Electoral Geography	F				●	●				○	●					
NRCan CCRS GeoAccess, National Atlas of Canada	F	●			○	●	●	○	○	○	●					
NRCan Centre for Topographic Information	F	●			●	●	●	●	○	○			●			○
NRCan Earth Observation Satellite	F	●			●	○	●	●	○				●			○
NRCan Geodetic Survey	F	●				○	●	●	○	○			●			
NRCan Geophysical Information Branch	F			●		○	●	●	○	○	●		●			
NRCan Legal Survey	F			●		●	●	●	○	○	●	●	●			
Statistics Canada–Geography Division	F			●		○	●	○	○	○		●	●		○	
Alberta Environment–Land Administration Division	P	●			●		●				●	●				
AltaLis	P	●		○	●			○	●			●		●		●
BC–Crown Lands	P			●	●	●	○				●	●				
BC–Geographic Data	P	●			●	○	●	○	●	○	●	●			○	○
Manitoba–Dept. of Conservation, LID (Info Utility)	P	●		●	●	●	●	●	●	●	●	●				
Newfoundland–Surveys and Mapping Division	P	●		○	●	○	○	●	○	○		●				
Service Nova Scotia and Municipal Affairs–LIS	P	●		●	●	●	●	●	●	●	●	●				
Nunavut, Department of Sustainable Development	P	●			○	○	○	○	○	○	●					
Ontario Ministry of Natural Resources	P	●			●	○	○	●	○	●		●			○	●
Ontario Ministry of Northern Development and Mines	P			○	●	●		○	●	○		○	○			
PEI, Provincial Taxation and Property Records	P	●		○	●	●	●	●	○	●	●	●				
Quebec Natural Resources–Photocartothéque Québécoise	P	●			●	○	○	○	○	○				○		●
Saskatchewan LIS Corp	P	●		●	●		○	●		○	●	●	●			●
Service New Brunswick–Topographical Mapping (IU)	P	●		●	●		●	●	●			●	●			
Teranet	P	●		●	●			●	●						●	●
Yukon Geology	P			○		●	●	●	●	●	●					
Cape Breton Regional Municipality	M	●					●	●	●			○	○			
City of London	M	●			○		●	○	○							
City of Montreal	M	●			●		●	●	●	●	●					
City of Toronto	M	●	●		●		●		○	○	●	○			○	
Halifax Regional Municipality	M	●			●		●	○	○	●		○	○		○	
Regional Municipality of Ottawa–Carleton	M	●			○		●	○	○	●		●	○		○	
Simcoe County	M	●			○		●	○	●	●	●	○	○		○	

● Primary or main focus/activity   ○ Secondary focus/activity

F = Federal   P = Provincial   M = Municipality

Source: Spears 2001, 221.

Alberta

In 1996, Alberta Environment Protection decided that it could not continue in the business of updating, storing, and distributing its digital base maps. They set up a new company, Spatial Data Warehouse (SDW), to carry out these tasks. SDW is an Alberta registered not-for-profit company owned by the following partners: Alberta Association of MDs and Counties, the Alberta Urban Municipalities Association, ATCO Electric, ATCO Gas and Pipelines, ATCO Pipelines, TELUS Services Inc, UtiliCorp Networks Canada (Alberta) Inc., and the Government of Alberta. At the outset of its activities, SDW decided that it did not have the expertise or the resources to re-engineer their business and selected AltaLis Ltd. to carry out this work (Spatial Data Warehouse 1998). AltaLis is a joint venture company formed by QC Data Ltd. and Martin Newby Consulting Ltd. AltaLis and SDW prepared a detailed business plan for its operations and signed a long-term joint venture agreement in December 1999. This enables them to implement new pricing and licensing options, as well as to introduce a Value Added Service Providers Agreement. AltaLis's activities revolve around the maintenance and distribution of four primary provincial data sets: urban cadastre, rural cadastre, topographic mapping (1:20,000), and small-scale mapping at scales of 1:250,000 and above *(www.AltaLis. com)*. The government of Alberta retains the copyright in this basic SDI framework data.

In January 2004, AltaLis announced a substantial reduction in the prices of its data products as a result of the increased use of SDW data and increased efficiencies within the initiative. As a result, the price of a rural cadastral map was reduced from 200 to 100 dollars (Canadian) per township, and the price of a 1:1,000,000 scale topographic map for the whole province fell from 800 to 400 dollars (Canadian). In addition to these reductions, AltaLis has been offering reduced prices through a variety of licensing options and volume discounts since March 2000.

Figure 5.8
The home page of
Service New Brunswick.

New Brunswick

Service New Brunswick (SNB) was originally established in 1990 under the title of the New Brunswick Geographic Information Corporation (Finlay 2000). It changed its name in April 1998 when it became the gateway for the electronic delivery of a wide range of basic government services. It is a Crown corporation owned by the Province of New Brunswick. Its duties are set out in the Service New Brunswick Act. This states that SNB is "the main provider, on behalf of government, of customer services, through physical offices, telephone and electronic channels." The act also sets out the corporation's responsibilities for coordinating geographic information services, real property assessment and registration, and the promotion of the geomatics industry in the private sector. In 2003, SNB was also given an eGovernment leadership role in the province's eNB strategy. It is fulfilling this role by making additional information available online, making information more readily available, and openly engaging citizens in public policy consultations. This is clearly evident from the content on its home page *(www.snb.ca)* *(figure 5.8).*

In 2003, SNB employed 640 staff members in thirty-five communities and generated revenues of fifty million Canadian dollars in the year 2002–2003 as against nearly forty million in expenses (Service New Brunswick 2003). Its mission is "making government services more available to citizens and businesses, and being stewards for authoritative information" (Service New Brunswick 2003, 9).

SNB has four main lines of business:

1. Property assessment: assessment of all land, buildings, and associated improvements to provide the basis for property taxation for municipalities and the province

2. Registries: real and personal property registries that provide land and personal property information to the public and the Corporate Affairs registry that contains information on corporations, partnerships, and business names registered in the province

3. Government service delivery: a gateway for the public to 176 government services offered through a network of thirty-six service centers located through the province, as well as over the phone and on the Internet. These services include motor vehicle registration renewals, parking permits for people with disabilities, address changes on driving licences, and Medicare files

4. Government information infrastructure: creation and maintenance of the province's control survey network and base mapping data

David Finley has almost thirty years of experience in geomatics—first as a data collector and end-user working in exploration geology, and more recently as a developer and facilitator of SDI implementation and evolution. Dave has been active in promoting and advancing the geomatics profession through various roles on the executive of the New Brunswick Branch of the Canadian Institute of Geomatics since 1997, and a number of committees including the Canadian Council of Geomatics. He has published numerous articles related to geomatics and SDI, has lectured in GIS, and has been involved in GIS curriculum review.

In his view,

"We have been fairly successful in establishing the base infrastructure—a number of databases exist, technology has evolved, the focus has shifted from base mapping to application development—but the infrastructure must be maintained. While GIS is becoming ubiquitous, many users are unaware of the role geomatics plays in solving their problems.

The challenge we face is to ensure the SDI continues to evolve and get funded. We'll be successful if we can promote geomatics, so it receives the recognition it deserves as a foundation and fundamental tool to allow improved decision-making … [and] change the way we do business.

If we can learn a lesson from the computing sector, it would be to understand how some companies have successfully embedded computers into everything we now do, and we all recognize that fact. Geomatics and SDI need to receive similar recognition."

Box 5.4   Profile of David Finley, Manager, Topographic Infrastructure, Service New Brunswick, Fredericton, New Brunswick.

COMPARATIVE EVALUATION

THE EXPERIENCES OF THE UNITED STATES, Australia, and Canada in implementing multilevel SDIs highlights three main features: (1) the shift that is taking place from coordination to new models of SDI governance, (2) the shift that is also taking place from single level to multilevel implementation structures, and (3) the emergence of new types of organizational structure to facilitate SDI implementation.

The governance of SDI implementation

One feature that emerges from this analysis is the increasing attention that is now being given in NSDI implementation to the development of commercial opportunities for private-sector companies. This is particularly evident in Canada through the work of the Geomatics Industry Association of Canada. This well-established body played an important role in the formation of the CGDI. The growing importance of the private sector can also be seen in the Australian Ministry of Industry's Spatial Information Industry Action Agenda. One consequence of the Action Agenda was the formation of ASIBA in 2001. ASIBA is already playing a major role in the ASDI as the lead agency for the implementation of the Action Agenda.

These developments are reflected in the changes that are currently taking place in the arrangements for SDI coordination in the United States and Australia. Although there are still marked differences between the three countries in the style of NSDI leadership, there are signs in both the United States and Australia of a move toward more inclusive forms of governance. There is still a strong coordination dimension to the work of the U.S. FGDC. Although its composition is broad in scope, its current membership is restricted to federal government agencies and the U.S. federal government. However, this could change if the FGDC implements the ideas put forward in its Future Directions Project regarding the creation of a new governance model that includes representatives of all stakeholder groups to guide the NSDI.

The existing position in Australia is similar in some respects to that of the United States, but it is more inclusive in terms of representation. ANZLIC is essentially an umbrella organization consisting of representatives from both the commonwealth and state-level government public-sector coordination bodies. However, it plans to work closely in the future with ASIBA and the Spatial Sciences Institute to implement Australia's SDI.

This brings these bodies more in line with more inclusive bodies such as GeoConnections in Canada. The lead Canadian agency, GeoConnections, has always been a cooperative organization that seeks to bring together all levels of government, the private sector, and academia. These interests are reflected in the composition of its management board and also in the membership of the nodes in its policy advisory network. It sees itself as a catalyst for successful implementation. There is also a strong industry connection in the CGDI through the Geomatics Industry Association of Canada.

The example of MetroGIS also shows that effective SDI implementation at the state level requires a more proactive multistakeholder operation. The same is the case with respect to the most recent Victorian Spatial Information Strategy that explicitly shifted its priorities to a more comprehensive "whole of industry" approach to the acquisition of spatial information.

This is not the case in either New Brunswick or Alberta in Canada. New Brunswick has taken on an eGovernment role, but remains exclusively a government corporation, albeit with a remit from the provincial government to consult widely with its customers. Alberta has outsourced important SDI framework activities. Once again, this may not matter as much as it may seem at first sight, provided that the provincial government and the local authorities together with private-sector companies and academia in the province are themselves actively involved in the CGDI.

All of these developments are a response to the challenges of operating in a multistakeholder and a multilevel environment. This also poses new challenges for leadership, and it is interesting to note the use of the term "governance" in this respect in the Future Directions report and the ANZLIC Action Plan. Governance "can be seen as the exercise of economic, political and administrative authority to manage a country's affairs at all levels. Governance encompasses the state, but transcends it by including the private sector and civil society organizations. Good governance is, among other things, participatory, transparent and accountable" (Rabinovitch 1999, 230).

Given the appropriateness of this definition as a description of the issues discussed above, it seems reasonable to talk about the governance of multilevel SDI implementation. This definition of governance means far more than coordination. It requires both proactive leadership and vision, but it also requires the continuing commitment of the stakeholders over time.

The multilevel structure of NSDI implementation

The impression given by many NSDI documents is that they abide by the principle of "one size fits all." In other words, they suggest that the outcomes of SDI implementation in a particular country will be uniform. However, the evaluation of the experiences of the United States, Australia, and Canada demonstrates the extent to which such a product must also take account of the aspirations and capabilities of many different stakeholders at the subnational, as well as the national level, as well as those of the private sector and academia. Although the lead agency in NSDI formulation is usually the national/federal government or a body such as a national GI association, its effective implementation lies, to a considerable extent, in the hands of the state and local government agencies who act as lead agencies at the subnational level.

The example of the Geodata Alliance and the I-Teams in the United States shows some of the ways in which the federal government can provide incentives to promote state- and local-level initiatives to implement the U.S. NSDI. However, it should also be noted that the extent to which such initiatives are taken up is likely to vary considerably from state to state. Given that the distinctive feature of these initiatives is the creation of self-organizing and self-authorizing geographic information consortia, it is also likely that there will be differences between what happens in each state.

Consequently, it is unlikely that the outcomes will be uniform. The outcomes of such processes are likely to be that the nature of SDI implementation will vary considerably from state to state and from local government to local government. Consequently, the SDI that emerges from this process will be a collage of similar but often quite different elements that reflect the commitments and aspirations of the different subnational governmental agencies. Some measure of consensus will be essential to ensure interoperability and integratibility (to use the phrasing of the ANZLIC Action Plan); but within this agreed framework there must also be room for diversity.

Similar processes can be seen in Canada and Australia. The CGDI will have to incorporate not only the very different approaches that have been adopted at the provincial level in Alberta and New Brunswick, but also those of the other Canadian provinces. The case of Victoria also highlights the proactive role that a state agency can play in promoting data exchange and data sharing between the state and its seventy-eight local government agencies. Its Property Information Project (PIP) drastically reduces the amount of duplicative database maintenance work that occurs within the state and at the same time ensures a high level of consistency between the data being used by state and local government agencies.

The emergence of new organizational structures

The multilevel nature of NSDI implementation also requires the creation of new kinds of organization. These can take various forms. The findings of this study show some of the different kinds of organizational structures that have emerged in the three case-study countries to facilitate NSDI implementation. At least five different types of partnerships are in operation *(table 5.1)*. These range from the restructuring of existing government agencies to the establishment of joint ventures involving different combinations of the key stakeholders.

TYPE	STATUS	DRIVING FORCE	EXAMPLE
Restructuring	Within government structures	Creation and maintenance of an integrated land information database	Land Victoria
	External to government structures	Delivery of wide range of eGovernment services	Service New Brunswick
Joint ventures	Consortium of data producers	Integration of data sets held by state and commonwealth agencies	Public Services Mapping Agencies Consortium
	Joint venture by key data users	Maintenance and dissemination of core data sets	Spatial Data Warehouse
	Joint venture by wide range of data producers and users	Creation and sharing of core data sets	MetroGIS

Table 5.1
Examples of organizational
structures created to facilitate
NSDI implementation.

The simplest case of organizational restructuring is the merger of various government departments with responsibilities for various activities based on geographic information. The driving force for this kind of restructuring is typically the perceived administrative benefits to be derived from the creation of an integrated database for the agency as a whole. This can be seen in the creation of Land Victoria in 1996. It is the product of merging various state government entities with responsibilities for various aspects of land administration. The basic objective of this merger was to establish an integrated land administration agency with a shared geographic information resource for the State of Victoria.

An alternative strategy is to set up a special government agency outside the existing governmental structure with a specific remit to maintain and disseminate core data sets. Service New Brunswick is a good example of such a strategy. It is a Crown Corporation owned by the State of New Brunswick. It was originally set up to deal with matters relating to land transactions and topographic mapping for the province as a whole. Since 1998, it has shifted its position to become the gateway for the delivery of a wide range of basic government services, as well as NSDI implementation. Consequently, its current driving force is the need for more effective service delivery within the context of electronic government in the emerging information society.

There are also some interesting examples of joint ventures between different groups of the stakeholders in SDI implementation. The simplest case is the data-producer-driven joint venture involving the Australian public-sector mapping agencies that was originally set up to create an integrated national digital basemap for the 1996 Census of Population. The driving force behind this partnership was the recognition that the whole is worth more than the sum of the parts in that there are clear economic and social benefits for the nation to be derived through the assembly and delivery of national data sets from the data held and maintained by the consortium members. Since then the range of derived products has expanded and the PSMA consortium became a government-owned corporation in 2001.

The other two types of joint ventures involve more complex structures. Unlike the PSMA consortium, Alberta's SDW is very much a data-user-driven initiative. It is a not-for-profit joint venture between key data users including the state itself, the local government associations, and the utility groups to facilitate the continuing maintenance and distribution of four primary provincial data sets. From the outset in 1996, the partners recognized that they had neither the expertise nor the resources to maintain and disseminate the existing databases. Consequently, they negotiated a long-term joint venture agreement with two private-sector companies in 1999 to carry out these tasks. This covers the reengineering of the databases and also makes it possible to implement new pricing and licensing options.

Initiatives such as the MetroGIS that bring together a large number of data producers and data users are both more ambitious and more open ended in their potential for development than either of the other joint ventures. The distinctive feature of this initiative lies in its insistence on voluntary, open, flexible, and adaptive collaborations, which optimize the interdependencies between citizens and organizations. Unlike the other initiatives *(table 5.1)*, MetroGIS has no legal standing and relies on an informal voluntary structure where the members themselves collaborate to develop and implement regional solutions to common GI needs.

SUMMARY

TWO MAIN ISSUES HAVE BEEN EXPLORED in this chapter with reference to the experiences of the United States, Australia, and Canada. The first of these was the nature of SDI implementation and the second concerned the notion of multilevel SDIs that operate from the national to the local levels and vice-versa. The findings of the analysis of SDI implementation indicate that a shift is beginning to take place from the central government coordination of SDI activities toward more inclusive models of governance. This reflects both the increasing importance that is attached to the creation of commercial opportunities for the private sector through SDI development and the need to involve all the stakeholders in the management of the SDI process. The analysis of multilevel SDI structures suggests that the outcomes of NSDI implementation are likely to take the form of a collage of similar but often quite different elements that reflect the commitments and the aspirations of the various subnational participants involved. Another outcome of SDI implementation is the creation of new types of organizational structures. In some cases, these may operate alongside existing structures, while in others they may supersede them. This is particularly likely to be the case where multilevel or multi-agency collaboration is concerned and can take the form of joint ventures by consortiums of either data producers or data users, or joint ventures involving both data producers and users.

CHAPTER 6

SDI bodies at the regional level
The European Umbrella Organisation for Geographic Information

The case for transnational SDIs is less clear than that for the national and subnational levels. But cogent arguments can be put forward for transnational development in situations where concerted actions are required to deal, for example, with the nine riparian countries of the Nile river basin (Latham et al. 2002) or integrated mountain development in the Hindu–Kush Himalayan region (Shrestha and Bajracharya 2001). The absence of established governmental authorities makes transnational SDI development more difficult. Not only are there few administrators with experience at this level, but also there is a lack of appropriate resources to carry out SDI development. For this reason, Rajabifard (2002) has pointed out that the problems associated with developing regional SDIs are even more challenging than those associated with the establishment of national ones because of the extent to which regional SDI developers depend on voluntary multi-national collaboration.

At the thirteenth United Nations Regional Cartographic Conference for Asia and the Pacific, which was held in Beijing in May 1994, it was resolved that the "directorates of national survey and mapping organizations in the region form a permanent committee to discuss and agree on geographical information system standards and infrastructure, institutional development, and linkages with related bodies throughout the world." As a result of this resolution, the Permanent Committee on Geographic Information for Asia and the Pacific (PCGIAP) was formally established at its inaugural meeting in Kuala Lumpur, Malaysia, in July 1995. The members of the PCGIAP are directorates of national survey and mapping organizations or equivalent national agencies of the fifty-five member nations of the UN Economic and Social Commission for Asia and the Pacific. A large part of the activities of the PCGIAP revolve around its four working groups on the institutional framework, technical standards, fundamental data sets, and the access network. The PCGIAP is also working toward the implementation of an Asia Pacific Spatial Data Infrastructure (APSDI). This is based on the premise that people need to share spatial data to avoid duplication of expenses associated with generation and maintenance of data and its integration with other data.

Box 6.1   An alternative regional SDI model: The Permanent Committee on Geographic Information for Asia and the Pacific.
Sources: Masser et al. (2003), Permanent Committee on Geographic Information for Asia and the Pacific (1998).

Notwithstanding these difficulties, regional (i.e., multi-national) institutions have been created in Europe, Asia and the Pacific, the Americas, and Africa to promote SDI development. The oldest of these bodies are the European Umbrella Organisation for Geographic Information (EUROGI) and the Permanent Committee on Geographic Information for Asia and the Pacific (PCGIAP), which date back to 1993 and 1995, respectively. In contrast, the Permanent Committee for the Americas (PC IDEA) and the United Nations Economic Commission for Africa Committee on Development Information (CODI-GEO) have only been in existence since 2000 and 2003, respectively. The four regional bodies have similar objectives and share a similar commitment to the promotion of SDIs within their regions (Masser et al. 2003). For example, EUROGI's mission "to maximize the use of GI for the benefit of citizens, good governance and commerce" has much in common with PCGIAP's mission "to maximize the economic, social and environmental benefits of geographic information in accordance with Agenda 21." EUROGI's efforts to promote a European SDI also have strong similarities to those of the PCGIAP to promote an Asia and the Pacific SDI through its working groups on the institutional framework, technical standards, fundamental data sets, and the development of an access network (Permanent Committee on Geographic Information for Asia and the Pacific 1998).

Nevertheless, there are important differences between the four regional organizations that reflect their origins and the institutional environment within which they operate. Both PCGIAP and PC IDEA are closely linked to the United Nations Regional Cartographic Conferences, and their membership is largely limited to representatives of the national mapping agencies of the countries involved. CODI-GEO is closely linked to the UN Economic Commission for Africa and draws its membership from a wider range of government agencies than the Asian and American institutions. EUROGI, on the other hand, is based on a different model. It was initially set up with assistance from the European Commission as an umbrella organization to represent the interests of the wider European GI community. For this reason, its members are either national geographic information organizations such as the British Association for Geographic Information (AGI) (see chapter 4) or pan-European bodies such as the Urban Data Management Society (UDMS).

EUROGI also differs from the other regional bodies in that it is independent from any national or intergovernmental body. It supports a full-time secretariat from the subscriptions of its members. In contrast, the two PCs are an integral part of the intergovernmental structures of the United Nations *(box 6.1)*. They rely heavily on the voluntary input of their members who take it in turns to provide a secretariat to support the activities of their various working groups (see, for example, Rajabifard 2002).

Dozie Ezigbalike was educated at the University of Nigeria, Enugu Campus, Nigeria (BSc Hons, Surveying); Ahmadu Bello University, Zaria, Nigeria (MSc Land Surveying); and the University of New Brunswick, Fredericton, Canada (PhD Land Information Management). Prior to joining the Economic Commission for Africa, he lectured at the University of Zimbabwe (1988–1990), the University of Melbourne (1990–1998), and the University of Botswana (1998–2000). He also spent some time at the Sasol Centre for Innovative Environmental Management (SCIEM) of the University of Witwatersrand, South Africa, as a visiting scholar in 2000–2001, where he was involved in the early metadata activities of Safari 2000, an international scientific initiative.

Dozie joined the Economic Commission for Africa in May 2001, where he is in charge of the Geoinformation Team in the Development Information Services Division (DISD). In this position, he coordinates activities to strengthen geoinformation resources in African countries, with emphasis on establishing spatial data infrastructures, under the umbrella of the African Information Society Initiative (AISI). Dozie's Geoinformation Team provides the secretariat for the geoinformation subcommittee (CODI-GEO) of the Committee on Development Information (CODI), which oversees and advises on Economic Commission of Africa's (ECA) implementation of AISI. Dozie also serves as the coordinator of the Knowledge Management Pillar of ECA's Institutional Strengthening Programme (ISP).

Box 6.2 Profile of Chukwudozie (Dozie) Ezigbalike, Senior Geographic Information Systems Officer, United Nations Economic Commission for Africa, Addis Ababa, Ethiopia.

The other main difference between EUROGI and the other three bodies is in terms of the institutional environment within which it operates. As of May 1, 2004, twenty-five European countries with a combined population of nearly 450 million are members of the European Union (EU). The EU is not a state that is intended to replace existing states, but it is also more than another international organization. It is a unique body in that its member states have set up common institutions to which they delegate some of their sovereignty. This enables member states to make decisions on specific matters of joint interest democratically at the European level. As a result of these developments, a strong impetus has been built up over the last half century toward a European-wide perspective. This is evident in the creation of a wide range of European-level institutions and the availability of funds to support a variety of regional policies. This has been an important factor in the emergence of a European perspective in the geographic information field during the last ten years.

Table 6.1 summarizes main features of the EU countries and the other European countries. Over three quarters of Europe's 2001 population of 585 million lived in the twenty-five EU countries. These countries accounted for 70 percent of the total European land area. The countries that formed part of the old USSR have been excluded from the table, while Turkey has been included because it has applied for EU membership.

All of the fifteen EU members prior to 2004, together with Iceland, Norway, and Switzerland, fall into the World Bank's high-income category, whereas all ten new EU members and Croatia fall into the upper-middle-income band. The three countries whose applications for membership are currently under consideration together with all but one of the remaining countries fall into the lower-middle category, while the other country (Moldova) falls into the low-income category.

This chapter considers the development of EUROGI in the context of ongoing developments at the EU and European level. The discussion is divided into four parts:

1. The development of EUROGI

2. Some current activities

3. A profile of EUROGI's national GI association members

4. An exchange of letters between the president of EUROGI and the president of the European Commission

	2001 POP. (MILLIONS)	LAND AREA SQ. KMS (THOUSANDS)	GNP IN $ PER CAP 2001	STATUS
European Union				
EU6 (1957)				
Belgium	10	31	23,850	HI
France	59	562	22,730	HI
Germany	82	357	23,560	HI
Italy	58	301	19,390	HI
Luxembourg *				HI
Netherlands	16	42	24,330	HI
Additional members (up to 2004)				
Austria	8	84	23,940	HI
Denmark	5	43	30,600	HI
Finland	5	338	23,780	HI
Greece	11	132	11,430	HI
Ireland	4	70	22,850	HI
Portugal	10	92	10,900	HI
Spain	41	506	14,300	HI
Sweden	9	450	25,400	HI
United Kingdom	59	243	25,120	HI
New members (May 2004)				
Czech Republic	10	79	5,310	UMI
Cyprus *				UMI
Estonia	1	45	3,870	UMI
Hungary	10	93	4,830	UMI
Latvia	2	65	3,230	UMI
Lithuania	3	65	3,350	UMI
Malta *				UMI
Poland	39	323	4,230	UMI
Slovak Republic	5	49	3,760	UMI
Slovenia	2	20	9,760	UMI
EU subtotal	**449**	**3,990**		

	2001 POP. (MILLIONS)	LAND AREA SQ. KMS (THOUSANDS)	GNP IN $ PER CAP 2001	STATUS
EU Applications in progress				
Bulgaria	8	111	1,650	LMI
Romania	22	238	1,720	LMI
Turkey	66	775	2,530	LMI
Other European countries				
Albania	3	29	1,340	LMI
Bosnia/ Herzegovina	4	51	1,240	LMI
Croatia	4	57	4,550	UMI
Macedonia	2	26	1,690	LMI
Moldova	4	34	400	LI
Norway	5	324	35,630	HI
Switzerland	7	41	38,330	HI
Yugoslavia Fed. Rep.	11	102	930	LMI
Combined total	585	5,778		

GNP refers to gross national product per capita.

* Countries with less the one million population.

The last column of the table indicates the status of each country according to the ranking system of the World Bank: HI refers to high-income countries with GNP per capita incomes of more than $9,206; UMI to upper-middle-income countries with GNP per capita incomes of $2,975–$9,206; LMI to lower-middle-income countries with GNP per capita incomes of $746–$2,975 ;and LI to lower-income countries with GNP per capita incomes of less than $746.

Source: World Bank 2003, table 1.1, 14–17.

Table 6.1

Some key indicators for the European countries.

THE DEVELOPMENT OF EUROGI

THE ORIGINS OF EUROGI GO BACK TO 1991
when Directorate General XIII (now DG Information Society)
of the European Commission set up an enquiry into the desir-
ability and feasibility of establishing a European association for
geographic information to promote the development and use of
geographic information at the European level. Four prominent
members of the European geographic information community
carried out the enquiry. These were Michael Brand (director
and chief executive of Ordnance Survey Northern Ireland and
founding president of the European Division of AM/FM), Peter
Burrough (professor of Physical Geography at the University of
Utrecht), François Salge (director of the Permanent Technical
Group of the European association of mapping agencies), and
Klaus Schueller (a consultant in the GIS field and a member of
the AM/FM International European Division Board).

This team presented its initial findings at a Forum in
Luxembourg in October 22–23, 1992. They argued that there
was a strong European-wide demand for an organization that
would further the interests of the European geographic information community. They also presented a vision of EUROGI
as an organization that would not "replace existing organizations but … catalyse effective cooperation between existing
national, international, and discipline oriented bodies to bring
added value in the areas of Strategy, Coordination, and Services" (Burrough et al. 1993, 31).

The team then set about preparing detailed proposals for the establishment of a European Umbrella Organisation for Geographic Information. These were presented at another meeting in Luxembourg on November 25–26, 1993, that was attended by delegates from fourteen different European countries and six pan-European organizations (Commission of the European Communities DG XIII 1994, 4). These delegates formally resolved to set up EUROGI at this meeting and elected Michael Brand as its founder president together with an eight-person executive committee. They produced a work plan to address some of the most important issues that had been identified by the team. It was also agreed that EUROGI should be established as an independent European Foundation under Dutch law and that its secretariat would be housed in the new offices of the Dutch National Council for Geographic Information (RAVI) at Amersfoort in the Netherlands.

EUROGI held its first general board meeting in Luxembourg on May 19–20, 1994. Delegates at this meeting approved its statutes, budget, and a work plan for 1994. The work plan for its first year of operation focused on the following issues: standards, legal issues, assistance for central and east European countries, conference coordination, and the creation of a number of directories to establish a baseline for future activities (European Umbrella Organisation for Geographic Information 1995). An important first result of the EUROGI conference coordination initiative was the decision to hold the first Joint European Conference in March 1995 under the combined auspices of three well-established European conference organizations (AM/FM International Europe, European GIS Conference, or EGIS, and UDMS). The secretariat was placed on a firm footing in September 1994 by the secondment of Christian Chenez from IGN France to EUROGI.

The 1999 strategic review

Five years after the establishment of EUROGI in 1994, the executive committee decided to carry out a strategic review of its activities. The findings of this review were presented at its general board meeting in Luxembourg in March 1999. The timing of the review also coincided with the end of Michael Brand's term as founder president and Christian Chenez's secondment as secretary general.

The strategic review assessed the achievements of EUROGI during its first five years. It was divided into six sections: mission and objectives, structure, European activities, global activities, funding, and the position of the secretariat. Its main findings with respect to each of these sections can be summarized as follows:

⤏ Mission and objectives: EUROGI's mission statement and its objectives needed to be modified to take account of the changes that had occurred at both the European and global levels over the previous five years.

⤏ Structure: the original two-college membership structure needed to be revised to take account of EUROGI's success in stimulating the development of geographic information associations in most European countries at the national level and its relative lack of success in attracting or retaining full members from pan-European associations.

- European activities: a number of important changes had taken place that has affected the range of activities undertaken by EUROGI. These included the emergence of the GI2000 initiative *(box 6.3)*, the decision to abandon the Joint European Conferences in 1997, and the growing commitment of the resources of the secretariat to EU cofunded projects.

- Global activities: EUROGI has also played a key role in the Global Spatial Data Infrastructure initiative that was launched in Germany at the first of a series of worldwide conferences in 1996.

- Funding: after the end of the start-up grant provided by DG XIII, EUROGI has been dependent on the subscriptions of its members and the proceeds from projects to support its activities.

- Secretariat: the secretariat moved from Amersfoort to Marne la Vallee near Paris in 1997. It was recognized that the future location and staffing of the secretariat would depend on the choice of the new secretary general.

EUROGI *at the millennium*

In March 1999, Ian Masser took over from Michael Brand as president. He had extensive experience of EUROGI affairs prior to taking over this position. He had participated in the two foundation meetings in 1992 and 1993 and became the British Association for Geographic Information member on the executive committee in March 1998. He had also played an active part in the discussions surrounding the GI2000 and the Global Spatial Data Infrastructure initiatives. In his election manifesto, he argued that a number of important changes were likely to take place in Europe over the next few years. These were likely to have a big impact on the future development of the organization. To meet these challenges he called for a refocusing of EUROGI's core activities and a greater involvement of its member bodies in them.

One of the first tasks facing the new president was to oversee the changes in the secretariat as a result of the departure of Christian Chenez. EUROGI was fortunate to persuade the Dutch Kadaster to second Anton Wolfkamp to the position of secretary general for two and a half years from November 1999. Anton Wolfkamp's professional background was in law and public administration. As a result of this appointment, the secretariat moved from Marne la Vallee to Apeldoorn in December 1999, and EUROGI began the new millennium at its new base at the Kadaster in Apeldoorn in the Netherlands with a new secretary general and a new assistant secretary general, Karen Levoleger, who took up her post in January 2000.

The changeover at EUROGI coincided with a period of major changes within the European Commission. In March 1999, the president of the European Commission and all the commissioners were forced to resign in the face of mounting criticism regarding their conduct of European Union affairs.

It was not until September 1999 that the new commissioners began to take up their positions under the presidency of Romano Prodi. Ian Masser wrote to Mr. Prodi in September 1999 to express EUROGI's concern about the continuing failure of the commission to establish an appropriate policy framework for geographic information at the European level. The text of this letter together with the reply from the president of the European Commission can be found at the end of this chapter. Despite the assurances given by Mr. Prodi in his reply to this letter, it had become increasingly clear by the end of 1999 that the GI2000 initiative would be put on the shelf together with many other projects launched by the commission. These developments were largely due to the pressure of other work in the commission and the relative low priority given to this initiative by senior officials. Consequently, EUROGI also began the millennium with a major change in the circumstances surrounding geographic information in Europe.

The most important outcome of the strategic review was the proposal to change the statutes and bylaws of EUROGI to create two new classes of membership. This proposal was approved at the general board meeting in Luxembourg on April 3–4, 2000. It abolished the old distinction between the national and pan-European association colleges and sought to widen the range of representation of the European geographic information community within EUROGI.

Delegates at the board meeting also approved a revised mission statement for EUROGI and an expanded set of strategic objectives (European Umbrella Organisation for Geographic Information 2000). The new mission statement stressed the importance of increasing the use of geographic information for many different purposes: "To maximize the effective use of geographic information for the benefit of the citizen, good governance and commerce in Europe and to represent the views of the geographic community."

GI2000: TOWARDS A EUROPEAN POLICY FRAMEWORK FOR GEOGRAPHIC INFORMATION
A Communication from the Commission to the Council, to the European Parliament, to the Economic and Social Committee and to the Committee of the Regions

The starting point for discussions about the European Geographic Information Infrastructure was the meeting convened by DG XIII in Luxembourg in February 1995. This brought together key people representing GI interests in each of the member states to discuss a draft document entitled *GI2000: Towards a European Geographic Information Infrastructure.* The main conclusion of this meeting was that DG XIII should initiate and support a widespread consultation process within the European GI community with a view to the preparation of a policy document for the Council of Ministers. The basic argument underlying this initiative was the concern that "Europe is in danger of missing out on an important opportunity to exploit the potential of GI to contribute to social and economic development." Consequently, action was needed at the European level to coordinate the GI initiatives coming into being at the national level to ensure that EU-wide objectives could be met as well.

The original document went through various drafts during the consultation process until the final draft was released in September 1999. Its main recommendation was for the creation of a high-level working party to provide the leadership that was needed for coordination purposes. It was argued that this should include representatives from both the public and private GI sectors, including users, and that it should be chaired and facilitated by the commission. Although never embodied directly into EU policy, GI2000 did a great deal to create a climate of opinion within the European GI community that was favorably disposed to the development of an overall GI strategy.

Box 6.3 GI2000.
Sources: Masser and Salge (1997), Longhorn (2004), *www.ec-gis.jrc.it.*

 Anton Wolfkamp holds a degree in Law and Public Science from the University of Amsterdam. From 1991 until 1999 he held a number of positions in the Dutch Cadastre (the Cadastre and Public Registers Agency from The Netherlands) including director of one of the regional branches. Through the Dutch Cadastre he developed a strong interest in matters relating to geographic information and international relations. In 1999, he was seconded by the Cadastre to become secretary general of EUROGI. As secretary general he was responsible for the day-to-day running of EUROGI. He also represented EUROGI within the European Commission and acted as a liaison for the broader GI community. He was involved in the GSDI, especially the preparations of the GSDI 6 in Budapest, September 2002, which he continued after his retirement that year. Within the framework of the Geographic Information Network in Europe (GINIE) project, he carried out studies of the role and position of national GI associations and the nature of the European-level GI organizations.

Bearing in mind the outcomes of the GINIE reports, opinions about the role of geographic information institutions, and the developments within the European Commission related to legislation, Anton sees the biggest challenges for organizations like EUROGI in the near future as

» creating added value for the members by informing them about developments that happen at the European level and encouraging them to participate

» supporting member participation in initiatives taken by the European Commission (PSI, INSPIRE)

» encouraging cooperation between pan-European GI organizations by supporting the creation of a European Geographic Information Network

» supporting the European GI Industry to become more visible

Box 6.4   Profile of Anton Wolfkamp, Secretary General (1999–2002), EUROGI, Apeldoorn, Netherlands.

EUROGI (2000) published a consultation paper in October 2000 entitled *Towards a strategy for geographic information in Europe*. The starting point for this paper was the belief that positive steps were needed to fill the void with respect to GI strategy at the European level following the demise of GI2000. This identified five strategic objectives for EUROGI:

1. Encouraging greater use of geographic information in Europe: This is the overarching goal, as it is vital to ensure that GI is used as widely as possible in both the public and private sectors, as well as by individual citizens in the interests of open government.

2. Raising awareness of GI and its associated technologies: There is a continuing need to raise awareness in the community as a whole regarding the importance of recent advances in both technology and their potential for an increasing range of applications.

3. Promoting the development of strong national GI associations: An important element of EUROGI's strategy is to create the institutional capacity to take a lead in SDI formulation and implementation. This is particularly important given the need for national associations to maintain some measure of independence from government.

4. Improving the European GI infrastructure: Although many of the main elements of a European infrastructure are already in place in different countries, there is a lack of effective mechanisms at the European level to promote greater harmony and interoperability between countries in this respect.

5. Representing European interests in the global spatial infrastructure debate: In an era of increasing globalization, it is essential that Europe does not evolve in isolation.

Following the publication of this paper, a proposal was submitted to the European Commission (EC) as an accompanying measure under its Fifth Framework for Research and Development. This involved EUROGI, together with the Joint Research Centre of the EC, the Open GIS Consortium Europe, and the University of Sheffield. The main objectives of the resulting GINIE project, which took place between November 2001 and January 2004, *(www.ec-gis.org/ginie)* were to

⇥ develop a deeper understanding of the key issues and actors affecting the wider use of GI in Europe

⇥ articulate a strategy that was consistent with major policy and technological developments at the European and international levels.

To achieve these objectives, the project coordinators organized a series of specialist workshops, commissioned analytical studies, collected numerous case studies of GI in action, and disseminated widely its findings across Europe and beyond in more than ten different European languages. Through its activities, GINIE involved more than 150 senior representatives from industry, research, and government in thirty-two countries, and contributed to building up the knowledge necessary for an evidence-based geographic information policy in Europe. The project consortium presented its findings to a high-level audience of senior decision makers in government, research, and industry at its final conference in Brussels in November 2003. A summary of the main findings of this project was also published in book form entitled *Geographic Information in the Wider Europe* (Craglia et al. 2003).

During the lifetime of this project, two important developments took place at the EC level. The first was the debates leading up to the adoption by the Council of Ministers and the European Parliament of a directive on the reuse of public-sector information *(box 6.5)*. EUROGI was very active in the lead up to the adoption of the directive and will continue to be involved in monitoring its implementation with respect to geographic information. The second was the launch of the INfrastructure for SPatial InfoRmation in Europe (INSPIRE) initiative by the European Environmental Agency, Eurostat, and the Commission's Joint Research Centre to create a European spatial data infrastructure *(box 6.6)*. EUROGI has strongly supported this initiative from the outset and encouraged its members to participate in its various activities. The emergence of this initiative during the lifetime of the GINIE project also gave an extra momentum to its own work program.

DIRECTIVE 2003/98/EC OF THE EUROPEAN PARLIAMENT AND OF THE COUNCIL
of November 17, 2003, on the reuse of public-sector information

The public-sector information debates within DG Information Society ran in parallel during the late 1990s to those concerning GI2000. The rationale behind these debates was the recognition that the public sector is the largest single producer of information in Europe and that the social and economic potential of this resource has yet to be tapped. Although geographic information is only one type of information that is produced by the public sector, it is regarded as one with considerable potential for the development of digital products and services. The basic objective of the directive is to increase access to the information that is collected by the public sector throughout Europe with a view to stimulating the internal market. The directive sets out a framework for the conditions governing the reuse of public-sector information. These cover matters such as available formats, principles governing charging, transparency, and licenses. The adoption of this directive has important implications for the future development of the geographic information field because the measures that it contains are mandatory on all the EU member states who have until July 2005 to incorporate them in their respective national legislation.

Box 6.5   The reuse of public-sector information directive.

Sources: Commission of the European Communities (2003), Pira International Ltd., University of East Anglia, and Knowledge Ltd. (2000).

The INSPIRE initiative was launched in December 2001 with a view "to making available relevant, harmonised and quality geographic information to support formulation, implementation, monitoring and evaluation of Community policies with a territorial dimension or impact." INSPIRE is seen as the first step toward a broad multisectoral initiative that focuses initially on the spatial information required for environmental policies. It is a legal initiative of the EU that addresses "technical standards and protocols, organisation and coordination issues, data policy issues including data access and the creation and maintenance of spatial information."

Important outputs from the INSPIRE initiative during 2002 included position papers prepared by its working groups on common reference data and metadata (led by Eurostat), data policy and legal implications (led by the UK Environment Agency), architecture and standards (led by the Joint Research Centre), and funding and implementation structures (led by the Swedish Land Survey), as well as the state-of-play study of NSDIs throughout described in chapter 3.

A draft directive to "establish an infrastructure for spatial information in the Community" was published in July 2004 and the European Environment Agency, together with Eurostat and the Joint Research Centre, are currently engaged in a process that should lead to its approval in late 2006 or early 2007. When approved, the governments of all twenty-five member states will be required to modify existing legislation or introduce new legislation to implement its provisions within a specific time period.

Box 6.6   The INfrastructure for SPatial InfoRmation in Europe (INSPIRE) initiative.
Source: Commission of the European Communities (2004), van der Haegen and de Groof (2004), *inspire.jrc.it.*

Current developments

Anton Wolfkamp retired as secretary general of EUROGI in May 2002 and was replaced by Bino Marchesini. Bino Marchesini trained as a lawyer and came to EUROGI with more than twenty years experience at the Dutch Kadaster. His appointment meant that the EUROGI secretariat continued to be based in the cadastral offices at Apeldoorn, thereby avoiding the disruption caused by the need to relocate its operations as a result of the appointment of a new secretary general from another European country.

Ian Masser's term of office as president came to an end in March 2003, and Jean Poulit from France was elected as his successor. M. Poulit came to EUROGI with many years experience in the operational use of GI for land planning and the environment. He was the former general director of IGN France and president of IGN France International. He was also president of CERCO (now EuroGeographics) for two years and is currently a member of the French National Council for Transportation and Planning and serves as an advisor to the president of the French National Space Agency. In his manifesto, M. Poulit expressed his strong belief that special attention should be given to promoting the benefits of GI to society at large and argued that this can best be done by demonstrating its potential for applications in key fields such as transport, buildings, and natural space.

Figure 6.1
National members of EUROGI.

In March 2004, EUROGI had twenty-one national and two pan-European members. Its membership included representatives from all fifteen EU countries prior to May 2004 together with Iceland, Norway, and Switzerland *(figure 6.1)*. Of the ten new EU members, Hungary and Poland have been full members of EUROGI for some time, and the Czech Republic is a candidate member. Only two pan-European bodies were associate members of EUROGI in March 2004. These were the European Association of Remote Sensing Companies and the Urban Data Management Society conference organization. However, EUROGI has built up strong links over the years with most of the other pan-European bodies in the field and acts as the convenor for an annual Pan-European Associations Forum of these bodies. These include Eurogeographics, the Association of GI Laboratories in Europe (AGILE), the Council of European Geodetic Surveyors (CLGE), the European Association of Remote Sensing Laboratories (EARSEL), and the European Organization for Spatial Data Research (EuroSDR). One of the proposals arising out of the GINIE project is the establishment of a European GIS network with an expanded membership. EUROGI also has a Memorandum of Understanding with the EU's Joint Research Centre for various joint activities, including the organization of specialist workshops, and another with Eurogeographics.

The activities of EUROGI are currently managed by its secretariat in conjunction with an executive committee elected by its members. This is chaired by the president and meets four times a year. In March 2004, the nine seats on this committee were held by representatives from the British, French, German, Hungarian, Italian, Polish, Portuguese, Swedish, and Swiss national GI associations. Under its statues and bylaws, EUROGI must convene a general board meeting once a year to approve its work plan and budget. The meeting also approves any proposed changes in the statutes and bylaws and elects its president (every two years, with one possibility for a further two year extension) and its executive committee (on a three year rotational basis).

STRENGTHS	WEAKNESSES
Independent status	Legitimacy has to be earned
Diversity of membership	Diversity of membership
Permanent secretariat	Dependency on subscriptions for funding

Table 6.2

Some strengths and weaknesses of EUROGI as an organization.

Source: Masser et al. (2003, 75).

Table 6.2 summarizes some of the main strengths and weaknesses of EUROGI as a regional institution.

EUROGI's strengths lie in its independent position. This enables it to criticize national and regional governments if necessary and makes it possible to lobby for support of its ideas. Its member associations include most of the main stakeholders in spatial data infrastructure activities, and its permanent secretariat facilitates the flow of information between its members and also between them and the European Commission. This is reflected in high levels of attendance at meetings. Two-thirds of its full members have also actively participated in the work of its executive committee, which meets four times a year.

However, each of these strengths can be regarded as weaknesses. EUROGI's independent status also means that it has to make constant efforts to sustain its legitimacy to its members, as well as to policy makers in the EU and Europe as a whole. The diversity of its membership also means that it can be difficult to find a common position among the competing and sometimes conflicting interests of its members, and the overhead costs of maintaining a permanent secretariat are relatively high given its small number of members. This means that EUROGI must be always looking for support to sustain its activities.

SOME CURRENT ACTIVITIES

RECENTLY, EUROGI WORK REFLECTS ITS five strategic objectives (discussed previously). To encourage greater use of GI in Europe, it has disseminated information about applications through publications, and presentations at workshops and conferences. Also, it has stimulated investment in research and development activities. In particular, there is a need for a greater emphasis on geographic-information-related research topics in the European Commission's Framework Programs for Research and Technology Development.

To raise awareness of GI and its associated technologies, EUROGI has developed an integrated lobbying strategy that involves putting into place and maintaining a logistical infrastructure that supports a sustainable coordinated lobbying program. This program complements those of the EUROGI members at the national level and other pan-European representative bodies.

EUROGI has also begun to inform the population as a whole. European GI strategy must seek to facilitate the diffusion of knowledge and experience between different countries, professional groups, and application fields. An important tool in this respect is EUROGI's strategy for developing a GI Case Study Service. This has been further developed in the context of the WebCastle service that has been developed by a team at the Technical University of Ostrava in the Czech Republic as part of the GINIE project *(gis.vsb.cz/webcastle)*.

EUROGI has also developed strong national GI associations by promoting the comparative analysis of national GI policies. In its early years, EUROGI commissioned comparative studies of copyright and commercialization in various European countries. In November 1999 and June 2001, EUROGI, Joint Research Centre, European Commission (JRC), and DG InfoSoc organized workshops on data policy (Craglia, Annoni, and Masser 2000) and cadastral issues relating to agri-environmental policies (Waters and Dallemand 2002).

A further data policy workshop organized primarily by EUROGI during the GINIE project provided a useful opportunity to make an input to the INSPIRE initiative *(box 6.6).*

EUROGI pooled the experience of the national associations themselves as an instrument for national capacity building. A lot can be learned from the positive (and negative) experiences of different national associations. (Some of the findings of the studies of national member associations commissioned by EUROGI and the outcomes of the follow up studies undertaken as part of the GINIE project will be described in the next section of this chapter.)

To improve the European SDI, EUROGI created a forum for new members and potential EU members to discuss their accession requirements in terms of geographic information. A joint EUROGI/JRC workshop to explore these issues was held in Brussels in November 2000 (Craglia and Dallemand 2001), and a follow up workshop in Prague was primarily organized by EUROGI as part of the GINIE project (Pauknerova et al. 2003).

Additionally, EUROGI worked with other organizations to improve the quality of metadata services, given that lack of information as to what data is available in different European countries is a major barrier to many transnational applications. A good example of this is the European Territorial Management Information Infrastructure project (ETeMII) coordinated by Associazione GISFORM. EUROGI and a number of other key stakeholders, including GI such as the JRC, OGC Europe, and AGILE, as well as the French, German, and Portuguese national GI associations worked together on this project (European Territorial Management Information Infrastructure 2002).

Finally, to represent European interests in the GSDI debate, EUROGI is playing a full role in the organization of GSDI activities. Until the launch of the GSDI Association in 2004 (see chapter 7), the GSDI structure was loosely organized around the periodic rotation of responsibilities between its regional bodies. EUROGI was in charge of the GSDI Web site up to June 2000 and organized the GSDI 6 conference in Budapest in September 2002.

EUROGI has also been participating in several working groups that have been set up under the auspices of the GSDI. These groups are essentially virtual working groups in that they rely on the exchange of information and opinions over the Web rather than face-to-face meetings.

A PROFILE OF EUROGI'S NATIONAL GI ASSOCIATION MEMBERS

ONE OF THE MOST DISTINCTIVE FEATURES of EUROGI is the national GI associations that make up the majority of its members (see table 6.3 for the dates of the foundation of these associations in different European countries). Associations already existed in ten European countries at the time EUROGI was founded: Belgium, Finland, France, Italy, Luxembourg, the Netherlands, Norway, Portugal, Slovenia, Sweden, and the United Kingdom. The oldest of these bodies, Norway's GeoForum, dates back to 1969.

An important principle underlying the structure of EUROGI membership is the assumption that there should be only one national GI association for each country. Since its foundation, EUROGI has implemented this principle by setting up national GI associations in twelve more countries, with plans to set up associations in five more *(table 6.3)*.

YEAR	COUNTRIES
1969	Norway
1986	Belgium, France, Sweden
1989	United Kingdom
1990	Italy, Portugal
1991	Slovenia
1992	Luxembourg
1993	Finland, Netherlands
1994	Germany, Hungary, Iceland, Switzerland
1995	Denmark, Ireland, Russia
1996	Poland
1997	Czech Republic
1998	Austria, Greece
2002	Slovakia
Plans for national GI association	Bulgaria, Cyprus, Lithuania, Malta, Turkey

Table 6.3

The establishment of national GI associations in Europe.

Source: Wolfkamp (2003, 10).

In practice, these associations often differ considerably from one another. A survey of EUROGI member associations (van Biessen 2001) explored in some detail the variations between the organizational models adopted by different European countries. Subsequently, the profiles of these bodies have been updated and extended in coverage by Wolfkamp (2003) in the context of the GINIE project. These association studies identified five distinguishing factors:

1. The national environment: this determines the reason for the existence of the association, the resources that it has at its disposal, and the nature of its organizational structure

2. The mission of the association: this provides direction and meaning to its activities

3. The financial resources at its disposal: these are very much dependent on the national environment and determine the level of support that is available to sustain its activities

4. The organizational structure: this gives direction to the ways in which activities are undertaken

5. The activities of the association: these are dependent on the resources and the organizational structure of the association, which in turn reflect the national environment

The findings of these studies also suggest that the extent of a government's involvement in the nature and activities of the national GI associations is relative to the extent of its influence on the association's affairs. Luxembourg's national association, for example, is a working group established by the government that consists of representatives from all the main departments that deal with geographic information. In most other countries, the national associations have been set up as a counterpart to government. For example, Ireland's IRLOGI is recognized by the government as an independent national body representing all sectors of the GI industry. Similarly, Hungary's Association for Geo-Information (HUNAGI) is recognized as an independent body that cooperates with government as a non-governmental organization (NGO).

Some of the consequences of the national environment can also be seen in terms of the size of the membership of these bodies *(table 6.4)*. The combined total members represented by EUROGI as a whole is more than 6,500 public- and private-sector organizations and individuals. There are also considerable differences between the national associations in terms of the size of their membership, which reflects to some extent the degree to which individual members are permitted to join them. However, it should be noted that the association with the largest number of members, Norway's GeoForum, is based in one of the smaller countries in Europe with respect to population. In contrast, the national association in Europe's largest country with respect to population, Germany, has only ninety members. Overall, there is a marked difference between Norway's GeoForum, the United Kingdom's AGI, and Denmark's Geoforum, each of which has more than five hundred members, and the associations from Austria, Belgium, Luxembourg, and the Netherlands, each of which has fifty or fewer members.

Austria	Austrian Umbrella Organisation for GI	48
Belgium	Coordination committee for Digital GI	50
Czech Republic	Czech Association for Geoinformation	163
Denmark	Geoforum Denmark	575
Finland	Finnish Association for GI	237
France	French Association for GI	67
Germany	German Umbrella Association for GI	90
Greece	Hellas GI	289
Hungary	Hungarian Association for GI	63
Iceland	Organisation for GI in Iceland	128
Ireland	Irish Organisation for GI	131
Italy	AM/FM GIS Italy	100
Luxembourg	Inter Ministerial Working Group on GIS	12
Netherlands	RAVI Foundation	8
Norway	GeoForum	2,150
Poland	National Land Information System Users Association	149
Portugal	Portuguese GI Users Association	500
Spain	Spanish Association for GI	234
Sweden	Swedish Development Council for Land Information	213
Switzerland	Swiss Organisation for Geoinformation	129
United Kingdom	Association for GI	1,200
	COMBINED TOTAL	6,536

Source: Wolfkamp (2003, 17–18).

Table 6.4
National GI association names and
combined membership.

The findings of Wolfkamp's analysis also show that there is some measure of agreement between most of the national associations regarding their missions. This is generally articulated in a simple one sentence statement such as that of the United Kingdom's Association for Geographic Information, which seeks "to maximize the use of GI for the benefit of the citizen, good government and commerce." Most associations list some or all of the following as their fields of interest in order of importance:

- awareness raising
- networking
- information dissemination
- lobbying
- promotion of standards
- policy formulation
- education and training (see also, van Uden 2003).

There are substantial differences in the financial resources that are at the disposal of the national associations. The wealthiest associations are the United Kingdom's AGI, the Dutch RAVI, and Norway's GeoForum, each of which has an annual turnover of more than half a million Euros. In contrast, Belgium's Coordination Committee and Luxembourg's Working Group reported no income at all.

As might be expected, the organizational structures that have emerged in these associations reflect the resources at their disposal. As a result, wealthier organizations such as the United Kingdom's AGI and the Dutch RAVI are able to support a substantial full-time secretariat, whereas most of the poorer associations are dependent on voluntary or, at best, part-time support for their activities. These activities mainly include conferences, seminars, lobbying, projects, workshops, and publications.

AN EXCHANGE OF LETTERS

THE EXCHANGE OF LETTERS BETWEEN THE president of EUROGI and the president of the European Commission in the summer of 1999 illustrates the nature of the relations between the two organizations at a critical point in time. The letter from EUROGI highlights the deep concern felt by the European geographic information community regarding the lack of progress in connection with the GI2000 initiative. It draws attention to the strategic importance that is attached to geographic information and the need for the European Commission to establish an appropriate policy framework for its exploitation based on the GI2000 document. It points out the economic benefits that are linked to such a framework in terms of the competitive position of European business and the benefits the Commission itself will experience when such an initiative is implemented.

As might be expected, the reply from the incoming president of the European Commission looks very much to the future and identifies two activities of importance for the European geographic information community. The first of these refers to the Committee on Geographic Information (COGI) that was set up by Eurostat in 2000 to manage the needs for GI among the commission services. This has subsequently played a major role in the development of the INSPIRE project, which in some respects is the natural successor to the GI2000 initiative. The second activity mentioned in the letter is the Public Sector Information green paper that eventually led to the EU directive on the reuse of public-sector information, which was approved by the Council and the European Parliament in December 2003.

EUROGI
Marne le Vallee
France
8 September 1999

Dear Mr. Prodi,

I am writing to you, as incoming president of the European Commission, to draw your attention to the concerns expressed by members of my organization regarding the failure of the commission to create the policy framework that is required for them to exploit the potential of modern geographic information technologies. EUROGI represents the interests of more than thirty national and European sectoral associations in Europe with a combined membership of more than 2,000 public- and private-sector agencies.

It is generally accepted that geographic information has a vital role to play in the creation of the Information Society as 80 percent of all information has some form of geographic reference attached to it. For this reason, it has considerable potential to improve decision making at all levels in both government and business. However, this potential cannot be fully exploited at the European level in the absence of an appropriate policy framework.

The importance of a policy framework of this kind has already been recognized by two of Europe's leading competitors, the United States and Japan. Both these countries have taken steps at the highest political levels to establish National Spatial Data Infrastructures for this purpose. Many governments within the EU are also embarking on similar initiatives at the national level.

The failure of the EU to take action at the European level has important economic consequences with respect to both the competitiveness of European business and the effective conduct of the business of the commission itself. Geographic information services and products constitute a small but dynamic component of the information sector of the European economy. At the present time their global market share is relatively small in comparison with their North American counterparts. This is largely because of the absence of a truly European market. Consequently, the creation of a European policy framework would help them to expand their activities within Europe and compete more effectively in the global market.

A major customer for these services and products is the European Commission itself. Geographic information is an important input to decision making in most of the commission's directorates, especially in the fields of agriculture, environment, regional policy and transport. The lack of an overall European policy framework is felt particularly when decisions have to be made that require cross-national spatial data, as is the case in many of the cross-border initiatives that are now under way in various parts of Europe.

To deal with these matters, EUROGI wants to see a high-level working group set up as soon as possible to prepare an action plan for a European policy framework. Its membership should be drawn from all the main stakeholders in government, business, and academia. Because of the extent to which geographic information matters transcend the responsibilities of any one directorate, EUROGI feels that this must be handled at the highest level within the commission.

In making this proposal, EUROGI is well aware that a similar recommendation is contained in a draft communication prepared by DG XIII that has been circulating within the commission since September 1996. EUROGI played an important role in the preparation of this document and strongly supports its main recommendations. However, it believes that the continuing failure to turn them into actions is principally due to the fact that they require strategic decisions within the commission at a higher level than that of a particular directorate.

I hope that you will respond positively to these proposals and would be pleased to elaborate them at greater length if required. As an indication of our commitment to the idea of high-level working group, I would also like to offer the services of the EUROGI secretariat to support its activities.

Yours sincerely,

Prof. Ian Masser
President of EUROGI

COMMISSION OF THE EUROPEAN COMMUNITIES
Brussels
7 October 1999

Dear Prof. Masser,

Thank you for your letter of 8 September 1999 in which you propose that the EU should establish a European policy framework for geographic information to help realize the potential at European level.

As you know, this issue was initiated under the previous commission. After extensive consultation with the major actors, DG XIII prepared a draft communication (GI2000) to launch a political debate in council and Parliament on how to deal with geographic information at European level. Several member state's ministers wrote to the commission in support of this initiative. In September 1998, a member of the European Parliament put an oral question to the commission asking when it will present GI2000. The commission answered that, in fact, it intended to adopt GI2000 shortly. This was, however, prevented by the resignation of the previous commission.

In the coming weeks, the new commission will be looking into all pending issues to determine if and how they fit into its political priorities. Independently of the outcome hereof, two other activities of importance to European geographic information are in any case underway:

Firstly, an internal working group cutting across all relevant directorates general is being set up to examine the needs for European geographic information within the commission services and how these needs could be satisfied in a co-ordinated and cost-effective way.

The second activity is the follow-up of the Green Paper on Public Sector Information, which was issued for consultation in the beginning of the year. It contains substantial reference to issues relating to geographic information and many organizations with a stake in geographic information have responded. A further document, including the results of this consultation and follow-up actions envisaged by the commission is in preparation. This will most certainly include actions which will be highly relevant for geographic information in Europe.

Yours sincerely,

Romano Prodi
President of the European Commission

SUMMARY

THIS CHAPTER HAS DESCRIBED THE WAYS
in which EUROGI has developed as an organization to promote SDI development in its region during the ten years since
its foundation in response to changing circumstances within
the European Union and the rest of Europe. As a result of
these developments, EUROGI has emerged as an independently funded European organization that seeks to develop a
European approach toward the use of geographic information
technologies. It works closely with its national and pan-
European members and is able, as a result, to draw upon the
combined skills and experiences of more than 6,500 public and
private bodies and individuals who belong to these organizations. The range and diversity of these activities demonstrates
what can be done by an active organization, albeit with limited
resources at its disposal.

The profiles of EUROGI's members indicate the diversity of its
national member organizations within Europe. This in turn
reflects the different institutional circumstances within which
they have come into being and have to operate. The role that
these associations can play in the development of national
thinking about SDIs was highlighted in an earlier chapter on
the evolution of SDIs in the United Kingdom.

CHAPTER 7

*SDI bodies at the
global level*
The global spatial data infrastructure

At the global level, the position is even more complex than at the regional level. The United Nations has set up the UN GI Working Group *(ungiwg.org)* to promote interagency cooperation, but this is not in any sense a global SDI (GSDI). Nevertheless, there have been some noteworthy successes at the global level. Some of the most interesting of these are sectoral initiatives such as the Global Map program *(www.iscgm.org)* and environmental research initiatives such as the International Geosphere–Biosphere Programme *(www. igbp.kva.se)*.

Under these circumstances, the rationale for a global SDI can be questioned. O'Neil (2004), for example, posed the following questions at the Bangalore GSDI conference. What is the purpose of a global SDI? Who are its potential users? How can we monitor its progress? For some people the answers to these questions are to be found in conspiracy theory. Dale (2003, 33), for example, claims that Hans Christian Anderson's story about the Emperor's new clothes may also be an allegory for GSDI with more sinister intentions. "The drive behind GSDI appears to be from three sources—academics who dream of a brave but unrealistic new world, vendors who see this as a great marketing opportunity for their hardware and software, and the military. The latter are caught between wanting spatial data for anywhere they might have to conduct operations but not wanting others to have access to it."

In contrast to this position, others see a GSDI as a stepping stone to a truly digital earth (Foresman et al. 2004) or as an inevitable and largely beneficial consequence of recent technological developments and the emergence of a global information society. "SDI is a natural step in the evolution of the use of GIS. Knitting together geographic data to support decision making leads to the birth of a societal GIS. It is my view that GIS does and will continue to profoundly influence people's lives. It is inevitable that GIS will be seen as a fundamental infrastructure" (Dangermond 2004, 13).

This chapter considers the GSDI concept in three parts:

1. The evolution of the GSDI concept from the first GSDI conference in 1996 to the establishment of the GSDI Association and the election of its first board of directors in February 2004

2. A profile of the GSDI Association that has emerged in terms of its structure and membership

3. An evaluation of the GSDI Association's achievements so far, the immediate challenges that face the fledging organization, and the questions raised above about its rationale

THE EVOLUTION OF THE GSDI

THE FIRST GSDI CONFERENCE WAS HELD in Bonn, Germany, in September 1996. This was followed by six more conferences at intervals of slightly more than one year until the GSDI 7 in Bangalore, India, in February 2004. The eighth and ninth GSDI conferences will take place in Cairo, Egypt, in April 2005, and in Santiago, Chile, in October 2006.

Table 7.1
GSDI conferences.

GSDI 1	Bonn, Germany	September 1996
GSDI 2	Chapel Hill, North Carolina	October 1997
GSDI 3	Canberra, Australia	November 1998
GSDI 4	Capetown, South Africa	March 2000
GSDI 5	Cartegena, Colombia	May 2001
GSDI 6	Budapest, Hungary	September 2002
GSDI 7	Bangalore, India	February 2004
GSDI 8	Cairo, Egypt	April 2005
GSDI 9	Santiago, Chile	October 2006

There is a clear sequence in the global choice of locations for these conferences that reflects the desire of the organizers to raise awareness of the strategic importance of geographic information and spatial data infrastructures in all parts of the world. GSDI 1 took place in Europe and was followed by GSDI 2 in North America. The third conference was held in the Asia and Pacific region, the fourth in Africa, and the fifth in Latin America. In 2002, the conference returned to Europe and then moved again to Asia and the Pacific in 2004 and back to Africa in 2005.

There has also been a shift in emphasis in the choice of conference locations during the lifetime of the GSDI. The first three conferences were held in relatively developed countries such as Germany, the United States, and Australia, whereas the recent conferences have taken place in less-developed countries or countries in transition such as South Africa, Colombia, Hungary, India, Egypt, and Chile. This shift reflects the changing GSDI policy agenda following the widespread diffusion of SDI initiatives to all parts of the world (Masser 2004a).

Early days

The first GSDI Conference in Bonn was attended by sixty-three invited individuals from a wide range of organizations in twenty countries. The underlying agenda of the meeting was outlined by EU Commissioner, Martin Bangemann, past chair of the commission's high-level working group on Europe and the Global Information Society, in the following terms: "An ever expanding list of data, and the tools required to put those data to good use are being demanded by the global information society. Accordingly, all professionals in all disciplines are being called upon to participate and contribute to advancing our understanding and use of data of all types. A new level of cooperation and sharing between all nations is required to accelerate our future successes" (Bangemann 1996).

These sentiments were echoed in the opening remarks of the three main organizers: Michael Brand, the president of EUROGI; Fritz Petersohn, the president of the Atlantic Institute; and Klaus Barwinski, the president of the German national GI association (DDGI). The main outcomes of the meeting included a general consensus among those present that it was time to start thinking globally about spatial data infrastructures *(table 7.2)*. It was also felt that this would be facilitated by the creation of a global forum to promote the exchange of ideas and encourage joint activities at the global level.

The second GSDI conference took place at Chapel Hill, North Carolina, under the patronage of the U.S. Secretary of the Interior and Chairman of the Federal Geographic Data Committee (FGDC), Bruce Babbit, as well as EU Commissioner Bangemann. It was co-chaired by Michael Brand and the Science and Technology Advisor to the Governor of the State of North Carolina, Jane Smith–Paterson. It was similar in both scale and format to the Bonn conference.

Table 7.2
The evolution of GSDI.

EARLY DAYS	
GSDI 1	**Bonn, Germany**
	Time to start thinking about the GSDI concept
	Need for a global forum to facilitate the exchange of ideas and development of joint activities
GSDI 2	**Chapel Hill, North Carolina**
	Need to get support from decision makers in business, government, and academia
	Establish an organizational nucleus to promote SDI at all levels
INITIAL FORMALIZATION	
GSDI 3	**Canberra, Australia**
	Creating an organizational framework: steering committee and working groups
	Importance of capacity building in developing countries and countries in transition
GSDI 4	**Capetown, South Africa**
	First edition of SDI cookbook
	U.S. FGDC offers to host interim secretariat
TOWARD A GSDI ASSOCIATION	
GSDI 5	**Cartegena, Colombia**
	Moving beyond a conference organization to a GSDI Association
	Launch of ESRI GSDI/Global Map Grant program
GSDI 6	**Budapest, Hungary**
	Board of directors tasked to create a GSDI Association
	Launch of Intergraph Open Interoperability Grant program
FORMALIZING THE GSDI ASSOCIATION	
GSDI 7	**Bangalore, India**
	First council meetings
	Elections to the board of directors

The conference delegates were addressed by a number of senior decision makers from different levels of government. These included the governor of North Carolina, the under global secretary for management at the U.S. Department of State, the director of the National Imagery and Mapping Agency, and the director of the Division for Economic and Social Development and Natural Resources Management at the United Nations.

In the final session, the participants concluded, "It is necessary to seek involvement and support of decision makers at the highest levels of business, government, and academia in establishing the GSDI, and to generate support at the local, national, regional, and international levels. In particular, it is important to involve the G6 countries, the UN Institutions, and the World Bank in the creation and use of the GSDI."

To achieve these objectives, they tasked Jane Smith–Paterson to chair an interorganizational initiative to establish an organizational nucleus "to encourage the creation, development and linkage of local, national, regional and global geospatial data infrastructures."

Initial formalization

The theme of the third GSDI conference in Canberra was "Policy and organizational frameworks for a GSDI." In its opening session, the chair of the GSDI steering committee, Jane Smith–Paterson, said that it was now time to tackle the big issues and move forward toward a global organizational structure and commitment to support this initiative.

A theme paper by Michael Brand considered some of the policy and organizational issues involved in setting up a GSDI organization. He argued that a GSDI should aspire to the following principles:

- be inclusive of all stakeholders
- add value
- build on, facilitate, and support existing initiatives
- command respect and authority
- support sustainable development
- be flexible and adaptable to change
- command support and financial resources
- facilitate new initiatives, especially those relating to the use and sharing of data
- be as simple, transparent, open, and democratic as possible
- enhance democratic decision-making processes
- engender partnerships (Brand 1998, 6)

Three different kinds of organizational model could be used for these purposes. The first of these was the governmental model. The advantage was that it could easily obtain official recognition, but the disadvantage was that it would exclude most of the stakeholders. The second model was the business model. This might be better resourced, but would also exclude large sections of the GI community. Consequently, it was argued that the umbrella model "has the potential to involve all the GI community, at different levels of involvement, speed, and commitment. In other words, it can be designed to be very flexible and inclusive. Potentially, it is less threatening to existing initiatives, which in many cases will need facilitation and support especially to ensure implementation" (Brand 1998, 7).

With this in mind, the conference participants resolved that a global SDI should aim to become an independent global umbrella organization in the long run, and a GSDI steering committee was set up for this purpose. This consisted of the past, present, and future chairs of the steering committee, representatives from each of the four regions of the world (i.e., Asia/Pacific, Europe, Africa, and the Americas), as well as a number of members at large from the GSDI stakeholder community (Holland 1999). Four working groups were also established

+ to oversee the implementation of the umbrella organization

+ to advise the steering committee on the technical aspects of GSDI

+ to advise the steering committee on the economic, legal, and funding mechanisms underpinning the GSDI

+ to promote the GSDI concept in the wider world

To facilitate these developments, the Australian Surveying and Land Information Group (AUSLIG) volunteered to provide secretarial support during the period between GSDI 3 and 4.

The participants at the Canberra conference also thought that it was important for the GSDI to encourage capacity building in developing countries and in countries in transition so they could effectively participate in its activities. This was reflected in the theme of "Engaging emerging economies" at the fourth GSDI Conference in Capetown in March 2000. GSDI 4 marked a departure from the format of earlier conferences in that it was an open conference with both invited speakers and presentations resulting from a widely publicized call for papers. This resulted in a substantial increase in the number of delegates to a total of more than 180.

GSDI 4 also departed from previous conferences in that it included presentations based on projects commissioned by the GSDI steering committee and its working groups. The most important of these projects was the presentation of the first draft of the *SDI Cookbook* by the chairman of the Technical Working Group, Douglas Nebert (2000). This was the outcome of an ongoing international collaborative project by its members to share current experiences about building SDIs in different parts of the world. From the outset, this book was envisaged as a constantly updated "living" document that would be made available in both printed and digital format to ensure its widest possible diffusion throughout the world. Version two of this cookbook was released in January 2004 (Nebert 2004).

Peter Holland from AUSLIG, the chair of the GSDI steering committee, presented the AUSLIG outcome of GSDI 3. This was the report of the scoping study into the business case for SDI that was carried out by the Centre for International Economics in Australia (Centre for International Economics 2000). This recommended that the main emphasis in any further work must be placed on the demand side in evaluating the need for a GSDI and that a great deal of effort should be devoted to clarifying the exact nature of the GSDI product. The outcomes of such a study would help the GI community to understand the process themselves, as well as helping them make their case to outsiders.

In the final session of the conference, the delegates at GSDI 4 approved a resolution to establish a secretariat made up of staff from one or more countries to provide the necessary support for future GSDI activities. Shortly after the meeting, the steering committee accepted the U.S. FGDC's proposal for the establishment of an interim secretariat based in Reston, Virginia for program coordination.

Toward a GSDI Association

The number of delegates at both GSDI 5 and 6 increased to more than 250, and both conferences made important steps toward the creation of an independent GSDI Association. Delegates at the Cartegena conference resolved to move toward the establishment of a public–private, not-for-profit organization "to guide the leadership activities for GSDI," and a task force chaired by Santiago Borrero was set up to draft bylaws for the governance of the new organization. Delegates at GSDI 5 also approved the extension to the previous definition of a GSDI that was discussed in the introduction to this book.

The findings of a study of ten examples of global organizations that had been successful in promoting global science and technologies were also made available to delegates at GSDI 5. This study was carried out by the RAND Science and Technology Policy Institute (2001) for the GSDI Secretariat.

On August 5th, 2002, the first steps were taken toward the incorporation of the GSDI Association in the state of Virginia and the first board of directors was appointed at the Budapest Conference in September 2002. Its members were the past, present, and future presidents [Santiago Borrero from the Colombian Geographical Institute (IGAC), Ian Masser, the president of EUROGI, and Mukund Rao from the Indian Space Research Organization] together with the chairs of the Technical and the Legal and Economic Working Groups (Douglas Nebert and Harlan Onsrud) and the current secretary, Al Stevens *(figure 7.1)*. This board was given the task of making the GSDI Association fully operational by GSDI 7 in February 2004.

Santiago Borrero was born in Bogotá, Colombia. In 1978, he was awarded the master of science at MIT. He has extensive experience in development, mainly in the production and application of spatial information to land administration and the strategic value of geographic information for developing nations. Internationally, Santiago has chaired the Global Spatial Data Infrastructure (GSDI), the Permanent Committee on SDI for the Americas (PC IDEA), the Colombian Spatial Data Infrastructure (ICDE), and the PanAmerican Institute for Geography and History (PAIGH) Cartographic Commission.

In Colombia, Santiago was director general of the "Agustin Codazzi" Geographic Institute (1994–2002), the senior geoinformation manager in the government of Colombia, the general manager of the Bogotá Water Supply and Sewerage Company, and the National Fund for Development Projects.

In Santiago's view, "we are living at a time where we have to share a common SDI vision, but this will be achieved by having a distributed system of responsibilities."

"There is urgent need to concentrate GSDI activities on how to (1) sustain and fund SDI activities in developing nations and regions; (2) develop and implement improved and innovative capacity building initiatives for SDI; and (3) achieve better levels of cooperation, coordination, and if viable, integration among the growing number of global projects related to the access and application of spatial data.

The vision of a GSDI provides a unique opportunity for all those interested in facilitating access and applicability of spatial data to promote new development alternatives and democracy, especially for developing nations. Being this inclusive, by recognizing the existence of a multidiverse society, the GSDI Association must be an exception in the context of current criticism to globalization processes.

In the case of developing nations, technology itself does not ensure the successful use and application of digital data, and information technology, infrastructure, and connectivity do not necessarily equate to information access and a real bridging of the digital divide."

Box 7.1   Profile of Santiago Borrero, Secretary General, Pan American Institute for Geography and History, Mexico City, Mexico (past president of GSDI, 2001–2002).

 Mukund Rao joined the Indian Space Research Organization at Ahmedabad in 1981 after obtaining a master in science (Geology) degree from Gujarat University. His research and work experience is in the field of Spatial Information Systems. He has been working on systems analysis and design and implementation of decision-support systems based on the use of earth observation images and GIS tools. Mukund has played the central role in the design and definition of the Indian Natural Resources Management System (NRIS) program and has carried out a number of NRIS projects in support of district planning, urban planning, and wasteland development. As program manager of NRIS, he has been involved in furthering its scope and concept as a natural resources information repository. He is also a key design person for the Indian National Spatial Data Infrastructure and is associated in its strategy and action plan development and implementation.

Mukund Rao was elected vice president of the Global Spatial Data Infrastructure (GSDI) Association in September 2002 and became president in February 2004. In his view,

"Any SDI has to be a national initiative and is envisioned to provide a standardized infrastructure for spatial data holdings of various spatial data generating agencies to be linked into a national system. It is about sharing and providing spatial data and applications services. It is about making spatial data accessible and available, and realizing that the more you make your data available, the more will be the demand for it and also for newer spatial data sets. It is a 'culture' that we will have to imbibe—a culture of standardization and formatting, declaring metadata, sharing, encouraging access and applications."

Box 7.2   Profile of Mukund Rao, Deputy Director, Earth Observations System Programme Office, Indian Space Research Organization (ISRO) Headquarters, Bangalore, India (president of the GSDI Association, 2004–2005).

Following the Budapest conference, extensive consultations took place in connection with the draft bylaws before they were approved by the interim council in early 2003. A part-time business director, Suzy Jampoler, was appointed to oversee the initial enrollment of founder members of the association in September 2003, and its new Web site *(www.gsdi. org)* became operational in November 2003.

At GSDI 6 delegates also affirmed the importance of working toward the goals contained in its draft bylaws to

- "support the *establishment and expansion* of local, national, and regional (multination) *spatial data infrastructures* that are globally compatible

- provide an organization to foster *international communication and collaborative efforts* for advancing spatial data infrastructure innovations

- support interdisciplinary *research and education* activities that advance spatial data infrastructure concepts, theories and methods

- enable better *public policy and scientific decision making* through spatial data infrastructure advancements

- promote the *ethical use* of and access to geographic information

- foster spatial data infrastructure developments in *support of important worldwide needs* such as

  - improving local to national economic competitiveness

  - addressing local to global environmental quality and change

  - increasing efficiency, effectiveness, and equity in all levels of government

  - advancing the health, safety, and social well-being of humankind in all nations"

Capacity building initiatives also featured prominently in both conferences (Borrero 2002). Delegates at GSDI 5 welcomed the establishment of a multimillion-dollar Global Map/GSDI Grant program by the president of ESRI, Jack Dangermond, in memory of the late Professor John Estes, the first chair of the International Steering Committee for Global Mapping. This program provides a useful resource for national mapping organization or spatial development organizations that are leading the effort to build NSDIs in their countries. More than one hundred countries have so far benefited from these grants *(www.gsdi.org)*. At GSDI 6, delegates also applauded the launch of Intergraph's own multimillion-dollar Open Interoperability Grant program. This seeks to stimulate the use of open interoperability standards through its support for organizations who wish to build Web services using Open GIS Consortium (OGC) standards, as well as organizations who wish to publish their data in XML/GML file format. So far, grants have been made to agencies as diverse as the East Midlands Development Agency in Britain, the city of Bochum in Germany, and the Military Geographic Institute of Chile *(www.gsdi.org)*.

Formalizing the GSDI Association

GSDI 7 in Bangalore attracted nearly four hundred participants. It was also the first GSDI conference to be organized alongside an exhibition. GSDI 7 was also the setting for the first meeting of the new GSDI Association Council on Monday, February 2, 2004. One of its main tasks was to elect the new vice president and president elect of the association, Harlan Onsrud, as well as the first board of directors. The board of directors met for the first time under the presidency of Mukund Rao on Friday, February 6, 2004. One of the matters discussed at this meeting was the association's response to the invitation extended by the chief minister of Karnataka State, S. M. Krishna, to establish its secretariat in Bangalore.

Delegates to GSDI 7 also welcomed the representatives of the UNECA CODI-GEO who were attending their first conference as the formal regional body for Africa. The establishment of CODI-GEO with GSDI help in May 2003 completed the global regional substructure of GSDI.

The last session of the conference was devoted to a discussion of the arrangements for GSDI 8 that will be held in Cairo in April 2005. This conference breaks new ground in that it is being held in conjunction with an International Federation of Surveyors (FIG) Working Week meeting.

THE GSDI ASSOCIATION:
A PROFILE

THE SHAPE OF THE GSDI ASSOCIATION that emerged at GSDI 7 has a lot in common with the umbrella model that was discussed at GSDI 3 in its intention to involve all sectors of the SDI community from all parts of the of the world. The basic structure of the association is set out in its bylaws *(www.gsdiassociation.org)*. These define three classes of membership: full, associate, and individual. Full membership is open to all organizations "with programs and missions consistent with the purposes of the GSDI Association." These include government agencies, industry organizations and private companies, academic bodies, not-for-profit organizations, and any other agencies that "are strongly affecting the development of spatial data infrastructures at the national, regional (multinational), and international levels." Each full member has a seat on the association council with full voting rights. Associate members pay a lower membership fee and may observe council meetings, while individual members pay an even lower fee. Neither associate nor individual members have voting rights.

The fees for all three categories of membership are differentiated according to the nature of the organization and the per capita income of the country involved as defined by the World Bank indicators used in chapters 2, 3, and 6 of this book. For example, a government agency or a private-sector company in a country with a high income per capita such as the United States or the United Kingdom pay $9,000 in dues annually for full membership. On the other hand, an academic body or a nonprofit organization in a country with a low income per capita such as India or Nigeria pays only $200 a year for the same status.

The first meeting of the GSDI Association Council took place in Bangalore in February 2004. One of the first tasks of the council was to elect the governing body of the association, the board of directors. The association's bylaws specify that the board should be made up of six different categories of member:

- the past, present, and future presidents of the association

- members appointed by the regional bodies concerned with spatial data infrastructure coordination

- a representative chosen by the GSDI Industry Advisory Council

- three members from the following sectors: government, academia, and nonprofit

- five members from the following geographic regions: Africa, Asia and the Pacific, Europe, North America, and South America

- three members from the following sectors: international geographic organizations, GSDI-related global initiatives, and international industry organizations

All the positions listed above have been filled as a result of the elections that were held at the council meeting in Bangalore. The Industry Advisory Council has yet to be formed, and it was agreed in Bangalore that the seat should for the moment be shared between the two current industry members. It should also be noted that the terms of office for the members vary over a three year time span in order to ensure a rotation of the council membership over time.

Figure 7.1

The GSDI Board of Directors in July 2003 (from left to right): Santiago Borrero, Ian Masser, Keith Thackrey, Doug Nebert, Harlan Onsrud, Mukund Rao, and Al Stevens.

When its finances permit, the association plans to hire a part-time or full-time executive director to manage its affairs, and it is seriously considering the possibility of establishing a secretariat in India. Notwithstanding the outcomes of these discussions, it is anticipated that the association will retain its American links through the activities of its business director and the continuing support that it receives from the FGDC. To facilitate these operations, John Moeller and Robert Samborski were appointed by the board of directors as the association's secretary and treasurer, respectively, in June 2004.

Table 7.3

Officers and members of the Board of the GSDI Association in June 2004.

OFFICERS	
President	Mukund Rao
Past president	Ian Masser
President elect	Harlan Onsrud
Secretary	John Moeller
Treasurer	Robert Samborski

BOARD OF DIRECTORS	
President	Mukund Rao, Indian Space Research Organization (ISRO)
President-elect	Harlan Onsrud, University Consortium for Geographic Information Science
Past president	Ian Masser, Emeritus

Members appointed by regional bodies

EUROGI	Bino Marchesini
PC IDEA	Mario Reyes–Ibarra
CODI-GEO	Chukwudozie Ezigbalike

GSDI Industry Advisory Council*

Carmelle J. Cote, Environmental Systems Research Institute (ESRI)
Terry Keating, Intergraph Corporation

Sectoral elected members

Government	Amitabha Pande, Department of Science and Technology, Government of India
Academia	Bas Kok, Delft University of Technology
Nonprofit	Gabor Remetey–Fulopp, Hungarian Association for Geo-information

Regional elected members

Africa	Chukwudozie Ezigbalike, UNECA
Asia/Pacific	Wang Chunfeng, State Bureau of Surveying and Mapping of China
Europe	Jarmo Ratia, National Land Survey of Finland
North America	David Coleman, Atlantic Institute
South America	Santiago Borrero–Mutis, PanAmerican Institute for Geography and History

Global elected members

Geographic Org.	Kate Lance, Mesoamerican and Caribbean Geospatial Alliance
GSDI related	Guo Huadong, International Society on Digital Earth
Int. Industry Org.	Mark Reichardt, Open GIS Consortium

* two members share one vote

Some indication of the way that the association would like to develop over time can be seen from the draft strategic plan that was circulated at GSDI 7 *(www.gsdi.org)*. This plan sets out a vision of the association that "supports all societal needs for access to and use of spatial data." It sees the association as working toward this vision through five main sets of activities:

1. Promoting and developing awareness and exchanges on infrastructure issues for all relevant levels from local to global

2. Promoting and facilitating standards-based data access/discovery/use through the Internet to enable interoperable sharing of these data

3. Promoting, encouraging, supporting, and conducting capacity building in terms of capacity assessment and capacity development

4. Promoting and conducting SDI development research

5. Establishing and supporting active programs for attaining funding and resources to accomplish its vision and goals

Under the heading of developing awareness and exchanges, the plan lists activities such as providing forums for SDI professionals, scientists, and application people to meet on a regular basis, collaborating with other global institutions, and maintaining the Web site and the cookbook. Possible standards-based data access/discovery/use activities include the creation of simple and effective catalog services and the use of standardized metadata that accurately defines the data, how to access the data, and the integrity of the data.

Under the heading of capacity building, the draft plan lists training for those who may be coordinating SDI activities within a particular country, working with national and regional organizations to provide on-site development and training programs throughout the world, and establishing an overall knowledge infrastructure (see also Stevens et al. 2004). Possible development research activities include the creation of a small grant program to support SDI-related research, the development of SDI research networks throughout the world, and the creation of an online library of SDI reference material.

The authors of the plan recognized that the first four sets of activities will require funding and resources. Consequently, the last of the five sets of activities describes some of the types of activity that will be required to make their plan possible.

Following the publication of the draft strategic plan, the GSDI secretariat carried out a survey of its members to find out more about their expectations. The findings of this survey generally confirm the main lines of action that were included in the strategic plan. These were the top ten responses from the members:

1. Host a global conference regularly for the association as an important place for professional networking and exchange of knowledge

2. Expand the membership of the GSDI Association

3. Increase networking among GSDI members and others interested in spatial data infrastructure concepts

4. Establish and maintain an electronic repository for GSDI produced reports and papers prepared for conferences, meetings, and workshops or developed by GSDI Association committees

5. Provide a voice for the global spatial data infrastructure community at international meetings and in international policy and technical forums

6. Solicit funding to accomplish projects and host workshops of benefit to the global spatial data infrastructure community

7. Fully engage members in planning through open communications and in accomplishing specific projects and tasks through the GSDI committee infrastructure

8. Publish a brochure explaining the benefits of joining the GSDI Association

9. Foster discussions with international development agencies of spatial data infrastructure issues

10. Pursue funding to allow personnel from developing nations to attend GSDI sponsored workshops and conferences

To stimulate SDI activities throughout the world, the association invited applications in May 2004 for small grants of up to $2,500 to help organizations that are contributing to or developing SDIs. There was a good response to this invitation, and ten awards were made to proposals from Argentina, Bhutan, Czech Republic, Jamaica, Malawi, Mexico, Mongolia, Namibia, Tanzania, and Zimbabwe.

EVALUATION

THE ACHIEVEMENTS OF THE GLOBAL Spatial Data Infrastructure and the GSDI Association so far have been considerable. The creation of a multisector, multidisciplinary body with representatives from all parts of the world is no mean achievement in its own right. Although its combined membership was only just over fifty in February 2004, it can be expected to grow steadily over time. In the process it will emerge as an independent, not-for-profit, global umbrella organization that represents the interests of the GSDI community as a whole.

In his presidential address to GSDI 7, Ian Masser (2004b) identified four immediate challenges for the new association. The first challenge, getting the association off the ground and achieving a high degree of inclusiveness in its membership, has already been partly achieved, but it will require sustained efforts over the next few years to make the association the umbrella organization for the GSDI community as a whole.

The second challenge is currently foremost in the mind of the new board of directors. The goal is to create a sustainable organization that is able to employ an executive director to manage its affairs and support its own secretariat.

The third challenge facing the new association is the need to consolidate its links with other global bodies. This is being tackled in various ways, including the granting of observer status at the meetings of its board of directors to the International Steering Committee of the Global Mapping and professional bodies such as the International Federation of Surveyors (FIG), the International Cartographic Association (ICA), and the International Society for Photogrammetry and Remote Sensing (ISPRS). It can also be expected that its links with FIG will be strengthened through the organization of GSDI 8 in Cairo alongside one of FIG's Working Week conferences.

The final immediate challenge is to ensure that the GSDI Association is in a position to represent its membership in global forums such as the World Summit of the Information Society that will take place in Tunis during 2005. This must be given high priority over the next few years.

With these achievements and intentions in mind, it is now possible to return to the questions posed by O'Neil (2004) discussed in the introduction to this chapter. The first question was, what is the purpose of a GSDI? This in turn begs another question: is the task of GSDI to build a global SDI or is it to promote the creation of SDIs throughout the world? From the discussion above, there can be little doubt that the GSDI has played a key role with respect to stimulating the diffusion of SDI concepts, and it has also been very active in global capacity building through its support for initiatives such as the ESRI and Intergraph grant programs. Nevertheless, the concept of a truly global SDI must be seen as a long-term objective that is very much dependent on the success of regional initiatives such as the Asia Pacific SDI and the European INSPIRE program.

O'Neil's second question refers to the potential users of a GSDI. In one sense, the answer to this question seems relatively simple in that the main users of a GSDI in the first place will be the global and regional (i.e., transnational) stakeholders. However, as O'Neil points out, this may not be as simple a task as it seems at first sight as "many of the data sets are not robust enough to support the processes and applications that downstream users are expecting to be possible." Consequently, it must be recognized that it will take time and effort before these problems can be satisfactorily resolved. In the meantime, however, there is a great deal that the GSDI Association can do to promote and disseminate more user-oriented best practices.

O'Neil's final question, how we can monitor GSDI progress, is both the easiest and the most difficult to answer. The simple answer is to refer to the diffusion of SDIs throughout the world over the last ten years that has been described in chapters 2 and 3. The more complex answer takes into account the extent to which the data sets contained in them are used in practice. That raises questions relating to access and pricing that have yet to be resolved in many countries. Until these and a number of other policy-related matters have been sorted out, this is likely to be one of the most important challenges that must be resolved in the future development of SDIs.

SUMMARY

THIS CHAPTER HAS TRACED THE EVOLUTION of the GSDI Association as a global institution for promoting SDI development since September 1996. It has shown how GSDI began as an informal conference organization, which has subsequently expanded its range of activities to become an independent not-for-profit global umbrella organization in February 2004. Parallel to these developments has been the shift in emphasis from relatively wealthy to less wealthy countries, which can be seen in the choice of conference locations and the increasing attention that is being given to capacity building activities of all kinds. The GSDI board of directors is also currently considering locating its secretariat in India. An important strategic objective for the new association is to make it an inclusive one in terms of its membership. With this in mind, a system of membership dues has been devised that differentiates between public- and private-sector bodies, academic entities, and not-for-profit organizations. This system also has differentiates between high-, upper-middle-, lower-middle-, and low-income countries through out the world. The response to the invitation to join the association as founding members has been positive, and sustained efforts are under way to make the GSDI Association a fully representative umbrella organization for the global SDI.

CHAPTER 8

Conclusions

The last chapter of this book evaluates the findings of the analysis that has been summarized at the end of each of the previous chapters. Its main objective is to put these findings into a broader perspective and to identify issues that would benefit from further research. The discussion highlights some of the trends in SDI thinking that emerge from the analysis and then focuses on the four main themes that were identified in the introduction to this book: SDI diffusion, evolution, implementation, and hierarchy.

SHIFTS IN SDI DEVELOPMENT

THE INNOVATORS/EARLY ADOPTERS (SEE chapter 2) constituted the first generation of national SDIs and the development of the second generation of SDIs began around 2000 as the early majority gained momentum (Rajabifard et al. 2003). Since then, there has been an important shift in emphasis from the first to the second generation, both in technological terms and also with respect to the key themes of SDI development. The shift in technological emphasis is due to the opportunities opened up by the development of the Internet and the World Wide Web. The U.S. Mapping Sciences Committee in their report on Distributed Geolibraries (National Research Council 1999, 31) acknowledged this shift saying, "the WWW has added a new and radically different dimension to its earlier conception of the NSDI, one that is much more user oriented, much more effective in maximizing the added value of the nation's geoinformation assets, and much more cost-effective as a data dissemination mechanism."

Rajabifard et al. (2003) argue that the most distinctive feature of the second generation of SDIs is the shift that has taken place from the product model that characterized most of the first generation to a process model of an SDI *(table 8.1)*. Database creation was to a very large extent the key driver of the first generation, and as a result, most of these initiatives tended to be data-producer and national-mapping-agency led. The shift from the product to the process model is essentially a shift in emphasis from the concerns of data producers to those of data users. The main driving forces behind the data process model are data sharing and reusing data collected by a wide range of agencies for a great diversity of purposes at various times. This change in emphasis is associated with a shift from the centralized structures that characterized most of the first generation of NSDIs to the decentralized and distributed networks that are a basic feature of the WWW.

There is also a shift in emphasis from SDI formulation to implementation over time *(table 8.1)*. This shift reflects the move from single level to multilevel participation within the context of a hierarchy of SDIs. Under these circumstances, it will be necessary to think in terms of more inclusive models of governance. These developments may also require new kinds of organizational structure to facilitate effective implementation.

From a product to a process model
    From data producers to data users
    From database creation to data sharing
    From centralized to decentralized structures

From formulation to implementation
    From coordination to governance
    From single-level to multilevel participation
    From existing to new organizational structures

Table 8.1
Current trends in SDI development.

THE DIFFUSION OF SDIs

MORE THAN HALF THE WORLD'S COUNTRIES
claim they are involved in some form of SDI development (see
chapters 2 and 3). However, these claims need to be treated
with some caution until they have been backed up by factual
evidence as it is likely that there is an element of wishful thinking in some of them. The Leuven study (Spatial Applications
Division, Catholic University of Leuven 2003a) notes that
only a handful of European countries had anything like a full-
blown SDI and most of these initiatives can better be described
as "SDI-like or SDI-supporting initiatives." Furthermore, the
fact that some countries have reported that they are engaged
in some aspect of SDI development does not necessarily mean
that this will translate into a fully operational SDI over time.

The most obvious SDI success can be measured in the establishment of clearinghouses and portals to disseminate metadata
(see figure 8.1 and Tang and Selwood 2005). The FGDC Clearinghouse registry, for example, lists nearly three hundred
registered nodes from the United States and other countries
(registry.gsdi.org/serverstatus). Similarly, Maguire and Longley
(2005) claim that there were on average 5,622 visits per week to
the U.S. Geospatial One-Stop portal site in April 2004.

Nevertheless, it is not enough to report that clearinghouses
and portals have been established without including some
information on their usage and the arrangements that have
been made for their upgrading and maintenance. For example, Crompvoets and his colleagues (Crompvoets et al. 2004)
suggest that the use made of some of these metadata services
may be declining over time rather than increasing. This is
due largely to unsatisfactory arrangements for continuing site
management.

Figure 8.1

Typical portal search engines (for example, Geospatial One-Stop) allow users to find data sets with respect to their location, content, or time. Image source: *www.geodata.gov*; *www.geo-one-stop.gov*.

While considering the extent to which the diffusion of innovations model is an appropriate one for the study of SDI diffusion, it is also worth noting that SDIs generally fit the definition of an innovation as "an idea, practice, or object that is perceived as new by an individual or unit of adoption" (Rogers 1995, 11). Although the findings of the above analysis suggest that the characteristics of the innovators, early adopters, and the early majority show most of the features described by Rogers, it will be interesting to see whether this is the case with respect to the late majority and the laggards.

It should also be noted that the diffusion of innovations model has been criticized for its pro-innovation bias (Rogers 1993). This can also be seen in the statements that are made in connection with SDI development that constantly stress its positive impacts in terms of promoting economic growth, better government, and improved environmental sustainability. These and other similar claims need to be rigorously examined in further research.

In the process, more attention should be given to identifying possible negative impacts arising out of SDI development. A useful example of this kind of work can be found in the four brave new GIS worlds scenarios that were developed by Wegener and Masser (1996). Their trend, market, big brother, and beyond GIS scenarios are easily translatable into the SDI field as can be seen from the Mapping Science Committee's Future of Spatial Data and Society project (National Research Council 1997).

It is not always easy to define with precision the moment in time when the idea was adopted. In some cases, there is a gradual transition from existing practices into a SDI. This happened, for example, in Australia and Finland where there was a tradition of SDI-like thinking before the SDI itself formally came into being. In other cases the position is complicated by differences in the terminology that is used to describe SDI like activities. When, for example, does a national GI system become a SDI?

Some of these problems can be resolved by developing more systematic ways for describing and classifying SDIs. The typology developed by the Leuven group that is used in table 3.1 is a step in the right direction, even though, in its current version, it gives rise to some ambiguities and overlaps in practice. However, this typology only takes account of the approach that has been adopted toward coordination and it may be worthwhile extending it to incorporate some of the other variables discussed in chapters 2 and 3.

Another matter that needs consideration in future SDI diffusion research is the extent to which cultural factors are likely to influence SDI adoption. An interesting example of this kind of research is van der Toorn and de Man's (2001) analysis of the role of culture in SDI development. This draws upon the four dimensional model developed by Hofstede (1997). As a result of extensive empirical research, Hofstede found that national cultures varied with respect to four main variables: power distance (from small to large), uncertainty avoidance (from weak to strong), masculinity versus femininity, and collectivism versus individualism. In an SDI environment, van der Toorn and de Man argue that cultures where there are large power distances are likely to use SDI to reinforce the hand of management, whereas those with small power distances will welcome their data sharing and accountability properties. Similarly, masculine cultures will be interested in SDIs because of their capacity to contribute to visible achievements, whereas feminine cultures will welcome their networking and relationship building properties.

THE EVOLUTION OF SDIs

GIVEN THE EVOLUTIONARY CHANGES IN the United Kingdom (see chapter 4), it is necessary to consider the notion of reinvention that is put forward in the diffusion of innovations model in more detail. Rogers (1995, 16–7) defines it as "the degree to which an innovation is changed or modified by a user, in the process of its adoption and implementation." He also notes that, while some innovations are difficult or impossible to reinvent, others are "more flexible in nature, and they are reinvented by many adopters who implement them in different ways." The degree of reinvention involved in GIS implementation in British local government led Campbell and Masser (1995, 109–110) to conclude that "the meaning of a technology such as GIS was constantly being reinvented at both the organizational and individual scales. This has important implications for studies of diffusion as it would appear that innovations such as GIS embrace a wide range of perceptions. These differences in emphasis are likely to lead to tensions and problems, which will complicate the implementation process. It is also likely that such systems will be used to undertake activities not originally anticipated by their inventors."

There are clear parallels between these findings and those relating to SDI evolution. Given that SDI implementation is likely to take place over a long period of time when the technologies are also changing, together with the external political and institutional circumstances that surround an SDI, it may be necessary to distinguish between two levels of reinvention in this case. The first of these concerns the processes needed to initially adapt the notion of an SDI to the local or national context to take account, for example, of the impacts that the allocation of administrative responsibilities and the style of government will have on the form of SDI development in each case. The second relates to processes that are involved in its evolution over time in response to changing political, institutional, and technological circumstances (for example, see chapter 4).

Given the extent to which SDIs can be expected to change over time, it will be necessary to set up research procedures to ensure that their progress is systematically monitored. Longitudinal studies will form an important part of this research strategy. To facilitate research of this kind, it will also be necessary to ensure that key documents are not lost when they become out of date. This is particularly a problem in SDI research, which relies to a great extent on gray literature in the form of unpublished reports and memoranda. As a result, it is heavily dependent on materials obtained from Web sites that are also changing constantly. This is already a matter of concern in some countries and the analysis of the National Geospatial Data Framework experience (see chapter 4) was made more difficult by the fact that many key documents are no longer readily available following the closure of the NGDF Web site in 2001.

SOME OF THE MOST CHALLENGING questions in the whole book are posed by the discussion of multilevel stakeholder participation (see chapter 5). The scale of these operations in large countries such as the United States is massive, given that more than 80,000 public bodies alone need to be involved in some way. This task is made even more difficult by a governance model that is based largely on consensus building and the extent to which organizations such as the FGDC in the United States and ANZLIC in Australia lack the powers to enforce their strategies or to impose sanctions on unwilling participants.

Implicit in much of the SDI literature is the idea that a bottom-up SDI differs markedly from a top-down one. While the top-down vision emphasizes the need for standardization and harmonization, the bottom-up vision stresses the importance of diversity and heterogeneity, given the very different aspirations of the various stakeholders and the resources that are at their disposal. Consequently, the challenge to those involved in SDI implementation is to find ways of ensuring some measure of standardization and uniformity while recognizing the diversity and the heterogeneity of the different stakeholders. This will involve a sustained mutual learning process on the part of all those involved during SDI implementation.

Data sharing among the participants on an unprecedented scale will be needed for SDIs to become fully operational in practice. This level of data sharing is likely to require considerable changes in the organizational cultures of the participants. Onsrud and Rushton (1995, 1) define the issues involved in data sharing in the following terms: "Sharing of geographic information involves more than a simple data exchange. To facilitate sharing, the GIS research and user communities must deal with both the technical and institutional aspects of collecting, structuring, analysing, presenting, disseminating, integrating, and maintaining spatial data."

For this reason, there is a pressing need for more research on the nature of data sharing in a multilevel SDI environment. The studies that have been carried out by Zorica Nedovic–Budic and Pinto (1999a and b) and Nedovic–Budic et al. (2004) in the United States provide a useful starting point for work in other parts of the world. The two earlier studies focus mainly on the motivations for data sharing, the coordination process, and the costs of coordination, whereas the more recent analysis of the responses of 245 respondents to a survey questionnaire produces some interesting quantitative indicators of the interactions mechanisms involved and the motivations of the respondents. Similarly, the findings of Harvey's (2002) survey of local governments in Kentucky demonstrates the complexity of the networks involved in collaborative environments of this kind.

Another example of this kind of research is Uta Wehn de Montalvo's (2003) study of spatial data sharing perceptions and practices in South Africa from a social psychological perspective. This study uses the theory of planned behavior and combines both quantitative and qualitative analysis. This theory suggests that personal and organizational willingness to share data depends on attitudes to data sharing, social pressures to engage or not engage, and perceived control over data sharing activities of key individuals within organizations. The findings of her quantitative analysis generally bear out the relationships postulated in this theory and give valuable insights into the factors that determine the willingness to share spatial data. They also show that there is only a relatively limited commitment among those involved to promote data sharing in high-profile initiatives such as the South African national SDI whose successful implementation is dependent on a high level of spatial data sharing.

More attention also needs to be given to research, which identifies the types of organizational structure that facilitate data sharing. Given the importance of these matters for SDI development and implementation, Warnest et al. (2003) have argued that it may be useful to examine how matters of this kind have been dealt with in the management literature. The work of Child and Faulkner (1998) on cooperation strategies and Lendrum's (2003) partnering handbook, for example, may be helpful in future discussions of SDI implementation.

THE HIERARCHY OF SDIS

HIERARCHY DOES NOT NECESSARILY IMPLY a top-down command structure when used in connection with SDI development. There is a bottom-up as well as a top-down dimension in SDI development and implementation (see chapter 5). In many cases, national bodies such as the FGDC work directly with local bodies without reference to the state level. Similarly, it should be noted that the absence of SDI initiatives at one level of the hierarchy does not necessarily inhibit their development at other levels. France is a particularly good example of a country that has no national SDI initiative, but it has several well-developed subnational initiatives (see, for example, Roche and Humeau 1999).

From a research perspective it may be worthwhile exploring hierarchy theory in greater depth in the context of SDI development. Rajabifard (2002), for example, has made use of hierarchical reasoning in his work on SDI structures. He has also identified three properties of hierarchies:

1. The part–whole property, which describes the degree to which higher-level entities can be subdivided into lower-level parts

2. The Janus effect, which relates to the relationships that an element has with the levels above and below it

3. The near decomposability property, which describes the nesting of systems within larger systems and the extent to which the interactions between the different systems decrease in strength with the distance between them

It is also important to bear in mind that different levels of the SDI hierarchy perform different tasks. The role of bodies at the regional and global levels is primarily to disseminate information about current developments and best practices to the levels below them, whereas local SDIs are primarily concerned with the operational needs of day-to-day decision making. Despite these differences, all levels of the hierarchy are involved to some extent in the dissemination of information between the various levels. National level bodies perform a similar task with respect down to subnational, and upwards, regional bodies and state level bodies do the same with respect to local ones.

Many of these activities involve some measure of capacity building, and it is therefore worth looking at the notion of capacity building in more detail. The term "capacity building" can be used to include human resource development, organizational change, and societal transformation (see, for example, Pauknerova et al. 2003). Nevertheless, to some people it means essentially the training of SDI technicians and managers, although this definition is sometimes extended to include the education of politicians and the general public outside the geographic information industry (Hopkins 2004).

To others, including those involved in SDI development, it is necessary to take a much broader view of capacity building. If the term "environmental management" is replaced by "SDI development" in the quotation below it can be seen as a useful definition of some of the key strategic capacity building tasks involved in SDI implementation. "The contemporary view of capacity building goes beyond the conventional perception of training. The central concerns of environmental management-to manage change, to resolve conflict, to manage institutional pluralism, to enhance coordination, to foster communication, and to ensure that data and information are shared-require a broad and holistic view of capacity building" *(nrm.massey. ac.nz/changelinks/capacity.html)*.

Such a view is synonymous with organizational learning. This standpoint is reflected in the African Capacity Building Foundation's approach which argues that "capacity building should not only involve the creation of new human and institutional capacity, but also the effective utilization of existing capacity as well as the retrieval and regeneration of hitherto lost or decaying capacity" *(www.acbf-pact.org)*.

However, it is also important to bear in mind that capacity-building activities, like SDI development itself, can have a negative as well as a positive impact. This is particularly the case with some projects in less developed countries. Fukuda–Parr et al. (2002), for example, have shown how technical cooperation programs can adversely affect the development of local organizations as a result of two mistaken assumptions: "The first is that it is possible simply to ignore existing capacities in developing countries and replace them with knowledge and systems elsewhere—a form of development as displacement rather than development as transformation. The second assumption concerns the asymmetric donor recipient relationship—the belief that it is possible ultimately for donors to control the process and yet consider the recipients to be equal partners."

FINAL REMARKS

THE OVERVIEW OF SDI DEVELOPMENT that is contained in this book refers largely to a particular point in time (mid-2004) in a rapidly developing field. Just as some of the key features of current SDI development such as the extensive use that is now being made of Internet and the World Wide Web technologies would have been hard to predict ten years ago, the same is likely to be the case with respect to the technologies that are likely to be available in ten years time. This is not just a matter of technological change, but also new institutional and political developments. Over the next ten years, the trends from product to process models and from SDI formulation to implementation are also likely to be superseded by new and unexpected trends.

Nevertheless, the picture that has been painted in this book is one of a field at a particularly interesting stage in its development. About half the world's countries now claim to be involved in some aspect of SDI development, and for the first time, there is enough comparative literature available to be able to talk with some certainty about the picture in different parts of the world. The process of regional and global institutional building is now essentially complete with the establishment of CODI-GEO in 2003 and the inauguration of the GSDI Association on February 2004. There is also a growing body of SDI research, as this chapter shows, that draws widely on the economics, geography, management, and social science literature. It can be expected that the findings of this research will lead to more informed operational SDI development in the future. And lastly, with the publication of the draft SDI Directive in July 2004, there is a real chance of creating an operational SDI at the regional level for at least twenty-five European countries.

However, these achievements should not lead anybody to imagine that the next stages of SDI development are going to be straightforward. Some formidable challenges lie ahead and the task of sustaining the momentum that has been built up in recent years will not be easy. Nevertheless, it should be possible to look forward toward a very different kind of future for SDIs than anyone would have imagined ten years ago.

AGI Cymru. 2003. Geographical information strategy action plan for Wales. Cardiff: Welsh Assembly Government. *www.cymruarlein.wales.gov.uk/fe/fileupload_getfile.asp?filePathPrefix=613&fileLanguage=e.rtf*

———. 2002. Consultation paper for the national GI strategy for Wales. *www.agi.org.uk*

AGI Scotland. 2003. Towards a geographic information strategy for Scotland: Linking places and spaces to connect the faces of Scotland. *www.e-consultation.net/agiscot/agiscot_ consultation.pdf*

Al Thani, A. B. H. 1997. GIS in Qatar: An integral part of the infrastructure. Paper presented at GIS/GPS 1997 conference, Qatar.

Arnaud, A. M., L. T. Vasconcelos, and J. D. Geirinhas. 1996. Portugal: GIS diffusion and the modernisation of local government. In *GIS diffusion: The adoption and use of geographic information systems in local government in Europe*, eds. I. Masser, H. Campbell, and M. Craglia, 111–124. London: Taylor and Francis.

Association for Geographical Information (AGI). 2004. A geographic information strategy for England consultation document. Association for Geographic Information working group. *www.agi.org*

Australia and New Zealand Land Information Council (ANZLIC). 2004. Position paper on engagement with the spatial information industry. Canberra: ANZLIC. *www.anzlic.org.au*

———. 2003. *Implementing the Australian spatial data infrastructure: Action plan 2003–2004.* Canberra: ANZLIC.

———. 1996. *Spatial data infrastructure for Australia and New Zealand.* Canberra: ANZLIC.

———. 1992. *Land information management in Australasia 1990–1992.* Canberra: Australia Government Publishing Service.

Australian Spatial Industry Business Association (ASIBA). n.d. Policy brief, Canberra, Australian Spatial Industry Business Association. *www.asiba.com.au*

Bangemann, M. 1996. Foreword. In *Emerging global spatial data infrastructure.* Proceedings 1st GSDI conference, Bonn, Germany.

Barriga Vargas, R. 2004. The basic territorial information area: On the Chilean perspective for the development of a national geospatial data infrastructure. Proceedings 7th GSDI conference, Bangalore, India.

Blakemore, M., M. Craglia, K. Evmorfopolou, A. Fonseca, C. Gouveia, A. Lefevre, I. Masser, and P. Pekkinen. 1999. Comparative evaluation of national spatial data infrastructures. Methods for access to data and metadata in Europe (MADAME) project report. Sheffield: University of Sheffield.

Borrero, S. 2002. Taking advantage of best proved practices. *GIM International* 16 (August): 8–11.

———. 1998. Case study of transnational initiatives: Latin America. Proceedings 3rd GSDI conference, Canberra, Australia. *www.gsdi.org*

Brand, M. 1998. Global spatial data infrastructure: Policy and organisational issues, Proceedings 3rd GSDI conference, Canberra, Australia. *www.gsdi.org*

Brueggemann, H. 2004. The GDI NRW as a component of the German, European and Global Spatial Data Infrastructure. Proceedings 7th GSDI conference, Bangalore, India.

Budhathoki, N. R., and R. R. Chhatkuli. 2004. Building geographic information infrastructure at the national level: Nepalese experience. Proceedings 7th GSDI conference, Bangalore, India.

Burrough, P., M. Brand, F. Salge, and K. Schueller. 1993. The EUROGI vision. *GIS Europe* 2(3): 30–31.

Campbell, H., and I. Masser. 1995. *GIS and organisations: How effective are GIS in practice?* London: Taylor and Francis.

Canadian Geospatial Data Infrastructure (CGDI). 2001. Canadian Geospatial Data Infrastructure target vision. *Geomatica* 55: 181–185.

References

Centre for International Economics. 2000. *Scoping the business case for SDI development.* Canberra: Australian Surveying and Land Information Group.

Child, J., and D. Faulkner. 1998. *Strategies of cooperation: Managing alliances, networks and joint ventures.* Oxford: Oxford University Press.

Clarke, D. 2001. Development of the Australian spatial data infrastructure. Proceedings SDI workshop, Melbourne: University of Melbourne.

Commission of the European Communities, (CEC). 2004. Proposal for a directive of the European Parliament and the Council establishing an infrastructure for spatial information in the community (INSPIRE). COM (2004) 516 final, Brussels: Commission of the European Communities.

———. 2003. The reuse of public sector information, Directive 2003/98/EC of the European Parliament and of the Council. *Official Journal of the European Union* L345: 90–96.

———. 2000. *European Union enlargement: A historic opportunity.* Brussels: DG Enlargement.

Commission of the European Communities DG XIII. 1994. Setting up EUROGI, final report of the committee for investigating the feasibility of creating a European Umbrella organisation for Geographic Information, DG XIII-E2, Luxembourg.

Corbin, C. 2004. *GINIE progress report 1st November 2001 to 19th February 2004.* Apeldoorn: EUROGI.

Corey, M. 1998. The Canadian Geospatial Data Infrastructure. Paper presented at the ISO/TC 211 Conference, Victoria B.C., 4 March 1998.

Craglia M., A. Annoni, and I. Masser. 2000. Geographic information policies in Europe: National and regional perspectives. Report of the EUROGI–European Commission Data Policy Workshop, EC Joint Research Centre, Ispra.

Craglia, M., A. Annoni, M. Klopfer, C. Corbin, L. Hecht, G. Pichler, and P. Smits, eds. 2003. *Geographic information in the wider Europe.* Sheffield: University of Sheffield. *www.ec-gis.org/ginie*

Craglia, M., A. Annoni, R. S. Smith, and P. Smits. 2002. *Spatial data infrastructures in Europe: Country reports* 2002. Geographic information network in Europe project (GINIE) report. Sheffield: University of Sheffield. *www.ec-gis.org/ginie*

Craglia, M., and I. Masser. 2002. GI and the enlargement of the European Union. *URISA Journal* 14(2): 43–52.

Craglia M., and J. F. Dallemand. 2001. Geographic information and the enlargement of the European Union. Report of the EUROGI–European Commission Workshop, EC Joint Research Centre, Ispra.

Crompvoets, J., and A. Bregt. 2003. World status of national spatial data clearinghouses. *URISA Journal* 15(APA 1): 43–50.

Crompvoets, J., A. Rajabifard, A. Bregt, and I. Williamson. 2004. Assessing the world wide developments of national spatial data clearinghouses. *International Journal of GIS* 18: 1–25.

Dale, P. 2003. The emperor's new clothes. *GEOinformatics* (December): 33.

Dangermond, J. 2004. Data ownership is the biggest challenge. *Geospatial Today* Special issue on GSDI: Blueprint for development 2(5): 13

Department of Culture, Arts, and Leisure. 2002. A geographic information strategy for Northern Ireland: A consultation document, Department of Culture, Arts, and Leisure, Belfast.

Department of Industry, Tourism, and Resources (DITR). 2001. Positioning for growth: Spatial information industry action agenda. *www.industry.gov.au*

Department of Science and Technology (DOST). 2002. NSDI strategy and action plan, December 2002. New Delhi: Department of Science and Technology. *www.nsdiindia.org.*

Department of the Environment. 1987. Handling geographic information: Report to the Secretary of State for the Environment of the Committee of Enquiry into the Handling of Geographic Information. London: HMSO.

EIS-Africa. 2002. Geo-information supports decision making in Africa. EIS-Africa position paper, Pretoria: EIS-Africa. *www.eis-africa.org/publications.html*

Elliott, L. 2000. Unlocking geospatial information? Ask GIraffe for the key. Proceedings AGI 2000, London: Association for Geographic Information.

European Territorial Management Information Infrastructure (ETeMII). 2002. The road to Europe's future in spatial data infrastructure activities. *www.ec-gis.org/etemii*

European Umbrella Organisation for Geographic Information (EUROGI). 2000. Towards a strategy for geographic information in Europe: A consultation paper. Apeldoorn: EUROGI. *www.eurogi.org*

———. 1995. Annual report 1994. Amersfoort: EUROGI.

Executive Office of the President. 1994. Coordinating geographic data acquisition and access, the National Spatial Data Infrastructure, Executive Order 12906. *Federal Register* 59: 17,671–17,674.

Federal Geographic Data Committee (FGDC). 2004. NSDI future directions initiative: Towards a national geospatial strategy and implementation plan. Reston, Va.: Federal Geographic Data Committee. *www.fgdc.gov*

———. 2000. Improving federal agency geospatial data coordination. Reston, Va.: Federal Geographic Data Committee. *www.fgdc.gov*

———. 1997. A strategy for the national spatial data infrastructure. Reston, Va.: Federal Geographic Data Committee. *www.fgdc.gov*

———. 1994. The 1994 plan for the National Spatial Data Infrastructure: Building the foundations of an information based society. Reston, Va.: Federal Geographic Data Committee, USGS.

Finley, D. 2000. Service New Brunswick: The modernisation of a land information service. In *Geospatial data infrastructure: Concepts, cases and good practice,* eds. R. Groot and J. McLaughlin. Oxford: Oxford University Press.

Foresman, T. W., Gua Huadong, and H. Fukui. 2004. Progress with digital earth global infrastructure. Proceedings 7th GSDI conference, Bangalore, India.

Fritz, C. 2004. The JoGIS: Our experience. GISDECO Workshop on Statewide GIS, Universiti of Teknologi Malaysia, Johor, Malaysia.

Fukuda–Parr, S., C. Lopes, and K. Malik. 2002. *Capacity for development: New solutions to old problems.* London: Earthscan.

Geoplan Consultants. 1996. The development of an integrated Canadian spatial data model and implementation concept. Final report prepared for the Canadian Council on Geomatics.

Ghana Environmental Protection Agency and the World Bank. 1999. Ghana: Country at a glance (G-CAG). Data description and instructions for the use of the G-CAG. In *SDI Africa: An implementation guide,* UNECA. Addis Ababa: UNECA.

Giff, G., and D. Coleman. 2002. Funding models for SDI implementation: From local to global. Proceedings 6th GSDI conference, Budapest, Hungary.

Godfrey, B., P. Holland, G. Baker, and B. Irwin. 1997. The contribution of the Permanent Committee on GIS infrastructure for Asia and the Pacific to a global spatial data infrastructure. Proceedings 2nd GSDI conference, Chapel Hill, N.C.

Gouveia, C., Abreu, J., Neves, N., and Henriques, R. 1997. The Portuguese national infrastructure for geographic information: General description and challenges for the future. Paper presented at the GISDATA Conference on Geographic Information Research at the Millennium, Le Bischenberg, France.

Government Audit Office. 2004. Better coordination and oversight could help reduce duplicative investments. Testimony before the Subcommittee on Technology, Information Policy, Intergovernmental Relations, and the Census, Committee on Government Reform, House of Representatives, Washington, D.C.: Government Audit Office.

———. 2003. Geographic information systems: Challenges to effective data sharing. Testimony before the Subcommittee on Technology, Information Policy, Intergovernmental Relations, and the Census, Committee on Government Reform, House of Representatives, Washington, D.C.: Government Audit Office.

Government of Malaysia. 1997. Guidelines for the establishment of the national infrastructure for land information system (NaLIS), Public Administration Circular No. 1, Kuala Lumpur: Prime Minister's Department, Government of Malaysia.

Grant, D., and O. Hedberg. 2001. Public Sector Mapping Agencies—Australia: Concept to incorporation. Proceedings SDI workshop, Melbourne: University of Melbourne.

Guimet, J., 2004. Four rules to set up a basic SDI: The experience of the (local) SDI of Catalonia region. Proceedings 7th GSDI conference, Bangalore, India.

Hadley, C., and L. Elliott. 2001. National Geospatial Data Framework (NGDF): The UK model. *www.gisdevelopment.net/policy/gii/gii0004pf.htm*

Haegen, M. van der, and H. De Groof. 2004. A European SDI. In *Spatial data infrastructure and policy development in Europe and the United States,* eds. B. van Loenen and B. C. Kok. Delft: Delft University Press.

Hanson–Albites, F. A. 2004. Progress report on the spatial data infrastructure of Mexico (IDEMEX). Proceedings 7th GSDI conference, Bangalore, India.

Harvey, F. 2002. Potentials and problems for the involvement of local government in the NSDI. Proceedings 6th GSDI conference, Budapest, Hungary.

Henriques, R. G. 1996. The Portuguese national network of geographic information (SNIG network). In *Geographic Information: from Research to Application to Cooperation,* eds. M. Rumor, R. McMillan, and H. F. L. Ottens, 112–116. Amsterdam: IOS Press.

———. 1992. The Portuguese national geographic information system. Paper presented at GISDATA workshop on geographic data bases, Aix en Provence, France.

Heywood, I. 1997. *Beyond Chorley: Current geographic information issues.* London: Association for Geographic Information.

Hofstede, G. 1997. *Cultures and organisations: Software of the mind.* Beverly Hills, Calif.: Sage Publications.

Holland, P. 1999. The strategic imperative of a Global Spatial Data Infrastructure. Proceedings, Cambridge Conference for national mapping organisations, Cambridge, United Kingdom. *www.gsdi.org*

Holland, P., and S. Borrero. 2004. Global initiatives, In *Development of spatial data infrastructures: From concept to reality,* eds. I. Williamson, A. Rajabifard, and M. E. Feeney. London: Taylor and Francis.

Hopkins, F. 2004. Capacity building: The continuing challenge. *Geoinformatics* 7(1): 5.

House of Lords Select Committee on Science and Technology. 1983. *Remote sensing and digital mapping.* London: HMSO.

Hyman, G., and K. Lance. 2000. *Encuesta sobre infraestucturas nacionales de datos especiales en las Americas.* Calle: Centro Internacionale de Agricultura Tropical. *www.procig.org*

Instituto Geografico Agustin Codazzi (IGAC). 1999. *Infraestructura Colombiana de Datos Espaciales.* Bogota: Instituto Geografico Agustin Codazzi.

Jacoby, S. J., J. Smith, L.Ting, and I. Williamson. 2002. Developing a common spatial data infrastructure between state and local government. *International Journal of Geographical Information Science* 14: 305–322.

Johnson, R., and D. Arbeit. 2002. The MetroGIS initiative: Lessons learnt from a successful geospatial data collaborative. Proceedings 6th GSDI conference, Budapest, Hungary.

Johnson, R., Z. Nedovic–Budic, and K. Covert. 2001. Lessons form practice: A guidebook to organising and sustaining collaboratives. *www.geoall.net*

Keating, M. 2002. Devolution and public policy in the United Kingdom: Divergence or convergence? In *Devolution in practice: Public policy differences,* eds. J. Adams, and P. Robinson. London: Institute for Public Policy Research.

Kennedy, E. 2002. My objective is to make Canada a world leading exporter of geospatial information products and services *GISDevelopment* 6(8): 25–6.

Labonte, J., M. Corey, and T. Evangelatos. 1998. Canadian Geospatial Data Infrastructure (CGDI): Geospatial information for the knowledge economy. *Geomatica* 52: 194–200.

Lance, K. 2003. Spatial data infrastructure in Africa: Spotting the elephant behind trees. *GISDevelopment* 7(7): 35–41.

Latham, J., He Changchui, D. Kalensky, L. Alinovi, A. di Gregorio, H. Williams, and D. Poletto. 2002. FAO Africover project: Contribution to Africa SDI development. Proceedings 6th GSDI conference, Budapest, Hungary.

Lendrum, T. 2003. *Strategic partnering handbook: The practitioner's guide to partnerships and alliances.* New York: McGraw Hill.

Longhorn, R. 2004. Progress on the European SDI: GI2000 (1995) to INSPIRE (2004+). *www.geoinformatics.com.*

Maguire, D., and P. A. Longley. 2005. The emergence of geoportals and their role in spatial data infrastructures. *Computers Environment and Urban Systems* 29: 3–14.

Masser, I. 2004a. The making of GSDI. *Geospatial Today* 2(4): 10–13.

———. 2004b. GSDI: A progress report. Presidential address. Proceedings 7th GSDI conference, Bangalore, India.

———. 2001. The Indian National Geospatial Data Infrastructure. *GIM International* 15(8): 37–39.

———. 1999. All shapes and sizes: The first generation of National Spatial Data Infrastructures. *International Journal Geographical Information Science* 13: 67–84.

———. 1998. *Governments and geographic information.* London: Taylor and Francis.

Masser, I., and A. Stevens. 2003. GSDI: Moving forward, at the crossroads. Proceedings, Cambridge Conference for national mapping organisations, Cambridge, United Kingdom.

Masser, I., and A. Wolfkamp. 2000. EUROGI: Past, present and future. *GeoEurope* 9(8): 37–39.

Masser, I., and F. Salge. 1997. The European geographic information infrastructure debate. In *Geographic information research: Bridging the Atlantic,* eds. M. Craglia and H. Couclelis. London: Taylor and Francis.

Masser, I., S. Borrero, and P. Holland. 2003. Regional SDIs. In *Development of spatial data infrastructures: From concept to reality,* eds. I. Williamson, A. Rajabifard, M. E. Feeney. London: Taylor and Francis.

Mbaria, C. 2002. Experience towards establishment of a national spatial data infrastructure (NSDI) for Kenya. In UNECA, 2003.

MetroGIS. 2002. MetroGIS 2003–2005 business plan. Minneapolis–St. Paul, Minn.: MetroGIS. *www.metrogis.org*

Ministry of Construction and Transportation, (MOCT). 2003. National GIS in Korea, Seoul: Ministry of Construction and Transportation. *www.gsdi.org*

———. 1995. A master plan for National Geographic Information System (NGIS) in Korea, Seoul: Ministry of Construction and Transportation.

Ministry of Industry, Science, and Resources (MISR). 2001. *Positioning for growth: Spatial information industry action agenda.* Canberra: Ministry of Industry, Science, and Resources.

Nanson, B., and D. Rhind. 1998. Establishing the UK National Geospatial Data Framework. Paper presented at SDI 98, Ottawa.

Nanson, B., N. Smith, and A. Davey. 1996. A British National Geospatial Database: Part I–What it is and why we need it, and Part II–How it might be achieved. *Mapping Awareness* 10(3): 18–20 and 10(4): 38–40.

National Academy of Public Administration (NAPA). 1998. *Geographic information in the 21st century: Building a strategy for the nation.* Washington: National Academy of Public Administration.

National Framework for Geospatial Information Management, (NAFGIM). 2001. NAFGIM guidelines for spatial information and data policy. In *SDI Africa: An implementation guide,* UNECA. Addis Ababa: UNECA.

National Geospatial Data Framework. 1998. *Establishing the UK National Geospatial Data Framework: Strategic plan 1998.* Southampton: National Geospatial Data Framework.

National Land Information System (NALIS). 1996. Report of the NALIS task force on the establishment of the National Infrastructure for Land Information System (NALIS). Kuala Lumpur: National Land Information System.

National Land Survey. 1996. National geographic information infrastructure of Finland: Starting point and future objectives of the information economy, publication 2. Consultative committee for data administration in public administration. Helsinki: National Land Survey of Finland.

National Research Council. 2002. *Down to earth: Geographic information for sustainable development in Africa.* Committee on the Geographic Foundation for Agenda 21, National Research Council. Washington: National Academy Press.

——. 2001. *National spatial data infrastructure programs: Rethinking the focus.* Mapping Science Committee. Washington, D.C.: National Academy Press.

——. 1999. *Distributed geolibraries: Spatial information resources.* Mapping Science Committee, National Research Council. Washington, D.C.: National Academy Press.

——. 1997. *The future of spatial data and society.* Mapping Science Committee, National Research Council. Washington, D.C.: National Academy Press.

——. 1993. *Toward a coordinated spatial data infrastructure for the nation.* Mapping Science Committee. Washington, D.C.: National Academy Press.

National Spatial Information Framework (NSIF). 2000. Spatial data infrastructure. In Africa: A synopsis of SDI Africa survey questionnaires received. Proceedings 4th GSDI conference, Capetown, South Africa.

Nebert, D. D., ed. 2004. *Developing spatial data infrastructures: The SDI cookbook.* Version 2.0. Reston, Va.: FGDC. www.gsdi.org

——. 2000. *Developing spatial data infrastructures: The SDI cookbook.* Version 1.0. Reston, Va.: FGDC. www.gsdi.org

Nedovic-Budic, Z., and J. K. Pinto. 1999a. Interorganisational GIS: Issues and prospects. *Annals of Regional Science* 33: 183–195.

——. 1999b. Understanding interorganisational GIS activities: A conceptual framework. *URISA Journal* 11(1): 53–64. www.urisa.org/journal.htm

Nedovic-Budic, Z., J. K. Pinto, and L. Warnecke. 2004. GIS database development and exchange: Interaction mechanisms and motivations. *URISA Journal* (In publication). www.urisa.org/journal.htm

Nemoforum. 2001. *The national geoinformation infrastructure of the Czech Republic: Programme for the years 2001–2005.* Prague: Nemoforum.

Netherlands Council for Geographic Information (RAVI). 2002. Bsik proposal: Space for geographic information. Amersfoort: Netherlands Council for Geographic Information. www.ravi.nl

——. 1995. *The national geographic information infrastructure.* Amersfoort: Netherlands Council for Geographic Information.

——. 1992a. *Structuurschets vastgoedinformatie voorziening, deel 1: Bestuurlijke notitie.* Apeldoorn: Raad voor Vastgoedinformatie.

——. 1992b. *Structuurschets vastgoedinformatie voorziening, deel ll1: Inventarisatie en analyse.* Apeldoorn: Raad voor Vastgoedinformatie.

Office of Management and Budget, (OMB). 2002. Coordination of geographic information and related spatial data activities. Revised Circular A-16, Office of Management and Budget. Washington, D.C.: Executive Office of the President.

——. 1990. *Coordination of surveying, mapping and related spatial data activities.* Revised Circular A-16, Office of Management and Budget, Washington, D.C.: Executive Office of the President.

Oliver, A. 1996. Group dynamics: IGGI forges ahead on government geodata. *Mapping Awareness* 10(3): 26–28.

Oliver, A., and M. Havercroft. 2000. NIMSA: Mapping for the national interest. Proceedings AGI 2000. London: Association for Geographic Information.

O'Neil, R. A. 2004. The future: Can you see an SDI? Proceedings 7th GSDI conference, Bangalore, India.

Onsrud, H., and G. Rushton. 1995. Sharing geographic information. In *Sharing geographic information,* eds. H. Onsrud and G. Rushton. Piscataway N.J.: Centre for Policy Research, Rutgers University.

Open GIS Consortium. 2002. Geographic information for sustainable development. www.opengis.org/gisd

Ordnance Survey of Northern Ireland. 2002. *A geographic information strategy for Northern Ireland.* Belfast: Ordnance Survey of Northern Ireland.

Oxford Economic Research Associates, (OXERA). 1999. The economic contribution of Ordnance Survey GB. *www.ordnancesurvey.co.uk/oswebsite/aboutus/reports/oxera/contents.html*

Pauknerova, E., C. Corbin, M. Craglia, and K. Margoldova. 2003. SDI in accession and pre-accession countries. In *GI in the wider Europe,* ed. M. Craglia. Sheffield: University of Sheffield. *www.ec-gis.org/ginie*

Payne, S. 1999. NGDF progress report. *IGGI News* 10: 4–5.

Permanent Committee on Geographic Information for Asia and the Pacific, (PCGIAP). 1998. *A spatial data infrastructure for the Asia and the Pacific region.* PCGIAP Publication No.1. *www.gsi.go.jp/PCGIAP/tech_paprs/apsdi_cnts.htm*

Pira International Ltd., University of East Anglia, and Knowledge Ltd. 2000. *Commercial exploitation of Europe's public sector information.* Luxembourg: EC DG INFSO.

Podolcsak, A., and B. Jarolics. 2003. Local to regional at the Tisza basin. Paper presented at the GINIE Local to Global workshop, Rome.

Price Waterhouse. 1995. *Australian land and geographic information infrastructure benefits study.* Canberra: Australia Government Publishing Service.

Probert, M., and A. Wolfkamp. 2003. Key GI players in Europe. In *Geographic information in the wider Europe,* eds. M. Craglia et al. *www.ec-gis.org/ginie*

Rabinovitch, J. 1999. From urban management to urban governance: Towards a strategy for the new millennium. *City Development Strategies* 1: 23–25.

Rajabifard, A. 2002. Diffusion of regional spatial data infrastructures: With particular reference to Asia and the Pacific. PhD diss., Department of Geomatics, University of Melbourne.

Rajabifard, A., and I. Williamson. 2003. Asia–Pacific region and SDI activities. *GISDevelopment* 7(7): 30–34.

———. 2000. Report on analysis of regional fundamental data sets questionnaire. Melbourne: University of Melbourne.

Rajabifard, A., I. Williamson, P. Holland, and G. Johnstone. 2000. From local to global SDI initiatives: A pyramid building blocks. Proceedings 4th GSDI conference, Capetown, South Africa.

Rajabifard, A., M. E. Feeney, I. Williamson, and I. Masser. 2003. National spatial data infrastructures. In *Development of spatial data infrastructures: From concept to reality,* eds. I. Williamson, A. Rajabifard, and M. E. Feeney. London: Taylor and Francis.

RAND Science and Technology Policy Institute. 2001. *Lessons for the global spatial data infrastructure: International case study analysis.* Reston, Va.: GSDI secretariat. *www.gsdi.org*

Remetey–Fulopp, G. 1998. Facing the challenge of the EU accession: The emerging role of GI and RS technologies. Proceedings 4th EC-GIC workshop, Budapest.

Renong Berhad. 1995. Feasibility study for the National Land Information System: Final report. Kuala Lumpur: National Land Information System.

Rhind, D. 2000. Funding an NGDI. In *Geospatial data infrastructure: Concepts, cases, and good practice,* eds. R. Groot and J. McLaughlin. Oxford: Oxford University Press.

———. 1997a. Facing the challenges: Redesigning and rebuilding ordnance survey. In *Framework for the world,* ed. D. Rhind. Cambridge: Geoinformation International.

———. 1997b. Implementing a global geospatial data infrastructure. Proceedings 2nd GSDI conference, Chapel Hill, N.C. *www.gsdi.org/docs.html*

Roche, S., and J. B. Humeau. 1999. GIS development and planning collaboration: A few examples from France. *URISA Journal* 11(1): 5–14. *www.urisa.org/journal.htm* (last accessed July 10, 2004).

Rogers, E. 1995. *Diffusion of innovations.* 4th ed. New York: Free Press.

———. 1993. The diffusion of innovations model. In *Diffusion and use of geographic information technologies,* eds. I. Masser and H. J. Onsrud. Dordrecht: Kluwer.

Ryan, B., and N. C. Gross. 1943. The diffusion of hybrid seed corn in two Iowa communities. *Rural Sociology* 8:15–24.

Ryan, B. J., M. L. DeMolder, I. DeLoach, H. Garie, K Sideleris. 2004. A clear vision of the NSDI. *Geospatial solutions* 14(4).

Sarma, G. N. 2003. Financial strategy for the National Spatial Data Infrastructure. Paper presented at 3rd International Workshop on NSDI, India, Agra, India.

Schmid, G., and G. Keith. 2003. Towards a common geographic information framework for England, Proceedings GeoSolutions 2003. London: Association for Geographic Information.

Scottish Executive. 2004. *One Scotland, one strategy: A geographic information strategy for Scotland.* Edinburgh: Scottish Executive. *www.scotland.gov.uk/publications* (last accessed September 25, 2004).

Serpell, D. 1979. *Report of the Ordnance Survey review committee.* London: HMSO.

Service New Brunswick (SNB). 2003. Annual report 2002–2003. Fredericton: Service New Brunswick. *www.snb.ca*

Shrestha, B., and B. Bajracharya. 2001. ICIMOD's approach towards a regional geoinformation infrastructure (RGII) in the Hindu-Kush Himalayan (HKH) region. *www.gisdevelopment.net/policy/gii/gii008.htm*

Spatial Applications Division, Catholic University of Leuven (SAD). 2003a. Spatial data infrastructures in Europe: State of play during 2003. Summary report. *inspire.jrc.it/state_of_play.cfm* (last accessed July 10, 2004).

——. 2003b. Spatial data infrastructures in Finland: State of play spring 2003. *inspire.jrc.it/state_of_play.cfm* (last accessed July 10, 2004).

——. 2003c. Spatial data infrastructures in the Czech Republic: State of play spring 2003. *inspire.jrc.it/state_of_play.cfm* (last accessed July 10, 2004).

——. 2003d. Spatial data infrastructures in the United Kingdom: State of play spring 2003. *inspire.jrc.it/state_of_play.cfm* (last accessed July 10, 2004).

——. 2003e. Spatial data infrastructures in Hungary: State of play spring 2003. *inspire.jrc.it/state_of_play.cfm* (last accessed July 10, 2004).

Spatial Data Warehouse (SDW). 1998. *Alberta spatial data infrastructure initiative: An overview.* Calgary: Spatial Data Warehouse.

Spatial Technologies Industry Association (STIA). 2001. Phase 1 report on increasing the private sector awareness of, and enthusiastic participation in, the National Spatial Data Infrastructure. *www.fgdc.gov*

Spears, G. 2001. Geospatial data policy study. *Geomatica* 55: 208–222.

Stevens, A. 2004. SDI evolution in the U.S.: Solid technology, policy changes and just plain good luck. Proceedings 7th GSDI conference, Bangalore, India.

Stevens, A., K. Thackrey, and K. Lance. 2004. Global Spatial Data Infrastructure (GSDI): Finding and providing tools to facilitate capacity building. Proceedings 7th GSDI conference, Bangalore, India.

Suharto, L. 1995. Moves towards a national geographic information system. Paper presented at the 5th South East Asian Surveyors conference, Singapore.

Tamin, M. Y. 1997. The National Infrastructure for Land Information System (NaLIS): Applying information technology to improve the utilisation of land data in Malaysia. Paper presented at Oracle Open World Malaysia, Kuala Lumpur.

Tang, W., and J. Selwood. 2005. *Spatial portals: Gateways to geographic information.* Redlands, Calif.: ESRI Press.

Tarigi, R. C. S., and M. Al Malki. 2003. Nationwide GIS for Qatar. *GIM International* 17(12): 41–43.

Thompson, B., M. Warnest, and C. Chipchase. 2003. State SDI development. In *Development of spatial data infrastructures: From concept to reality*, eds. I. Williamson, A. Rajabifard, and M. E. Feeney. London: Taylor and Francis.

Tosta, N. 1997a. Data revelations in Qatar: Why the same standards won't work in the United States. *GeoInfo Systems* 7: 5.

——. 1997b. The U.S. National Spatial Data Infrastructure experience. Paper presented at the GISDATA Conference on Geographic Information Research at the Millennium, Le Bischenberg, France.

United Nations Economic Commission for Africa, (UNECA). 2003. SDI Africa: An implementation guide. Addis Ababa: UNECA.

Urban Logic. 2000. *Financing the NSDI: National Spatial Data Infrastructure. www.fgdc.gov*

van Biessen, K. T. 2001. *Models of national GI associations in Europe.* Apeldoorn: EUROGI.

van der Toorn, W., and E. de Man. 2000. Anticipating cultural factors of GDI. In *Geospatial data infrastructure: Concepts, cases and good practice,* eds. R. Groot and J. McLaughlin. Oxford: Oxford University Press.

van Uden, E. 2003. *The next decade of EUROGI.* Apeldoorn: EUROGI.

Warnest, M., A. Rajabifard, and I. Williamson. 2003. Understanding inter-organisational collaboration and partnerships in the development of National SDI. Paper presented at the Urban and Regional Information Systems Association Conference, Atlanta, Georgia.

Waters, R., and J. F. Dallemand. 2002. Cadastral data as a component of spatial data infrastructure in support of agri-environmental programmes. Report of the EUROGI–European Commission Workshop, EC Joint Research Centre, Ispra.

Wegener, M., and I. Masser. 1996. Brave new GIS worlds. In *GIS diffusion: The adoption and use of geographical information systems in local government in Europe,* eds. I. Masser, M. Craglia, and H. Campbell. London: Taylor and Francis.

Wehn de Montalvo, U. 2003. *Mapping the determinants of spatial data sharing.* Aldershot: Ashgate.

Weissbord, M., and S. Janoff. 2000. *Future search: An action guide to finding common ground in organisations and communities.* 2nd ed. San Francisco: Berrett–Koehler.

Whitefield, G. J. 2003. Local government and the NPLG: Are we nearly there yet? Proceedings GeoSolutions 2003. London: Association for Geographic Information.

Williamson, I. 2004. Building SDIs: The challenges ahead. Proceedings 7th GSDI conference, Bangalore, India.

Wolfkamp, A., 2003. National geographic information associations in Europe: Analysis and capacity building. *www.ec-gis.org/ginie*

World Bank. 2003. *World Development Indicators.* Washington: World Bank.

Yamaura, A. 1996. National spatial data infrastructure: An Asian viewpoint. Paper presented at the 1st GSDI conference, Bonn, Germany.

AGI	Association for Geographic Information, United Kingdom
AGILE	Association of GI Laboratories in Europe
AGINI	Association for Geographic Information Northern Ireland
AISI	African Information Society Initiative
AltaLis	Alberta Land Information System, Canada
AM/FM	Automated Mapping and Facility Management, United States
ANZLIC	Australia New Zealand Land Information Council
APSDI	Asia Pacific Spatial Data Infrastructure
ASDI	Australian Spatial Data Infrastructure
ASIBA	Australian Spatial Industry Business Association
AUSLIG	Australian Surveying and Land Information Group
CEC	Commission of European Communities
CGDI	Canadian Geospatial Data Infrastructure
CLGE	Council of European Geodetic Surveyors
CNIG	National Center for Geographic Information, Portugal
CODI-GEO	Committee on Development Information, UNECA
COGI	Committee on Geographic Information, European Commission
DANE	National Statistical Agency, Columbia
DCAL	Department of Culture, Arts, and Leisure, Northern Ireland
DDGI	German National GI Association
DG	Directorate General, European Commission
DISD	Development Information Services Division, UNECA
DSE	Department of Sustainability and Environment, Victoria, Australia
EARSEL	European Association of Remote Sensing Laboratories
EC	European Commission
ECA	(United Nations) Economic Commission for Africa
EGIS	European GIS Conference
EIS	Environmental Information System Program for Sub Saharan Africa
EPA	Environmental Protection Agency, Ghana
ETeMII	European Territorial Management Information Infrastructure project
EU	European Union

List of acronyms

EuroGeographics	European Association of National Mapping Agencies
EUROGI	European Umbrella Organisation for Geographic Information
EuroSDIR	European Organization for Spatial Data Research
FGDC	Federal Geographic Data Committee, United States
FIG	International Federation of Surveyors
FOMI	Institute of Geodesy, Cartography, and Remote Sensing, Hungary
GAO	Government Audit Office, United States
GI	Geographic information
GI2000	European Commission Initiative
GIAC	Geomatics Industry Association of Canada
GINIE	Geographic Information Networks in Europe project
GIS	Geographic information system(s)
GISDATA	European Science Foundation's scientific program
GNP	Gross national product
GSDI	Global Spatial Data Infrastructure
GVA	Gross value added
HUNAGI	Hungarian Association for Geo-Information
HUNGIS	Hungarian GIS Foundation
ICA	International Cartographic Association
ICDE	Colombia Spatial Data Infrastructure
I&DeA	Improvement and Development Agency, United Kingdom
IDEMEX	Mexican SDI
IGAC	Colombian Geographical Institute
IGBP	International Geosphere Biosphere Program
IGGI	Intragovernmental Group for Geographic Information, United Kingdom
IGN	French National Mapping Agency
INEGI	National Institute for Statistics, Geography, and Informatics, Mexico
INSPIRE	European Commission's Infrastructure for Spatial Information in Europe
IPO	Association of Provincial Agencies, Netherlands
IRLOGI	Irish Organization for Geographic Information
ISP	Institutional Strengthening Programme, UNECA
ISPRS	International Society for Photogrammetry and Remote Sensing

ISRO	Indian Space Research Organization
ITC	International Institute for Geoinformation Science and Earth Observation, Netherlands
I-Team	Implementation Team, United States
JRC	Joint Research Centre, European Commission
LGAs	Local government agencies
LINZ	Land Information New Zealand
MADAME	Methods for Access to Data and Metadata in Europe project
MEPAT	Ministry of Planning and Territorial Management, Portugal
MITI	Ministry of International Trade and Industry, Japan
MISR	Ministry of Industry, Science, and Resources, Australia
Mosaic	Northern Ireland GI Strategy
MSC	Mapping Sciences Committee, United States
NAFGIM	National Framework for Geospatial Information Management, Ghana
NaLIS	National Land Information System, Malaysia
NAPA	National Academy for Public Administration, United States
NGD	National Geospatial Database, United Kingdom
NGDF	National Geospatial Data Framework, United Kingdom
NGIIP	National Geographic Information Infrastructure Program, Nepal
NGIS	National Geographic Information System, Korea
NGO	Nongovernmental organization
NIMSA	National Interest Mapping Services Agreement, United Kingdom
NLIS	National Land Information Service, United Kingdom
NLPG	National Land and Property Gazetteer, United Kingdom
NRIS	Indian Natural Resources Management Systems
NSDI	National Spatial Data Infrastructure(s)
NSDS	National Spatial Data Strategy, Hungary
NSIF	National Spatial Information Framework, South Africa
NLS	National Land Survey, Finland
OGC	Open Geographic Information Systems Consortium, United States
OMB	Office of Management and Budget, United States
OSNI	Ordnance Survey Northern Ireland
PAIGH	PanAmerican Institute for Geography and History
PCGIAP	Permanent Committee on Geographic Information for Asia and the Pacific, Malaysia
PC IDEA	Permanant Committee on Geographic Information for the Americas
PIP	Property Information Project, Australia

PSI	Public sector information
PSMA	Public Sector Mapping Agencies, Australia
RAVI	Netherlands Council for Geographic Information (formerly Dutch Council for Real Estate Management)
REPELITA IV	Indonesia's sixth Five Year Plan
RIVM	The National Institute for Public Health and Environment, Netherlands
RRL	Economic and Social Research Council's Regional Research Laboratory initiative, United Kingdom
SAD	Spatial Applications Division of the Catholic University of Leuven, United Kingdom
SASDI	South Africa Spatial Information Infrastructure
SCIEM	Sasol Centre for Innovative Environmental Management, South Africa
SDI	Spatial Data Infrastructure(s)
SDW	Spatial Data Warehouse, Alberta, Canada
SNB	Service New Brunswick, Canada
SNIG	National System for Geographic Information, Portugal
SNIT	National Geographic Information System, Chile
SPEAR	Streamlined Planning through Electronic Applications and Referrals, Australia
STIA	Spatial Technologies Industry Association, United States
SYKE	Finnish Environmental Institute
UDMS	Urban Data Management Society, Europe
UK	United Kingdom
UKSGB	United Kingdom Standard Geographic Base
UNECA	United Nations Economic Commission for Africa
UNGIWG	United Nations Geographic Information Working Group
URISA	Urban and Regional Information Systems Association, United States
USGS	United States Geological Survey
V&W	Ministry of Transport, Public Works, and Water Management, Netherlands
VNG	Association of Dutch Municipalities, Netherlands
VROM	Ministry of Housing, Spatial Planning, and the Environment, Netherlands
VSIS	Victorian Spatial Information Strategy, Australia

A

African Capacity Building Foundation, 270

African Information Society Initiative (AISI), 184

AGI Cymru, 106, 123

AGI Northern Ireland (AGINI), 113, 123

AGI Scotland, 114–115, 124

Albania, 187

Algeria, 76, 77

AM/FM GIS Italy, 212

Argentina, 50, 67, 68, 247

Asia Pacific Spatial Data Infrastructure (APSDI), 182, 249

askGIraffe service, 102

Association for Geographic Information (AGI), 13, 106, 113, 114–115, 117, 118, 123, 124

Association of GI Laboratories in Europe (AGILE), 202, 206

Atlantic Institute, 226, 243

Australia New Zealand Land Information Council (ANZLIC), 32

    action planning, institutional applications, 151, 170, 171

    cost–benefit study and, 47

    development of, 41, 145

    implementation of, 147–151

    national demographic data and, 38, 39 (table)

    responsibilities of, 145–146

    scope of, 44, 45

    Victorian Spatial Information Strategy case example, 152–155, 170, 173, 174, 175

Australian Land Information Council, 128

Australian multilevel data infrastructures, 144

    Australian Spatial Industry Business Association, 150, 169

    CadLite and, 147–148, 148 (figure)

    current practices, 145–146

    custodian concept and, 146

    governance of, leadership/vision issues, 169–171

    implementation issues and, 147–151

organizational structures and, 172–177, 174 (table)

Public Sector Mapping Agencies Consortium and, 147–149, 174, 176

Spatial Information Industry Action Agenda and, 149–151

state/local implementation strategies, 152–155

user-oriented priorities and, 151

Victorian Spatial Information Strategy case example, 152–155, 170, 173, 174, 175

See also Australia New Zealand Land Information Council (ANZLIC)

Australian Spatial Data Infrastructure (ASDI), 32, 71, 72

development basis for, 42

early adopter characteristics and, 48–51, 50 (figure)

implementation mechanisms for, 47

scope of, 44

See also Australia New Zealand Land Information Council (ANZLIC); Australian multilevel data infrastructures

Australian Spatial Industry Business Association (ASIBA), 150, 169, 170

Australian Surveying and Land Information Group (AUSLIG), 32, 232

Austria, 61, 62, 186, 201, 209, 211, 212

Austrian Umbrella Organisation for GI, 212

Bangemann, M., 226

Barwinski, K., 226

Belgium, 61, 62, 186, 201, 209, 211, 212, 213

Benin, 76, 77

Bermuda, 50

Bhutan, 247

Blue Plan for the Mediterranean basin, 10

Bolivia, 50, 67, 68

Borrero, S., 233, 234, 242

Bosnia/Herzegovina, 187

Botswana, 76, 77

Brand, M., 188, 189, 192, 226, 229

Brazil, 67, 68

Bregt, A., 10, 57, 258

British Government Committee of Enquiry on Handling Geographic Information, 3

British National Geospatial Data Framework. *See* United Kingdom National Geospatial Data Framework

Bulgaria, 187, 209

Burkina Faso, 76, 77

C

Cadastral authorities, 5, 7

CadLite, 147–148, 148 (figure)

Campbell, H., 262

Canadian Council on Geomatics, 37, 42

Canadian Geospatial Data Infrastructure (CGDI), 9, 37, 156, 173

    development of, 42–43, 158, 169

    early adopter characteristics and, 48–51, 50 (figure)

    GeoConnections agency and, 125

    implementation mechanisms for, 46

    national demographic data and, 38, 39 (table)

    scope of, 43

    See also Canadian multilevel data infrastructures

Canadian Inter-Agency Committee on Geomatics, 42, 43

Canadian multilevel data infrastructures, 156, 157 (figure)

    current practices in, 158–159

    GeoConnections and, 158–159, 160, 170

    Geomatics Industry Association of Canada, 160, 169, 170

    GeoPartners program and, 160

    governance of, leadership/vision issues, 169–171

    implementation issues and, 160–161

    organizational structures and, 172–177, 174 (table)

    Policy Node and, 161

    Program Advisory Network, 160–161

    province/local implementation strategies, 162–167, 163 (figure)

    Service New Brunswick case example, 165–167, 165 (figure), 170, 173, 174, 175

    Spatial Data Warehouse case example, 164, 170, 173, 174, 176

    See also Canadian Geospatial Data Infrastructure (CGDI)

Capacity-building process, 231, 237, 245, 247, 269–270

Centre for International Economics in Australia, 232

Chaordic self-organization system, 137

Child, J., 266

Chile, 50, 67, 68, 81

Chilean Sistema Nacional de Informacion Territoriale (SNIT), 9

    development of, 69, 82, 84

    global conferences and, 224, 225

    scope of, 86

China, 71, 72

Chorley Report, 94, 96–99, 123

Clinton, W. J., 7, 8, 33, 40, 42, 100

Coleman, D., 88

Colombian Geographical Institute, 233

Colombian Infrastructura Colombiana de Datos Especiales, 9, 51, 52, 67–68

    early adopter characteristics and, 48–51, 50 (figure)

    global conferences and, 224, 225, 227

Colorado Plateau initiative, 138

Committee on the Geographic Foundation for Agenda 21, 75

Communication infrastructures, 75

Computer-based information technology, 3

    cadastral registers and, 5

    See also Geographic information systems (GIS); Internet resources

Cooperative structures, 137–138, 159, 264–266

Coordinating Geographic Data Acquisition and Access: The National Spatial Data Infrastructure, 8, 33, 40, 42, 100

Coordination Committee for Digital GI (Belgium), 212

Cory, M., 110

Costa Rica, 50, 67, 68

Council of European Geodetic Surveyors (CLGE), 202

Croatia, 187

Crompvoets, J., 10, 57, 258

Cuba, 50, 67, 68

Cultural factors, 28, 29, 40, 261

Cymru Conference, 106

Cyprus, 50, 186, 209

Czech Association for Geoinformation, 212

Czech Republic, 61, 62, 81, 186, 201, 202, 209, 212, 247

Czech Republic National Geoinformation Infrastructure, 65

    development of, 83, 84

    resource information on, 87

    scope of, 85, 86

D

Dale, P., 222

Databases. *See* Digital cartographic data

Data management practices, 3

    infrastructure development and, 4–5

    multidirectional information flows, 4

    See also Digital cartographic data

De Man, E., 261

Denmark, 62, 186, 201, 209, 211, 212

Developing nations, 73, 88, 231, 237, 247, 270

Diffusion of innovations model, 12, 26

    adopter categories in, 27–29, 28 (figure)

    communications channels and, 26

    innovations and, 26

    social system and, 28, 29, 40, 261

    uncertainty risk and, 29

    See also SDI diffusion process; SDI early majority adopters; Second-generation SDI

Digital cartographic data, 4

    cadastral registers and, 5, 7

    coordinated management of, 4

    data producer–user linkages and, 8, 20–21, 21 (figures)

    international data infrastructure and, 9–11

    market value of, 6

    national data infrastructure and, 7–8

    See also Global spatial data infrastructure; SDI (spatial data infrastructure)

Distributed Geolibraries, 256

Dominican Republic, 50, 67, 68

Dutch Council for Real Estate Information (RAVI), 20–21, 21 (figure), 34, 44–45, 49, 125, 189, 212, 213

    See also Netherlands National Geographic Information Infrastructure

Early adopters. *See* Diffusion of innovations model; SDI diffusion process; SDI early majority adopters

Early majority. *See* SDI early majority adopters

Economic valuation, 6, 8

    spatial data infrastructure stakeholders and, 18 (table), 19–21, 21 (figure)

    See also Policy formulation

Ecuador, 50, 67, 68

eGovernment services, 83, 117, 166, 170, 259

Egypt, 224, 225

El Salvador, 50, 67, 68

Emergency planning, 41, 143 (figure)

England, 104, 105, 117–119, 122–124

Environmental Information System Program for Sub Saharan Africa (EIS-Africa), 10, 75

Environmental Systems Research Institute (ESRI), 161, 243, 249

Estonia, 61, 62, 186

Ethiopia, 76, 77

Eurogeographics, 202

European Association of Remote Sensing Laboratories (EARSEL), 202

European Commission, 10, 59, 192, 216

European Environmental Agency, 198, 199

European Organization for Spatial Data Research (EuroSDR), 202

European Territorial Management Information Infrastructure (ETeMII) project, 206

European Umbrella Organisation for Geographic Information (EUROGI), 14, 90, 121, 181

    association members characteristics, 208–213, 209 (table), 212 (table)

    current activities of, 204–206

    development of, 188–189, 192–193

    European Territorial Management Information Infrastructure project and, 206

    features of, 183–184

    five-year strategic review of, 190–191

    foundations of, 182–183

    future of, 214–219

    governmental involvement in, 211

    INSPIRE initiative and, 198–199

    leadership of, 190, 192–193, 195, 200, 202, 216–219

    membership of, 201 (figure), 202, 206, 208–213

    national demographic data and, 185, 186–187 (table)

objectives statement for, 194, 196–197, 213

outcomes analysis for, 197–199

policy framework for, 216–219

public-sector information and, 197–198, 214, 216–217, 219

resources and, 213

strengths/weaknesses of, 203, 203 (table)

European Union (EU), 63–64, 83, 184–185, 198, 216, 218

Eurostat, 198, 199

Executive Order 12906 of 1994, 7–8, 33, 40, 42, 100

Ezigbalike, D., 184

Faulkner, D., 266

Federal Geographic Data Committee (FGDC), 33, 43, 131, 132–136, 169

FGDC Clearinghouse, 258

Finland, 50, 61, 62, 81, 186, 201, 209, 212

Finley, D., 167

Finnish Association for GI, 212

Finnish National Spatial Data Infrastructure, 65

development of, 84

scope of, 85, 86

First-generation SDI. *See* SDI diffusion process; SDI early majority adopters; Second-generation SDI

France, 50, 61, 62, 186, 209, 210, 212, 268

French Association for GI, 212

Friends of the Earth, 20

Fukuda–Parr, S., 270

Future Directions Project, 135–136, 169, 171

Future Search method, 109, 111, 121

Future of Spatial Data and Society project, 260

G6 countries, 228

GeoConnections, 125, 158–159, 160, 170

GeoData Alliance, 137–138, 172

Geoforum (Denmark), 211, 212

GeoForum (Norway), 211, 212

Geographic Information Network in Europe (GINIE) project, 59, 197, 204, 205

Geographic information systems (GIS):

    administrative procedures and, 5

    applications-driven nature of, 4–5

    definition of, 3

    digital data, management of, 4

    economic value of, 6

    international data infrastructures, development of, 9–11

    map production/utilization practices and, 3–4

    national data infrastructure, development of, 7–8

    policy/design decisions and, 5

    See also SDI (spatial data infrastructure); SDI diffusion process

Geographic Information in a Wider Europe, 197

Geomatics Industry Association of Canada (GIAC), 156, 160, 169, 170

GeoPartners program, 160

Geospatial One Stop, 134–135, 258, 259

German Umbrella Association for GI, 212

Germany, 50, 61, 62, 186, 201, 209, 211, 212, 224, 227

Ghana, 76, 77, 81

Ghana National Framework for Geospatial Information Managment (NAFGIM), 9, 79

    development of, 82, 85

    resources information on, 87

    scope of, 85, 86

GI2000: Towards a European Geographic Information Infrastructure, 194, 196, 214, 218

Giff, G., 88

GIgateway, 102

GINIE project. *See* Geographic Information Network in Europe (GINIE) project

GIS *See* Geographic information systems (GIS)

Global mapping, 222, 237, 249

Global spatial data infrastructure (GSDI), 191, 192, 222–223

    association development and, 233–237

    conference overview, 224–225

    developing nations, capacity-building and, 231, 237, 247

    development of, 224–238

early organization of, 226–228, 227 (table)

formalization initiatives, 229–232

organizational model for, 230–231

principles of, 229, 236

product clarification effort and, 232

SDI Cookbook and, 231

See also Global Spatial Data Infrastructure (GSDI) Association

Global Spatial Data Infrastructure (GSDI) Association, 10, 14, 16, 90

awareness/exchange development initiatives and, 245, 250

board membership categories and, 241–242, 243 (table)

capacity-building initiatives in, 237, 245

development of, 233–237

evaluation of, 248–250

funding activities for, 245, 246, 247

membership survey results, 246

objectives statement for, 236

organizational profile of, 240–247

strategic planning for, 244–245

See also Global spatial data infrastructure (GSDI)

Government role:

e-government and, 83, 117, 166, 170, 259

international spatial data infrastructure development and, 9–10

national spatial data infrastructure development and, 7–8, 40–41, 42, 211

spatial data infrastructure stakeholders, 18–19, 18 (table), 21 (figure)

See also Policy formulation

Greece, 50, 61, 62, 186, 201, 209, 212

Green Paper on Public Sector Information, 214, 219

Greenpeace, 20

GSDI. *See* Global spatial data infrastructure (GSDI); Global Spatial Data Infrastructure (GSDI) Association

Guatemala, 50, 67, 68

H

Harvey, F., 265

Hellas GI, 212

Hofstede, G., 261

Holland, P., 230, 232

Honduras, 50, 67, 68

Hong Kong, 71, 72

Humeau, J. B., 268

Hungarian Association for GI (HUNAGI), 211, 212, 243

Hungarian National Spatial Data Strategy, 9, 51, 53, 61, 62
 early adopter characteristics and, 48–51, 50 (figure)
 global conferences and, 224, 225, 227

Hungary, 186, 201, 202, 209, 211, 212

I

Iceland, 61, 62, 201, 202, 209, 212

IDEMEX (Mexico), 69

India, 50, 81

Indian National Spatial Data Infrastructure, 74
 development of, 84
 global conferences and, 224, 225, 227
 implementation mechanisms for, 86
 resources information on, 87
 scope of, 85, 86

Indian Space Research Organization, 233, 243

Indonesian National Coordinating Agency for Surveying and Mapping, 35

Indonesian National Geographic Information System, 35
 development impetus for, 41
 early adopter characteristics and, 48–51, 50 (figure)
 government mandate and, 42, 125
 national demographic data and, 38–39, 39 (table)
 scope of, 44

INfrastructure for SPatial InfoRmation in Europe (INSPIRE) initiative, 10, 59, 120, 122, 198–199, 214, 249

Innovation. *See* Diffusion of innovations model; SDI diffusion process

INSPIRE program. *See* INfrastructure for SPatial InfoRmation in Europe (INSPIRE) initiative

Institutional role, 7
 international spatial data infrastructure development and, 10–11
 multilevel infrastructure implementation and, 13–14, 15 (table)
 spatial data infrastructure stakeholders, 18 (table), 19–21, 21 (figure)

Instituto Geografico Portuguese, 125

Integrated systems. *See* Geographic information systems (GIS); SDI (spatial data infrastructure)

Intergraph Corporation, 243, 249

Inter Ministerial Working Group on GIS (Luxembourg), 212

International Cartographic Association (ICA), 249

International Federation of Surveyors (FIG), 249

International Geosphere-Biosphere Programme, 222

International Institute for Geoinformation Science and Earth Observation (ITC), 76

International Society on Digital Earth, 243

International Society for Photogrammetry and Remote Sensing (ISPRS), 249

International spatial data infrastructures, 9

    data producer–user linkages and, 20–21, 21 (figure)

    descriptive terminology of, 31

    extent of involvement in, 9–10

    institutional promotion of, 10–11

    subnational initiatives and, 10, 14

    transnational initiatives and, 10, 14

    See also European Umbrella Organisation for Geographic Information (EUROGI); Global spatial data infrastructure (GSDI); National spatial data infrastructure (NSDI); SDI (spatial data infrastructure); SDI diffusion process

International Steering Committee for Global Mapping, 237, 249

Internet resources:

    Electronic Conveyancing project, 153

    geodata collaboratives, 137–138, 159

    geodata discovery/distribution, 142

    global spatial data and, 16, 222, 237, 244

    Intragovernmental Group for Geographic Information site, 19

    metadata service, 102, 258, 259

    Service New Brunswick, 165–166

    spatial data infrastructure development, 10, 256–257

    United Kingdom spatial data agencies, 98–99

    WebCastle service, 204

Intra-governmental Group for Geographic Information (IGGI), 19, 98, 118

Iran, 71, 72

Ireland, 61, 62, 104, 105, 108–113, 122–124, 186, 201, 209, 211, 212

Irish Organisation for GI (IRLOGI), 211, 212

Islamic Republic of Iran, 71, 72

Italy, 61, 62, 186, 201, 209, 212

I-Team (implementation team) initiative, 138, 172

Ivory Coast, 76, 77

Jamaica, 50, 67, 68, 247

Japanese National Spatial Data Infrastructure, 36, 71, 72

 development impetus for, 41

  early adopter characteristics and, 48–51, 50 (figure)

  government mandate and, 42

  national demographic data and, 38, 39 (table)

  scope of, 44

Johnson, R., 139

Kenya, 76, 77, 81

Kenyan National Spatial Data Infrastructure, 79

 development of, 84

  resources information on, 87

  scope of, 86

Kiribati, 50, 71, 72

Korean Digital National Land, 125

Korean National Geographic Information System, 9, 36

 development impetus for, 40

  early adopter characteristics and, 48–51, 50 (figure)

  government mandate and, 42

  national demographic data and, 38, 39 (table)

  resources information on, 47

  scope of, 44

Lance, K., 75, 78, 87, 243

Land Informaion New Zealand, 72

Laos, 71, 72

Latvia, 61, 62, 186

Lendrum, T., 266

Lesotho, 76, 77

Leuven studies, 59–60, 61 (figure), 62 (table), 122, 161, 258

Lithuania, 61, 62, 186, 209

Local goverment GI Committee (LOGGIC), 118

Longley, P. A., 258

Lopes, C., 270

Luxembourg, 61, 62, 186, 201, 209, 211, 212

M

Macau, 50, 71, 72

Macedonia, 187

Madagascar, 76, 77

MADAME project. *See* Methods for Access to Data and Metadata in Europe (MADAME) project

Maguire, D., 258

Malawi, 76, 77, 247

Malaysian Center for Geospatial Data Infrastructure, 125

Malaysian National Land Information System, 35, 71, 72

    development impetus for, 41

    early adopter characteristics and, 48–51, 50 (figure)

    government mandate and, 42

    implementation mechanisms for, 46

    national demographic data and, 38–39, 39 (table)

    resources information of, 47

    scope of, 44

Maldives, 71, 72

Mali, 76, 77

Malik, K., 270

Malta, 61, 62, 186, 209

Mapping Sciences Committee (MSC), 4, 7, 134, 260

Maps:

    cadastral registers and, 5

    geographic information systems and, 3–4

    sieve maps, 5

updating functions and, 4

urban planning and, 4–5

See also Digital cartographic data

Masser, I., 9, 10, 25, 86, 192, 193, 200, 216–217, 233, 242, 243, 248, 260, 262

Mesoamerican and Caribbean Geospatial Alliance, 243

Metadata services, 102, 206, 258, 259

Methods for Access to Data and Metadata in Europe (MADAME) project, 59

MetroGIS case study, 139–142, 141 (figure), 143 (figure), 170, 174, 177

Mexican IDEMEX, 69

development of, 84

scope of, 86

Mexico, 50, 66, 67, 68, 81, 247

Minnesota case study, 139–143

Moeller, J., 242, 243

Moldova, 187

Mongolia, 50, 71, 72, 247

Mosaic program, 113

Multilevel spatial data infrastructures, 128

Australian infrastructures, 144–155

Canadian infrastructures, 156–167

comparative evaluation of, 169–177

governance issues in, 169–171

organizational structures and, 172–177, 174 (table)

second-generation SDI and, 264–266

U. S. infrastructures, 130–143

Namibia, 76, 77, 247

National Academy for Public Administration (NAPA), 6

National Land Information System Users Association (Poland), 212

National Land Survey of Finland, 243

National Spatial Data Council, 132

National spatial data infrastructure (NSDI), 7–8

data producer–user linkages and, 8

descriptive terminology of, 31

international development of, 9–11

Internet resources and, 256–257

utility of, 8

See also SDI (spatial data infrastructure); SDI diffusion process

Natural hazard planning, 41, 143 (figure)

Nebert, D., 231, 233, 242

Nedovic–Budic, Z., 265

Nemoforum. *See* Czech Republic National Geoinformation Infrastructure

Nepal, 50, 71, 72, 81

Nepal National Geographic Information Infrastructure Program (NGIIP), 74

    development of, 85

    scope of, 85–86

Netherlands, 186, 201, 209, 211, 212

Netherlands National Geographic Information Infrastructure, 34, 61, 62

    development basis for, 42

    early adopter characteristics and, 48–51, 50 (figure)

    national demographic data and, 38, 39 (table)

    scope of, 44–45

    Space for Geoinformation program and, 125

    See also Dutch Council for Real Estate Information (RAVI)

New Zealand, 71

    Land Information New Zealand, 72

    See also Australia New Zealand Land Information Council (ANZLIC)

Nicaragua, 50, 67, 68

Nigeria, 76, 77

Nongovernmental organizations (NGOs), 20, 211

Northern Ireland, 104, 105, 108–113, 122–124

Norway, 61, 62, 187, 201, 202, 209, 211, 212, 213

Not-for-profit organizations, 20

O

O'Neil, R. A., 222, 249, 250

Onsrud, H., 233, 242, 243, 265

Open GIS Consortium, 75, 243

Open Interoperability Grant program, 237

Ordnance Survey Great Britian, 6, 37, 96, 97, 101, 102

Ordnance Survey Northern Ireland (OSNI), 108, 110, 112, 113

Organisation for GI in Iceland, 212

Pakistan, 50

Panama, 50, 67, 68

PanAmerican Institute for Geography and History, 243

Peoples Republic of China, 71, 72

Permanent Committee on Geographic Information for Asia and the Pacific (PCGIAP), 182

Peru, 50, 67, 68

Petersohn, F., 226

Pinto, J. K., 265

Poland, 50, 61, 62, 186, 201, 202, 209, 212

Policy formulation, 5, 20

    Australian Spatial Industry Business Association and, 150

    Canadian Policy Node and, 161

    European Umbrella Organisation for Geographic Information and, 216–219

    global spatial data infrastructure and, 223

    MetroGIS case study and, 139–143

Portugal, 186, 201, 209, 212

Portuguese GI Users Association, 212

Portuguese National Center for Geographic Information (CNIG), 34, 45, 125

Portuguese Sistema Nacionale de Informacao Geografica (SNIG), 9, 34, 61, 62

    development impetus for, 41

    early adopter characteristics and, 48–51, 50 (figure)

    government mandate and, 42

    implementation mechanisms for, 45–46

    national demographic data and, 38, 39 (table)

    scope of, 44

Private-sector applications, 5, 8

    Australian Spatial Information Industry Action Agenda, 149–151

    Geomatics Industry Association of Canada, 156, 160

    spatial data infrastructures and, 18 (table), 19–21, 21 (figure)

    U. S. Spatial Technologies Industry Association and, 133–134

Prodi, R., 218–219

Producer–user linkages, 8, 20–21, 21 (figure)

Public-sector applications, 5, 8

    spatial data infrastructures and, 18–19, 18 (table), 21 (figure)

    See also Government role; Policy formulation

Public Sector Information Green Paper, 214, 219

Public Sector Mapping Agencies, 147–149, 174, 176

Qatar National Center for Geographic Information Systems, 45

Qatar National Geographic Information System, 33

    early adopter characteristics and, 48–51, 50 (figure)

    government mandate and, 42

    implementation mechanisms for, 45

    national demographic data and, 38, 39 (table)

    resources information on, 47

    scope of, 44

Rajabifard, A., 70, 122, 181, 256, 258, 266, 268

RAND Science and Technology Policy Institute, 233

Rao, M., 233, 235, 242, 243

RAVI Foundation. See Dutch Council for Real Estate Information (RAVI)

Republic of Palau, 71, 72

Rhind, D., 18, 101

Roche, S., 268

Rogers, E., 12, 26, 40, 48, 57, 90, 260, 262

Romania, 50, 187

Rushton, G., 265

Russia, 50, 209

S

Samborski, R., 242, 243

Schmid, G., 118

Scotland, 104, 105, 114–116, 122–124

SDI (spatial data infrastructure):

    definition of, 16

    international development of, 9–11

    multilevel implementation of, 13–14, 15 (table)

    principles of, 17

    stakeholders in, 18–21, 18 (table), 21 (figure)

    See also Global spatial data infrastructure (GSDI); National spatial data infrastructure (NSDI); SDI diffusion process; Second-generation SDI

SDI Cookbook, 231

SDI diffusion process, 25

    access to information and, 41

    Australian Spatial Data Infrastructure and, 32

    British National Geospatial Data Framework and, 37

    Canadian Geospatial Data Infrastructure and, 37

    descriptive terminology and, 31

    development impetus and, 40–41

    diffusion of innovations model and, 26–30, 28 (figure)

    early adopter characteristics and, 48–53, 50 (figure)

    early adopters, examples of, 30–37, 30 (table), 31 (figure)

    implementation mechanisms and, 45–46

    Indonesian National Geographic Information System and, 35

    Japanese National Spatial Data Infrastructure and, 36

    Korean National Geographic Information System and, 36

    Malaysian National Land Information System and, 35

    national demographic data and, 38–39, 39 (table)

    Netherlands National Geographic Information Infrastructure and, 34

    Portuguese Sistema Nacionale de Informacao Geografica and, 34

    Qatar National Geographic Information System and, 33

    resources information and, 47

    scope of information/representation and, 43–45

    social/cultural factors and, 28, 29, 40, 261

    status of systems origins and, 42–43

    U. S. National Spatial Data Infrastructure and, 33

    See also SDI early majority adopters; Second-generation SDI

SDI early majority adopters, 57

    African nations, 75–79, 81

    Asian/Pacific nations, 70–74, 81

    Central/South American nations, 66–69, 81

    Chile Sistema Nacionale de Informacion Territoriale and, 69

    Czech Republic National Geoinformation Infrastructure and, 65

    developing nations and, 73, 88

    development impetus and, 82–83

    early majority characteristics and, 90–91

    European nations, 59–65, 81

    European Union membership and, 63–64

Finnish National Spatial Data Infrastructure and, 65

Ghana National Framework for Geographic Information Management and, 79

implementation mechanisms and, 86

Indian National Spatial Data Infrastructure and, 74

Kenyan National Spatial Data Infrastructure and, 79

Mexican IDEMEX and, 69

national demographic data and, 80–81, 81 (table)

Nepal National Geographic Information Infrastructure Program and, 74

resources information and, 87–88

scope of information/representation and, 85–86

status of systems origins, 84–85

telecommunications infrastructures and, 75

typology of SDIs, 60, 61 (figure), 62 (table), 63, 66, 67 (figure), 68, 68 (table)

See also SDI diffusion process; Second-generation SDI

Second-generation SDI:

capacity-building and, 269–270

diffusion process and, 258–261

evolutionary changes and, 262–263

future research topics and, 260–261, 263

hierarchical structures and, 268–270

Internet technologies and, 256, 258–259

multilevel stakeholder participation and, 264–266

process vs. product model and, 256–257, 257 (table)

social/cultural factors and, 261

Senegal, 76, 77

Service New Brunswick (SNB), 165–167, 165 (figure), 170, 173, 174, 175

Sieve maps, 5

Singapore, 71, 72

Slovakia, 61, 62, 186, 209

Slovenia, 61, 62, 186, 209

Smith–Paterson, J., 226, 228, 229

Social factors, 28, 29, 40, 261

Solomon Islands, 71, 72

South Africa National Spatial Information Framework, 51, 52, 76, 77

early adopter characteristics and, 48–51, 50 (figure)

global conferences and, 224, 225, 227

South Korea, 50

Space for Geoinformation program, 125

Spain, 61, 62, 186, 210, 212

Spanish Association for GI, 212

Spatial Data Infrastructure Program of the Australian Surveying and Land Information Group (AUSLIG), 32

Spatial data infrastructure. See SDI (spatial data infrastructure)

Spatial Data Warehouse (SDW), 164, 170, 173, 174, 176

Spatial Technologies Industry Association (STIA), 133–134

Stevens, A., 233, 242

Sustainable development, 75, 82, 108, 111

Sweden, 50, 61, 62, 186, 201, 209, 212

Swedish Development Council for Land Information, 212

Swiss Organisation for Geoinformation, 212

Switzerland, 61, 62, 187, 201, 202, 209, 212

Tanzania, 76, 77, 247

Thackrey, K., 242

Thompson, B., 155

Tobago, 50

Togo, 76, 77

Toorn, W. van der, 261

Trinidad, 50

Tunisia, 76, 77

Turkey, 187, 209

Tuvalu, 50, 71, 72

Uganda, 76, 77

UN Economic Commission for Africa, 76, 88, 184

UN Economic Commission for Africa Committee on Development Information (CODI-GEO), 182, 183, 184

UN GI Working Group, 222

UN Regional Cartographic Conference for Asia and the Pacific, 182

United Kingdom, 186, 201, 209, 211

United Kingdom Association for Geographic Information, 211, 212, 213

United Kingdom National Geospatial Data Framework (NGDF), 37, 61, 62

    development of, 41, 43

    national demographic data and, 39 (table)

    scope of, 44, 45

    See also United Kingdom spatial data infrastructure

United Kingdom spatial data infrastructure, 94

    Chorley Report, impact of, 96–99

    comparative evaluation of strategies, 122–124, 122 (table)

    current state of, 104–119, 105 (table)

    development of, 97–99

    English geographic information strategy and, 117–119

    foundational organization of, 100–101

    Future Search method and, 109, 111, 121

    Intra-governmental Group on Geographic Information and, 98, 118

    Irish geographic information strategy and, 108–113

    lessons from, 120–121

    metadata service and, 102

    Mosaic program and, 113

    objectives of, 101–102

    review/reorganization of, 102

    Scottish geographic information strategy and, 114–116

    Welsh geographic information strategy and, 106–107

    See also United Kingdom National Geospatial Data Framework (NGDF)

University Consortium for Geographic Information Science, 243

Urban Data Management Society (UDMS), 183

Urban Logic report, 133

Urban planning, 4–5

    See also MetroGIS case study

Uruguay, 50, 66, 67, 68

User–producer linkages, 8, 20–21, 21 (figure)

U. S. Federal Geographic Data Committee (FGDC), 33, 43, 131, 132–136, 169

U. S. Mapping Sciences Committee (MSC), 4, 7, 256

U. S. multilevel data infrastructures, 130

    I-Team (implementation team) initiative and, 138, 172

    current practices in, 131–132

Federal Geographic Data Committee and, 131, 132–136

Future Directions Project and, 135–136, 169, 171

GeoData Alliance and, 137–138, 172

Geospatial One Stop program and, 134–135

governance of, leadership/vision issues, 169–171

implementation issues and, 133–136

MetroGIS case study and, 139–142, 141 (figure), 143 (figure), 170, 174, 177

National Spatial Data Council and, 132

organizational structures and, 172–177, 174 (table)

partnership programs and, 133–135

state/local implementation strategies, 137–143

U. S. National Digital Geospatial Data Framework, 13, 33

U. S. National Geospatial Data Clearinghouse, 33

U. S. spatial data infrastructure, 33

early adopter characteristics and, 48–51, 50 (figure)

global conferences and, 224, 225, 227

government mandate and, 42

implementation mechanisms for, 46

national demographic data and, 38–39, 39 (table)

resources information on, 47

scope of, 43

See also U. S. multilevel data infrastructures

Value-added estimate, 6, 8

Venezuela, 67, 68

Victorian Spatial Information Strategy (VSIS), 152–155, 170, 173, 174, 175

Wales, 104, 105, 106–107, 122–124

Warnecke, L., 265

Warnest, M., 266

WebCastle service, 204

Wegener, M., 260

Wehn de Montalvo, U., 266

Williamson, I., 70, 122, 258, 266

Wolfkamp, A., 192, 195, 200, 210, 213

World Bank, 38, 82, 83, 87, 185, 228, 240

World Summit of the Information Society, 249

World Summit on Sustainable Development, 75

Yugoslavia Federal Republic, 187

Zambia, 76, 77

Zimbabwe, 247

Books from

ESRI
Press

Advanced Spatial Analysis: The CASA Book of GIS *1-58948-073-2*
ArcGIS and the Digital City: A Hands-on Approach for Local Government *1-58948-074-0*
ArcView GIS Means Business *1-879102-51-X*
A System for Survival: GIS and Sustainable Development *1-58948-052-X*
Beyond Maps: GIS and Decision Making in Local Government *1-879102-79-X*
Cartographica Extraordinaire: The Historical Map Transformed *1-58948-044-9*
Community Geography: GIS in Action *1-58948-023-6*
Community Geography: GIS in Action Teacher's Guide *1-58948-051-1*
Confronting Catastrophe: A GIS Handbook *1-58948-040-6*
Connecting Our World: GIS Web Services *1-58948-075-9*
Conservation Geography: Case Studies in GIS, Computer Mapping, and Activism *1-58948-024-4*
Designing Geodatabases: Case Studies in GIS Data Modeling *1-58948-021-X*
Disaster Response: GIS for Public Safety *1-879102-88-9*
Enterprise GIS for Energy Companies *1-879102-48-X*
Extending ArcView GIS (version 3.x edition) *1-879102-05-6*
Getting to Know ArcGIS Desktop, Second Edition Updated for ArcGIS 9 *1-58948-083-X*
Getting to Know ArcObjects: Programming ArcGIS with VBA *1-58948-018-X*
Getting to Know ArcView GIS (version 3.x edition) *1-879102-46-3*
GIS and Land Records: The ArcGIS Parcel Data Model *1-58948-077-5*
GIS for Everyone, Third Edition *1-58948-056-2*
GIS for Health Organizations *1-879102-65-X*
GIS for Landscape Architects *1-879102-64-1*
GIS for the Urban Environment *1-58948-082-1*
GIS for Water Management in Europe *1-58948-076-7*
GIS in Public Policy: Using Geographic Information for More Effective Government *1-879102-66-8*
GIS in Schools *1-879102-85-4*
GIS in Telecommunications *1-879102-86-2*
GIS Means Business, Volume II *1-58948-033-3*
Hydrologic and Hydraulic Modeling Support with Geographic Information Systems *1-879102-80-3*
Integrating GIS and the Global Positioning System *1-879102-81-1*
Making Community Connections: The Orton Family Foundation Community Mapping Program *1-58948-071-6*
Managing Natural Resources with GIS *1-879102-53-6*
Mapping Census 2000: The Geography of U.S. Diversity *1-58948-014-7*
Mapping Our World: GIS Lessons for Educators, ArcView GIS 3.x Edition *1-58948-022-8*
Mapping the Future of America's National Parks: Stewardship through Geographic Information Systems *1-58948-080-5*
Mapping the News: Case Studies in GIS and Journalism *1-58948-072-4*
Marine Geography: GIS for the Oceans and Seas *1-58948-045-7*
Measuring Up: The Business Case for GIS *1-58948-088-0*
Modeling Our World: The ESRI Guide to Geodatabase Design *1-879102-62-5*

Continued on next page

When ordering, please mention book title and ISBN (number that follows each title).

Books from ESRI Press (continued)

Past Time, Past Place: GIS for History *1-58948-032-5*

Planning Support Systems: Integrating Geographic Information Systems, Models, and Visualization Tools *1-58948-011-2*

Remote Sensing for GIS Managers *1-58948-081-3*

Salton Sea Atlas *1-58948-043-0*

The ESRI Guide to GIS Analysis, Volume 1: Geographic Patterns and Relationships *1-879102-06-4*

Transportation GIS *1-879102-47-1*

Undersea with GIS *1-58948-016-3*

Unlocking the Census with GIS *1-58948-113-5*

Zeroing In: Geographic Information Systems at Work in the Community *1-879102-50-1*

Future titles from ESRI Press

Arc Hydro: GIS for Water Resources, Second Edition *1-58948-126-7*

Cartographies of Disease: Maps, Mapping, and Medicine *1-58948-120-8*

Charting the Unknown: How Computer Mapping at Harvard Became GIS *1-58948-118-6*

Children Map the World: Selections from the Barbara Petchenik Children's World Map Competition *1-58948-125-9*

Designing Better Maps: A Guide for GIS Users *1-58948-089-9*

Finding Your Customers: GIS for Retail Management *1-58948-123-2*

Fun with GPS *1-58948-087-2*

GIS Tutorial: Workbook for ArcView 9 *1-58948-127-5*

GIS Worlds: Creating Spatial Data Infrastructures *1-58948-122-4*

Mapping Our World: GIS Lessons for Educators, ArcGIS Desktop Edition *1-58948-121-6*

The ESRI Guide to GIS Analysis, Volume 2: Spatial Measurements and Statistics *1-58948-116-X*

Thinking About GIS: Geographic Information System Planning for Managers (paperback edition) *1-58948-119-4*

Thinking Globally, Acting Regionally: GIS and Data Visualization for Social Science and Public Policy Research *1-58948-124-0*

Ask for ESRI Press titles at your local bookstore or order by calling 1-800-447-9778. You can also shop online at www.esri.com/esripress. Outside the United States, contact your local ESRI distributor.

ESRI Press titles are distributed to the trade by the following:

In North America, South America, Asia, and Australia:
Independent Publishers Group (IPG)
Telephone (United States): 1-800-888-4741 • Telephone (international): 312-337-0747
E-mail: frontdesk@ipgbook.com

In the United Kingdom, Europe, and the Middle East:
Transatlantic Publishers Group Ltd.
Telephone: 44 20 8849 8013 • Fax: 44 20 8849 5556 • E-mail: transatlantic.publishers@regusnet.com

ESRI Press • 380 New York Street • Redlands, California 92373-8100 • www.esri.com/esripress

GIS Worlds: Creating Spatial Data Infrastructures

Copyediting by Tiffany Wilkerson

Book design, production, and illustration by Jennifer Galloway

Cartography by Bo King

Cover design by Suzanne Davis

Printing coordination by Cliff Crabbe